Duc Pho was a nightmare.

Less than two hours on the ground, and I felt like I'd been in the bush for a week. The tension grew until we could have cut it out of the air with a knife and served it up in large chunks.

Then the jungle exploded.

Automatic rifle fire poured over us so heavily, the leaves above rained down in chopped bits and pieces and kept on raining. In an instant, we were on the ground and facing uphill. Shouts and curses coming from above added to the confusion around me. In a state of near panic, I yelled at the men to get on line. Bullets were hitting everywhere in the trees and ricocheting off the rocks as the men scrambled on hands and knees to form a line.

My radio operator kept asking over and over what he was supposed to do, and I finally snapped at him to tell battalion we needed a gunship and to get it up now.

FIRST RECON— SECOND TO NONE

A Marine Reconnaissance Battalion 1967–1968

Paul Young

IVY BOOKS • NEW YORK

Ivy Books
Published by Ballantine Books
Copyright © 1992 by Paul Young

http://www.randomhouse.com

Library of Congress Catalog Card Number: 92-90616

ISBN 0-8041-1009-3

Manufactured in the United States of America

First Edition: November 1992

10 9 8 7

To my wife Roberta and our children, Jodi, Dan, Teri, and Brian, for all your love, support, and understanding.

ACKNOWLEDGMENTS

I would like to thank the following people for all the help and support they gave to make this book possible.

Col. Pete Badger, Capt. Ron Benoit, Capt. Dan Brophy, Capt. Joe Campbell, Sgt. Joe Cizek, Sgt. Mark Cleaves, Danny Crawford (Head, Reference Section, History and Museums Division. Headquarters Marine Corps), Capt. John Dunn (who got me into all this), Sgt. Budd Eckert, Col. Andrew Finlayson, Col. Richard Johnson (whose son Dick was killed while with Recon), Dr. Frank Osanka, Sgt. Ron Molnar, Lt. Dudley Porter, H.M. Robert "Doc" Stomp, 1st Sgt. Walter Webb. Nearly all of whom were wounded in Vietnam.

A special thanks goes to my mentor and never-ending source of encouragement, Jacqueline Buie—without whose kind words and constant prodding, I would have never a writer become.

1

January 21, 1967: Da Nang, Vietnam.

Recon couldn't have been farther from my mind as I sat outside the 1st Marine Division personnel office, wondering about my future. Hammering away at me was the fact that I had just argued my way out of a cushy job with a military police company and into a platoon leader's billet with an infantry battalion and couldn't believe I'd made such a stupid move. Working with the MPs, I could have safely spent the war in the "Greater Da Nang Vital Area," saluting each setting sun with a cold beer and listening to twenty-four-hour, nonstop rock 'n' roll spin from an army of state-of-the-art, guaran-damn-teed high-fidelity, won't-the-folks-back-home-crap-when-they-hear-how-much-they-don't-cost tape decks. Add to that the easy access to female companionship, USO shows, "Gunsmoke" nightly on the big screen, opportunities to dabble in an open, rampant black market, and an extra one hundred and ten dollars a month hazardous duty pay for no combat, and life in the rear equaled good.

Not ten minutes prior, I had said no to all that.

A tour of duty with an infantry battalion only offered the prospects of going home to my wife and daughter maimed or in a box. I did not want to return in either condition. But as a new second lieutenant with a military occupational specialty that spelled "infantry" and who had yet to prove himself on the field of battle, I believed that no greater honor could befall me than to be a combat Marine—a grunt, if you will.

1

Still, I was feeling uncertain about my decision not to go to the MPs, and a meeting with the division commanding general (CG) earlier that morning did nothing to calm that uncertainty. At 0900, five of us, all new in country, had been ushered into the office of Herman the German for a welcome-aboard speech—mandatory for all reporting officers. The welcome turned out to be a foaming-at-the-mouth lecture about the behavior and conduct becoming a Marine officer. "There will be no foul-ups in my command!" Herman swore, then proceeded to threaten us with being relieved of duty and sent home in disgrace should we fail to do our duty to God and country as Herman saw fit. When the meeting was over, I came away with the distinct feeling that the war had somehow taken a back seat to "conduct becoming" and that, by the very fact that I was present and accounted for in Vietnam, I had done something terribly wrong.

It was not a speech designed to instill confidence. As a matter of fact, as I sat outside the bunkered-down, dug-in, sandbagged, barbed-wired division command post (CP), I never felt more vulnerable in my life!

It was there, as I rummaged through the wilting atmosphere that had invaded my spirits, that recon entered my life for the second time.

A lieutenant colonel, followed by a brown bar like myself, rounded the far end of the headquarters building and started up the boardwalk in my direction. The men appeared to be close in age, and I knew the lieutenant had to be a mustang, a former enlisted man promoted to officer. The colonel was impeccably turned out in starched jungle fatigues and spit-shined boots. In contrast to his neat appearance, the lieutenant was dirty; his clothes were torn, and his face and hands bore traces of grease paint. He badly needed a shave, and his boots were covered with the red mud that seemed to carpet what little I had seen of Vietnam.

I jumped to my feet, saluted, and said good-morning to the colonel, who returned my salute. When they were abreast of me, the two stopped and began looking me up and down. For several seconds, no one said anything, and I began to wonder if I had somehow behaved in a manner unbecoming an officer and a gentleman and was about to receive my first reprimand.

Then the lieutenant spoke. "You want to go to recon? We lost an officer last night and need a replacement."

Something inside me sank like a stone. I shook my head and stammered a "no thank you" and explained that I had just been assigned to the 3d Battalion, 1st Marine Regiment, and would be leaving for wherever it was they were as soon as my orders were cut.

The lieutenant gave a knowing smile, and he and the colonel, who had not spoken, disappeared into the personnel office.

I wanted no part of recon.

In 1960, after serving eighteen months with a guard company in the Philippines, I pulled a tour with recon. For six months I climbed mountains and ran ridges from one end of Camp Pendleton to the other. When we weren't in the field, we were up at 0500 every morning for a half hour of physical training, followed by a five-mile run, then it was off to classes to learn map reading, escape-and-evasion techniques, scouting and patrolling, rappelling, and so on. At 1600, we fell out for another round of PT. We spent weeks in the field, melting under the hot California sun during the day and freezing in the wet cold at night. We lived on C rations while roaming the hills in teams of four to six men, hounding platoons and companies on training exercises, and hunting down and ambushing classes from the Scouting and Patrolling School as they tried to run patrols through us. During one exercise, we ambushed a SEAL team as it tried to work its way past us to a small stream. The team's route was protected by trees, thick brush, and large boulders, an ideal daytime approach. But we were there, waiting. When we sprang the ambush, the SEALs counterattacked with such force they quickly overran our position, and I was sure the guy coming at me with a knife was going to use it to pin me to a tree. My partner that day, Dean Carlton, was shot by a blank at such close range he was laid up in the hospital for ten days. Me, I came away with a healthy respect for the SEALs and a determination to give the next group more room before springing another ambush.

But as a private first class, who had just completed a year and a half flanking every mind-numbing post in the remote reaches of the Subic Bay Naval Base, the freedom to roam the open hills and valleys of Camp Pendleton was a small taste of heaven, and I loved it.

However, I also knew that working with a small group, far from any supporting units and relying solely upon the group for survival in the back country of Pendleton was one thing. In the real world of Vietnam, it would be entirely another.

A face wearing a devilish grin appeared in the door of the personnel office. It belonged to the lieutenant I'd met only moments before.

"Come here," the lieutenant said.

I went, knowing that a terrible wrong had just taken place in that office.

"You just had your orders changed. Welcome to recon," the lieutenant said, laughing.

My stomach knotted and rolled over.

"But what about 3/1?" I said, hoping that somehow my orders couldn't be changed without the approval of the battalion to which I had been assigned.

"They'll never know," the lieutenant said.

"My jeep's outside, Lieutenant," the colonel said, speaking for the first time. "Get your gear, and we'll give you a ride to the battalion area."

I gave the colonel an "aye-aye, sir," picked up my orders, and went outside to retrieve my seabag and Valpac, a large canvas and leather bag issued to officers and used in addition to the seabag to carry personal belongings.

As I struggled to keep up with the colonel, the lieutenant came alongside and took the heavy Valpac, which was crammed with extra clothing, books, shoe-polish tins, cans of spray starch, an iron, a pair of goggles, after-shave lotion, Brasso, a manicure kit, my own personal survival kit, a small tape recorder, and a few dozen other things I naively thought were needed to fight a war.

"My name's John Dunn. I've got the 2d Platoon of Bravo Company. Our call sign's Dutch Oven," the lieutenant said, introducing himself. "That's Colonel McKeon, the CO of 1st Recon," he added, nodding in the direction of the colonel, who was some distance ahead of us.

"I thought recon only took volunteers," I said, still looking for a way out.

"You just did," John replied.

We reached the jeep, and I threw my gear in the back and climbed in after it. The colonel got into the passenger seat, and John slid behind the wheel, started the engine, and we headed down the hill to Camp Reasoner, home of the 1st Reconnaissance Battalion.

On the ride to the camp, I learned that the man I was replacing, a Lieutenant Heilman, had been severely wounded the night before by a short round, the name given to an artillery round that doesn't get to where it's supposed to. Like any weapon, the accuracy of an artillery round decreases as it reaches its maximum range. When it approaches that range, there is a chance the round will fall short and detonate near or among the troops it was fired in support of. In this case, a large piece of shrapnel had hit Heilman in one leg, which the doctors didn't believe could be saved.

We reached the battalion area, which was only a short distance from division, and after dropping the colonel off at his quarters, John took me to the mess hall to eat. It was then I discovered that recon lived well while in the rear.

The mess hall, like all the buildings at Reasoner, was two-by-four framed, with walls sheeted halfway up with plywood then screened to the eaves. The roof was corrugated tin and the floors plywood. To keep the dust down, water was sprinkled on the floors several times a day. Insects were kept in check by long strips of flypaper hung from the ceiling, and small fuck-you lizards were encouraged to roam the walls. The food was excellent, and we actually ate off of plates at tables of four to six settings. Staff noncommissioned officers and officers ate together. The lower-ranking enlisted men ate in an adjoining building.

Having been led to believe that, at best, life would be lived in a tent and food served animal-like into a field mess kit, with cold potatoes and gravy over tapioca pudding and brussels sprouts, Camp Reasoner was a welcome surprise.

As we ate, John made a few introductions, but most of the men around us had either just come in off patrol or were preparing to go out and were too preoccupied with their own thoughts to pay much attention to the arrival of a lowly new second lieutenant.

After chow, John took me on a tour of the camp.

Reasoner was located on the lower slopes of the same hill occupied by division. Personnel, maintenance, and operations were down in a hollow, surrounded by living quarters, most of which were on the hills above the hollow. The Motor Transport Company was up near the main entrance to the camp and the road to the Freedom Hill Post Exchange (PX) and Dog Patch, about three miles away. The battalion was spread out over an area of about ten acres and included a landing zone, LZ Finch. A series of bunkers, which were manned only at night, ringed the compound.

From the hill above the LZ, the city of Da Nang, with its crowded, foul-smelling streets and nearby airbase, could be seen eight kilometers to the east. To the north lay the brooding, cloud-enshrouded Hai Van Pass, winding over mountains that reached into the South China Sea. Only ten kilometers away, the pass was fought over so often that only large, infantry-supported convoys used it, and recon ran a steady stream of patrols into the mountains around it to monitor and harass the enemy.

After dropping my orders off at the battalion personnel office, we went to the operations bunker, designated the S-3 shop, where I was introduced to the officer in charge, Major Welzant, and given a rundown on the workings therein. It was a busy place.

It was from the operations bunker that patrols were assigned their RAORs (Recon Area of Operational Responsibility), supporting arms were laid on, and the times, dates, and locations of insertions and extractions were fixed. Since almost all recon patrols were inserted into their RAORs by helicopter, the battalion relied heavily on them to carry out its mission, which was to act as the eyes and ears of the division. Both troop transport helicopters and gunships were used during each insertion and extraction. This normally called for a minimum of four helicopters, items not found in abundance on Marine Corps inventory lists. Although recon had a high priority on the helicopters, they were in big demand by everything from infantry units in the field to visiting dog and pony shows, and recon operations were sometimes postponed or cancelled because of flight commitments elsewhere. And, as I quickly learned, being left in the field an extra day or two because the birds weren't available for an extraction was a real sore point in the battalion.

Before a patrol could be inserted into its RAOR, artillery and air units had to be notified by the S-3 so that no indiscriminate shooting or bombing took place where the patrol was operating. Artillery units fired nightly harassing and interdicting fires (H & Is) on areas likely to be used by the enemy. These were plotted on the basis of chairborne guesswork, and I suspect that no more than one round in a thousand ever found its mark and killed a Vietcong. But they could be a real inconvenience to a patrol should it find itself in an area where H and I fires hadn't been lifted.

Friendly troops operating in or near a RAOR had to be contacted and radio frequencies exchanged to keep track of one another to avoid the possibility of an intramural firefight, which happened from time to time. Also, throughout Vietnam there were a number of free fire zones, where planes could unload their bombs and artillery could shoot any time of day or night. These zones shifted occasionally, and their whereabouts had to be kept current so a team wasn't accidentally put down in one and wiped out by friendly fire. The zones were established on the premise that everyone in them was hard-core Vietcong. How that premise was made was anyone's guess, and I suspect there was more magic wand involved than real intelligence work.

All radio messages from the field were monitored by the S-3 shop. Because the battalion shared Camp Reasoner with 1st Force Reconnaissance Company, there could be as many as ten or twelve patrols in the field at any given time, all coordinated by the one S-3 shop. Most of the patrols were assigned different radio frequencies, and all of them reported in hourly to a bank of radios manned by communicators standing eight-hour watches. Most hourly reports came in the form of a radio check or a notification that a patrol had changed location. When a patrol called in an enemy sighting, it was sent in as a SALUTE message (size, activity, location, unit, time, and equipment). The information from a SALUTE message was recorded and plotted on a series of overlapping topographic maps, covered with acetate and fixed to one wall of the shop. The information was then passed on to division intelligence and used to assess enemy activity within the division's TAOR (Tactical Area of Operational Responsibility). Once a patrol spotted an enemy unit, it usually tried to take it under fire, using supporting arms or by setting up an ambush.

When a patrol made contact with the enemy and a firefight ensued, it had priority over the network. During such times, both division and battalion would monitor the net, but it was the patrol leader who called the shots; bringing in arty, fixed wing or gunships, or calling for an emergency extraction or a medical evacuation. Division and battalion could expedite and advise, but it was advice the patrol leader could choose to accept or ignore. The patrol leader, and no one else, was in command on the ground. This rule was so strongly respected that on one patrol, while heavily engaged with the enemy and calling in supporting arms and moving his wounded to an LZ, Lt. Ron Benoit, leading Duckbill, received a radio message from a general at division, advising him to move to a particular hill where the general thought Ron could better defend his patrol. Ron snapped back at the general to get off the air and that he would get himself out of his own situation, thank you. No one ever reprimanded Ron, and the general later made himself the butt of his own joke about the incident.

In a nutshell, planning, coordination, and control of recon operations was the job of the S-3 and his staff.

After the briefing, I met with Colonel McKeon in his office, the back half of which served as his living quarters. He told me what he expected of a patrol leader and assured me I was in good hands, as most of the men in the battalion had a great deal of experience with reconnaissance operations and worked well together. On my first two patrols, he added, I would go in the capacity of an observer to learn what I could. He then assigned me to Bravo Company.

2

My company commander turned out to be a former All American football player named King Dixon. He gave me a rundown on what some of my duties would be and told me that the platoon I would be taking over was in the bush and wouldn't be back for several days. In the meantime, I was to settle in, draw my 782 gear—web belt and suspenders, magazine pouches, helmet, backpack, entrenching tool, bayonet, canteen, and poncho—and pick up a rifle from the armory. I was assigned to an officer's hooch, which differed from the enlisted quarters only in the number housed. Where six were billeted in the officers' hooches, twelve or more were in the enlisted. Like the officers, sergeants and staff NCOs lived in less crowded conditions. Company commanders lived alone in quarters in the rear of their company offices.

A lance corporal helped carry my luggage to the hooch, which was located on one of the hilltops overlooking the battalion area. Inside, I found an empty cot, dropped my gear next to it, and looked over my new home. A short, muscular lieutenant was asleep on a corner cot. The hooch measured fourteen by thirty feet, and like the mess hall, was built of two-by-fours, plywood, tin, and screens. The only difference here was that a cargo chute had been nailed to the rafters and draped in folds to form an insulating pocket below the roof. Without it, the room temperature would rise another ten to fifteen degrees, and the hooch would take on all the characteristics of an oven.

Recon had running water, but not all of the hooches were plumbed. This one was and came complete with a sink and faucet attached to the far end wall. I walked over to it, turned the faucet on, and sure enough, water ran out and down the drain. There was a brownish tint to it, but it was running water, suitable for washing and shaving and, who knew, maybe even drinking.

The furnishings were dusty and Spartan. Most of the shelves and cupboards were made from wood salvaged from shipping crates and ammo boxes then nailed to the walls. Cots and interior dividers were laid out according to the whims of the occupants, the arrangement lending a homey, lived-in touch to an otherwise drab rectangular box. Several of the officers had bought brightly painted wooden trunks from the Vietnamese to store personal belongings. What didn't fit into the trunks was stacked on the homemade shelves. A small table and four straight-backed chairs took up a corner near the sink, serving as a place to write letters or play cards. Each cot was covered with a mattress and mosquito net.

Grenades, flares, claymore mines, and rifle ammunition were haphazardly stored throughout the hooch. Being housed with enough explosives to wipe out a platoon did not exactly put me at ease, but my imagination told me they were needed to repel a Vietcong attack, which I had been led to believe was imminent. In reality, the battalion was located in a position that would have been very difficult to assault. That, plus it didn't offer much in the way of a target—not like the large, juicy Phantoms and C-130 transports roosting on the airfield at Da Nang.

The sleeping lieutenant and myself were not alone long when several patrol leaders came by to introduce themselves. One of them was Ken King, who in a few days would be taking me out on my first patrol. It was a battalion policy that all new patrol leaders bird-dog at least two patrols as part of a breaking-in process. By observing a patrol in the field, we were to learn the basics of a recon operation under combat conditions. I had been assured earlier by my company commander that Ken was a competent leader and I would benefit from his instructions.

Before chow, Ken took me by the armory, where I drew a .45-caliber pistol, an M-14 rifle, and a dozen magazines plus ammunition for both weapons. We dropped everything off at the hooch and headed for the mess hall.

On the way, I first heard then saw two CH-46s headed for recon's LZ Finch and asked about them. Ken said they carried a returning patrol, and we detoured to the hill overlooking the LZ to watch them come in. Several officers and men were gathered at the top of the hill, waiting to meet the patrol. The helicopters came in low, using most of the LZ to make a swooping approach that ended in a brief hover before setting down in a cloud of swirling dust. They dropped their ramps, and eight or nine Marines filed from the rear of each helicopter. All of the men in the returning patrol walked bowed forward to insure that their heads didn't come in contact with the spinning rotor blades—an episode that carried with it the guarantee of being dispatched immediately to the hereafter, a fate consigned to more than a few men in Vietnam, recon being no exception. As each man cleared the radius of the blades, he straightened up slightly, but continued to walk in a peculiar, pitched-forward gait, from which he had to tilt his head up and back if he wanted to look above the lower half of the man in front of him. The gait was accounted for by the large, heavy packs riding on their backs. All the water, food, ammunition, and pyrotechnics needed to sustain them for four to six days went into those packs, and they weighed from fifty to sixty pounds apiece.

Cuts and scrapes covered the arms, necks, and faces of the men, and many had the knees and seats torn out of their green jungle fatigues. All of them were unshaven, unwashed, and weary. However, as soon as a bantering between the returning patrol and the men on the hill began, spirits lifted, and large, toothy grins appeared on the dirty faces below.

As they started up the hill, those waiting on top went down to help carry their rifles and packs. The patrol leader stayed at the base of the hill, checking the chamber of each weapon as the men filed past. It was his job to insure that no loaded weapons were carried up the hill. Rule number one of Herman the German's surefire method for being relieved of command was to have your weapon or that of a subordinate discharge accidentally in an area designated as secure. Rule number two said that should the missile leaving the muzzle of that weapon strike another Marine, one's career was considered terminated. Herman hadn't mentioned anything about it hitting army or navy personnel, so I had to think he must have a sense of humor after all.

The helicopters didn't waste any time hanging around and soon departed in a cloud of blade-driven dust, which caused everyone at the bottom of the hill to stop what they were doing and turn away from the flying dirt and debris. Once the birds lifted off, they headed for the field at Da Nang.

As the men in the patrol reached the top of the hill and filed by me, I couldn't help but notice the distant look in their eyes. It was a sort of staring into a great unknown.

That night after chow, I cleaned my newly issued rifle and pistol and added a few items to my survival kit, which I hoped would serve me should the need to escape and evade ever arise. The kit was a pint-size plastic container, with a lid held in place by a pair of metal clips. In addition to fishing hooks, line, and sinker, there was now a small signal mirror, a razor blade, a bottle of water-purification tablets, some flint, and an extra firing pin and ejector spring for the rifle I had drawn.

After lights out, I took a shower beneath a two-hundred-gallon belly tank mounted on a wooden scaffold. During the day, the water in the tank was heated by the sun to hide-blistering temperatures, and it was only at night after the water had cooled down that most of us showered. Clean and smelling of soap for the first time in two days, I crawled onto my cot and dropped the mosquito net. Tired as I was, sleep failed to come. Adapting to the tropics, with its sweat inducing humidity, its sounds and smells, takes time, and the first few nights of tossing and turning to the accompaniment of a hundred unfamiliar sounds are followed by very little sleep.

A small fuck-you lizard crawled up one side of my mosquito net and took up its post on a supporting crossbar. These lizards had liberally inhabited the walls of our barracks in the Philippines, and the appearance of one on my cot was not cause for alarm. Its name came from the tiny croaking call it made that sounded a lot like, "fuck you," to which no one took offense. From its strategically located position, the lizard would spend the night picking off mosquitoes buzzing near the net.

Off toward Da Nang, bright illumination flares were being dropped from an orbiting plane, the light causing the shadows in the hooch to rise and creep along the walls as the flares descended under their oscillating parachutes.

It was then the fact that I didn't have to be in Vietnam drifted back to me, like it had so many times in the last few weeks.

In 1957, high school over with and suffering from an incurable itch for adventure, I enlisted in the Marine Corps for three years, hoping to cure the itch. After twelve weeks of boot camp and a month of infantry training, I was assigned to a guard company at the Marine Air Wing, El Toro, California. Boot camp and infantry training had been fast-paced and exciting, and I yearned for the adventure that was sure to follow. However, at El Toro, the reality that adventure was not going to come in the form of checking liberty cards and waving cars through the main gate quickly set in. I wanted something else. I began making weekly treks to the company office to request a transfer to a line company on Okinawa. Weekly, my requests were turned down. Six months went by. Thinking I would never get out of El Toro and see the world, I jumped at an opening in a guard company in the Philippines and got it.

Wet, green, unlike any place I had ever been to, the Philippines fulfilled my every dream of what an exotic island country would be like; adventure had to be just around the corner.

It didn't come.

While the Philippines always intrigued me, the duty did not. After a few months of flanking every post in the naval magazine area and some that weren't, I became convinced that a monkey with an M-1 rifle strapped to his back and a bayonet belted to his ass could, except for reporting in hourly by phone, do the job as well as I could. I still longed for a tour with an infantry company.

It was there at the Marine Barracks Cubi Point, after a run-in with the first sergeant, that my rank of private first class became terminal. We called our first sergeant Doom-Pat, a name given to him because of the curious slapping sound a game foot made when it hit the deck as he stalked the barracks. Hostile, aggressive, long on remembering, his arrival in the squad bays invariably signalled the pat of doom for some luckless soul. Couple Doom-Pat and his penchant for referring to us all as "No good, yellow-bellied sons a bitches" with a bird colonel, who had a passion for locking men up for the slightest infraction of the Uniform Code of Military Justice, and we had a difficult situation. Several of the staff NCOs and all of the officers fell right into line with the punitive atmosphere that pervaded our barracks. As a result, there was a time when things got so bad, we had nearly as many men in the brig as we did standing duty, and we converted to running guard status for six weeks, on twenty-four hours and off twelve. Mine had not been an offense punishable by court-martial, and I did not go to jail. I merely had a heated exchange with the first sergeant that ended all hopes of making corporal.

When my eighteen months were up, I was glad to go home, leaving on a World War II Liberty ship on the second of December, 1959, and arriving in San Francisco on the thirty-first.

After spending two weeks at home on leave, I reported to Camp Pendleton where I was assigned to 1st Recon for a taste of what the Marine Corps was really like. The work was hard, but I loved being in the field, and the officers and NCOs were among the finest I had ever served with. However, when the offer of a promotion to corporal was made if I extended my service time, the memory of the barracks at Cubi Point with its abusive sergeants and endless hours of flanking post was too strong. I took my discharge and went home to San Gabriel, California.

I tried college for a few weeks, failed, and went back to work at my old job as a grocery clerk in the village market, while living at home with my parents. The days grew tedious and long.

Determined to make something of myself, I returned to college with the intentions of becoming a teacher. This time, I took a serious interest in my classes and studied hard. However, my love life suffered horribly. After eighteen months in the Philippines, being adored by the women of Olongapo when I wasn't completely broke, I found it hard to relate to college girls who kept insisting I join a fraternity and upgrade from a Volkswagen before they would go out with me. Eventually, I took up with an older woman who was glad to have me.

Then, when the school year of 1962 began, the hometown paper ran a series of pictures of the newly hired teachers in our district. Among them was a second grade teacher, fresh out of college, a slender, smiling brunette whom I fell instantly in love with. Her name was Roberta Hernandez, and she had been assigned to the school where my mother taught. Through my mother, I arranged an introduction, and Roberta and I were soon dating. She liked my Volkswagen.

In the summer of 1963, we were married and set up housekeeping in a small, two-bedroom rental in a nice neighborhood. Roberta supported us both while I went to school. We were supposed to have two kids, a quiet life of teaching, and a home in the country.

A year went peacefully by.

Far away, a country I had always known as French Indochina was stirring and convulsing, and something inside me grew restless. I knew what it was; the adventure I had missed the first time around in the Corps was now out there waiting. I wanted to see that elephant I'd been hearing about since I was a kid. I wanted to save the world. And I wanted that parade down Broadway.

My junior year in college, Roberta four months pregnant,

a part-time job in a factory driving me up a wall, I decided I'd had enough of civilian life. Without telling my wife, I called a Marine recruiter and asked about the Officer Candidate Program—he'd be happy as hell to see me!

When I broke the news of my decision to go back into the Marine Corps and make a career of it to Roberta, she was afraid at first and cried. Realizing I wasn't going to change my mind, she dried her tears and became completely supportive. The summer of 1965, I went through the twelve-week Platoon Leaders' Class at Quantico, Virginia, and finished near the top of my class. In the fall, I began my senior year in college with renewed enthusiasm. After all, I was about to become a second lieutenant and save the world.

Only, as I lay on my cot watching the flares descend over Da Nang, the world looked too damn big to save, and that elephant was starting to take on a horror of its own.

I thought about my wife and daughter and how much I already missed them. Little things, like a shopping trip or a Sunday drive, taken for granted a few weeks ago now seemed important. The hard reality of leaving and possibly never seeing them again hadn't set in until a few days before my time to ship out came. I had just completed the six-month-long officers Basic school and I was home on leave with my family when we decided to go for a picnic in a nearby park. Roberta was four months pregnant with our second child, and Jodi, our daughter, wasn't quite two years old. I had taken an eight-millimeter camera along to record our day in the park and was shooting pictures of Jodi when a feeling of dread and loneliness came on me with all the subtlety of a dropped piano. There she was in her red jump suit, laughing and chasing after a flock of ducks, her light brown curls bouncing and catching the sun, and me following her every move with the camera, when the world suddenly stopped. The fear of never seeing her again caused me to double over in pain, and I had to lie down on a bench until the feeling passed. Later, I tried to shake it off, but something inside me had changed. The driving force to be a Marine in combat had been replaced by a glimpse at a future that was tenuous at best, and I realized I was not prepared to die fighting for the glory and sovereignty of the valiantly struggling people of the Republic of South Vietnam. I wanted to be present and accounted for when my kids graduated from college and to delight in the antics of my grandchildren and not exist merely as a memory dragged up at all suitable after-dinner occasions and mentioned as having been killed in a far-off, forgotten place, fighting for a cause no one seemed to remember.

Thinking about it while listening to the hammering of an artillery battery down the road did not help me get to sleep, and it was far into the night before I finally dozed off.

The next morning, the sun was out, and the world was still there. I shaved, dressed, and headed for chow, where I had breakfast with John Dunn, who was on his way back out to the bush. Before leaving, John introduced me to the patrol leader who had come in the afternoon before. He was a short, grinning, career Marine named Joe Campbell, who kept up a constant line of chatter as we walked back from the mess hall. Joe took me to his hooch and gave me a pencil flare and set of colored flares to go with it. "You might need this," he said, digging the set out of a box filled with tiny flares and the pencillike tubes used to fire them. "Hang onto it. They're hard to come by," he added. Joe then sat down on the edge of a cot, took a beer from a small, Japanese-made refrigerator, and offered it to me. I thanked him for the flares but declined the offer of a beer. The flare gun was the first of many gifts I was to receive from veteran patrol leaders, who readily shared the extra items they had squirreled away among their standard-issue equipment. Many of those items came from the army, whose supply system ranked as a supermarket compared to the mom-and-pop store run by the Marine Corps. The army had unparalleled access to the goodies in the system, and it was the duty of every good Marine to get his hands on them. Hence the pencil flare.

"You'll like recon," Joe said, after he had taken a few sips from his can of beer. "Remember when you were a kid and loved to play hide-and-go-seek? Well, that's how it is in the bush, only with bullets. Just make sure you tag the other guy first!'' Joe then let out a long howl of laughter that brought tears to his eyes. "And you want to keep a low profile while you're out there. Like this," he said, picking up a helmet and placing it over a pair of boots. "That's exactly how I look when I get off the birds." Joe almost fell off his cot over that one. The best I could do was make a nervous croaking sound. To me, the bush was still the great unknown, and even approaching it in thought was done with trepidation—uncontrolled laughter was not yet included on the agenda.

When recon Marines spoke of the bush, the word was applied in a generic sense to mean being in the field. Whether a patrol was operating on a bald hill or in dense jungle, it was in the bush. The term had nothing to do with what grew on the mountains and in the valleys of Vietnam.

After Joe had passed on a few more words of wisdom, I left, dropped by my hooch to pick up my rifle and several magazines full of ammo, and walked down to the LZ to test fire the M-14. A long, sandbagged bunker, dug into the side of the hill, served as a test site. I got in line behind a group of Marines firing their weapons into the hill. The sandbags served to prevent rounds from being accidentally discharged up, which would put them in the direction of division, God forbid, or to the right or left, which would cause the colonel some concern on one side and anyone traveling the road to Da Nang on the other. There was an unexplained gap in the roof of the bunker that did allow an occasional round to ricochet high over the hill and into a wild flight above the battalion area. These rounds must have been considered harmless, because ricochet they did for as long as I was at Reasoner. However, anyone stopping a ricochet would probably think otherwise.

When my turn came, I stepped up to the bunker and began slow firing through the first magazine. Then I turned the selector to automatic and fired the next two magazines in bursts of three and four rounds. Satisfied the rifle was in working order, I returned to the hooch and spent an hour stripping, cleaning, and inspecting each part of the weapon.

There were no burred or damaged pieces, but most of the
bluing was worn off, and the barrel was shiny from having
been cleaned too often with steel wool—a method frowned
on by the Marine Corps but the only one that quickly removed rust. Since the rifling was unpitted and the bolt and
operating rod worked smoothly in the receiver, I didn't return the rifle to the armory and request a new, freshly blued
one. I zeroed the windage and cranked the elevation up to
eight clicks. There wouldn't be a chance to range fire the rifle
before going on my first patrol, so I went by the book and
hoped the eight clicks of elevation would put me on target
for anything up to two-hundred meters.

  Finished, I put the rifle away, changed into a pair of shorts
and tennis shoes, and went for a long, hard run.

3

My fourth day with the battalion dawned foggy, overcast, and not likely to improve. It was the morning I was scheduled to make my first patrol. The night before, I had spent several hours organizing, cleaning, and stowing my gear in the lightweight frame pack issued by battalion supply. Unlike the small, high-riding, World War II–field pack, with its web straps designed to destroy the shoulders, the frame pack was built to carry larger, heavier loads by distributing most of the weight to the hips. Thirty percent of the weight was still borne by the shoulders but without the painful chafing and numbing effect left by the old-style packs.

I packed with an eye toward water and firepower: ten canteens of water and over four hundred rounds of ammunition for the M-14. For food, I stuck to those C rations that didn't need to be heated before they were eaten—fruit cocktail, high-energy candy bars, peanut butter, John Wayne crackers, and a can of beans and franks, which didn't congeal in the can like many of the other "heavies" did. If I stuck to the menu, there would be enough food to last five days. In addition to food, bullets, and water, there were four grenades, a poncho, a pop-up flare, two illumination grenades, a stick of grease paint, toilet paper, mosquito repellent, a P-38 can opener attached to a shoelace tied to the pack frame, three large compress bandages, and a toothbrush for cleaning my rifle. Some of the ammunition was carried in magazines in pouches attached to a web belt supported by suspenders. Also attached to the belt were two canteens and more hand grenades. To the suspenders, I had taped a small pouch hous-

21

ing my compass (secured by another shoelace), a smoke grenade, and the pencil-flare kit Joe had given to me. My dog tags were taped together and hung on a chain around my neck.

Ken King would be leading the patrol. The area assigned to us was known to harbor several Vietcong units, and our chances of making contact with one or more of them were high. I had a topographic map of the area and had gone over it in detail with Ken. On it, he penciled in the primary and alternate routes through our RAOR. We were to be inserted on a ridge, high above the southwest end of Antenna Valley, so named for the extensive radio communications network the enemy had established in the region. Our mission was to locate any VC units operating in the area, report on their activities, and bring them under fire with supporting arms or draw them into an ambush if we could. At the end of four days, we would be extracted near the valley floor.

The ridge we would be working was indistinguishable from a thousand others like it that had no end or beginning and twisted and turned their way from Vietnam to Laos and beyond.

I was given a list of radio frequencies and call signs for battalion, two artillery batteries, and division. These I kept with the map in a waterproof packet. The patrol would be carrying two PRC-25 radios, one on a battalion frequency and the other on the frequency of our primary supporting artillery unit. Which in this case was a 105 battery, capable of lobbing rounds out to 11,500 meters. The backup 155 battery could shoot out to 14,500 meters.

Ken's call sign was Eyelet; battalion's was Beacon Light. Since patrols were referred to by call sign rather than platoon or squad, the patrol leaders were also referred to by call sign. All unit commanders, regardless of the size of the unit, had the number six appended to their call signs. Thus, Ken was Eyelet Six.

That morning, I got up early, took a shower under the wing tank, and shaved. There weren't any spare jungle fatigues or boots available in the battalion, so I dressed in my regular

Stateside issue, which were both heavy and hot and slow to dry out when wet. Also, the leather boots had a tendency to hold water and had to be removed and drained several times a day during the monsoon season in order to prevent immersion foot, a serious problem in the tropics that could lead to crippling if allowed to go untreated. After I dressed, I rubbed a handful of mosquito repellent onto my face, then coated it with black-and-green grease paint. I did the same for my hands and arms, first applying the repellent, which broke down the paint and made it go on thicker and easier. The repellent also ate most plastics, and I often wondered what it did for my skin.

Prepared for battle, I went off to the mess hall, only to discover that I couldn't eat prior to going on patrol. Just looking at the food on the serving line made me sick to my stomach. I took a piece of toast and a cup of coffee and sat down at a table. The coffee went down all right, but I only ate half of the toast before pushing it away.

Back at the hooch, Ken gave me a few last-minute instructions and told me once again that my job was to observe and learn and I was to listen to and follow the directions of the lowest ranked man in the patrol. We gathered up our gear and went down to the LZ.

The morning fog had burned off, but the sky was overcast with a low ceiling. Our ride would be late.

A total of fourteen of us made up the patrol. Included was a gunnery sergeant who had been assigned to look after me.

With the monsoon season still on, it was difficult to get patrols in and out of the bush. Full platoons were going out rather than squad-size patrols, the thinking being that a large patrol would have a better chance of surviving if it ran into serious trouble and the weather prevented help from reaching it. However, a recon platoon is smaller than an infantry platoon—twenty-four men versus a thundering forty or more. Due to casualties, rotation, R & R, and illness, few platoons anywhere in Vietnam were up to full strength. That morning was no exception, and the fourteen, including myself, were all that mustered for the patrol.

We sat, leaned back into our packs with our feet sprawled

in the dirt, and waited. It drizzled, then it got hot, then it drizzled some more, and the wind came up, and it got cold.

No birds.

For the tenth time that morning, the gunny started down his list of dos and don'ts.

"Lieutenant, you gotta keep your eyes open. You gotta look in the trees; you gotta look down the trail; you gotta look in the bushes. The last thing you want to do is walk into an ambush and get your men killed. If anybody's gonna be surprised, make sure it's the gooks, not you. You understand, Lieutenant?"

My head bobbed up and down as I took in everything he said.

"Going in can turn into your worst nightmare. If the gooks catch you in the birds on the approach to the LZ, they'll make hamburger out of you. If the bird crashes because the pilot suddenly drops dead, or there's a loss of power, or you hit a downdraft, or an engine fails, your ass has probably had it. But if you're still alive, don't hang around pickin' your nose. Get out and regroup fast because Charlie isn't going to cut you any slack on account of half your men are barbecuing in a burning bird. You got to move and keep thinking. You get careless, you adopt a don't-give-a-shit attitude, and you're gonna die, Lieutenant."

As he spoke, visions of going up in a ball of fire on my first patrol hovered before me.

"Now, on this particular LZ, there's a big rock. Once we're in, stay away from it because it's probably booby-trapped; recon's used the LZ before. When we start moving, watch out for any branches or vines across a trail. Don't touch or pick up anything unless one of us hands it to you. Put your feet down where the man in front of you puts his down. Look where he looks, go where he goes. Don't talk in anything above a whisper and then keep it to a minimum. Learn to communicate with your hands. 'Swift, Silent, Deadly,' it's the battalion motto, and it's the key to survival."

The gunny's list was long, and in between deliveries, he

fell into long periods of brooding silence. He obviously didn't want the death of a green second lieutenant on his hands.

We waited right up until lunchtime. By then, my stomach had settled, and when we went to chow, I was able to eat without feeling sick.

Back on the LZ, the afternoon went about like the morning. The S-3 bunker kept sending down messages that the overcast was about to lift and the birds would come any minute. But such was not the case.

At 1700, we were told to secure.

Being shut out by the weather was not uncommon, but according to the gunny, being left in the bush an extra day or two happened more often than being left in the battalion area. "We lucked out with another day in the rear," he said, grinning, as we climbed the hill and headed for the showers.

The next morning, the ceiling was above two thousand feet, and I was certain we would go out. I put on my war paint and headed for chow, which once again was toast and coffee.

At 0800, we saddled up and went down to the LZ, where the gunny went through his litany of dos and don'ts and warned me again about the rock on the LZ, which by now had taken on a sinister aspect of its own. "Beware the rock," my mind kept telling me.

I was determined to give it a wide berth.

At 0830, the helicopters arrived. There were two CH-46 transports, trailed by a pair of Huey gunships to provide fire support. The gunships would go in first to check out the LZ, draw fire, or shoot up any position likely to hold the enemy. In the event VC were on or near the LZ, an alternate one would be used.

The birds landed and shut down. The pilots got out, and Ken and the gunny went over for a briefing that lasted fifteen minutes. In the meantime, the rest of us filed on board the 46s according to a prearranged order. I was to ride with the gunny and five other men; Ken would be in the lead bird with the rest of the patrol.

I climbed the ramp and took a seat halfway along one of the bulkheads. The seats were unpadded nylon stretched over aluminum frames and strictly utilitarian. I sat with my pack on, leaned forward, and planted the butt of my rifle on the deck for support.

Briefing over, the pilot and copilot boarded, climbed into their seats, and cranked up the engines. The crew chief closed the ramp, then quickly ran through a preflight check. Satisfied everything was in working order, he gave the pilot a thumbs-up and took a seat next to a .50-caliber machine gun mounted in a forward window. The gunny sat opposite, near a second gun. For protection, the crew members wore flak jackets of thick, armored plates, while we wore neither flak jacket nor helmet, items considered to be too heavy and cumbersome for recon work. I was acutely aware of the fact that our fatigues and soft covers didn't measure up to the task of stopping bullets and was more than envious of the armor-clad crew.

The noise of the engines made it impossible to carry on a conversation, and the only way to get a message across was to yell in a listener's ear while executing a vigorous sign language. Usually, I never understood a word anyone said and spent most airborne trips in contemplation.

None of the porthole-shaped windows had Plexiglas in them, all having either been shot out or removed by the crew to provide firing ports for the men inside.

The pilot increased the RPMs, and we lifted off. Nose angled slightly downward, we shot across the LZ and the rice paddies beyond.

The Hueys were already airborne and rose to make a pass over the battalion area before taking the lead of our small armada. Near Da Nang, we turned south to avoid the traffic around the airfield, the pilot keeping the bird at about two hundred feet. Tearing along at close to one hundred knots at that level is an exhilarating experience, and I twisted around to get my face near a porthole and look out. Below, villages of thatched huts, clustered around flooded rice fields worked by peasants in conical straw hats, flashed by. A flock of ducks began a panic-driven run for the safety of a nearby stream, with their keeper running after them, angrily shaking his long herding pole at us. A group of Marines in line outside a shack in Dog Patch looked up, some giving us the finger. The man next to me laughed and indicated they were waiting to get laid. We raced down the Song Cau Do, dotted with fishing boats carrying tall, graceful outrigger nets that dipped and rose from the muddy waters of the river. Then we were up and over a railroad bridge that had been blown and rebuilt so many times it looked like Issie's Junkyard back home. We left the river, and the birds began to gain altitude as we came to the edge of the vast Dai Loc plain and all its violent uncertainties. The ground below was secure only as long as Marines trod it, and then they'd better watch where they put their feet down.

Once we reached two thousand feet, we leveled off and began the forty-kilometer run to Geo Coc and the rock on the LZ. Houses were now small squares and people ants, riding or walking to wherever the morning took them. The whine of the turbine engines began to sing a strange, high-pitched song that seemed to call from some faraway place, beckoning. It was a song that would burn itself into my memory and haunt me through one sweat-soaked nightmare after another in the years to come. It was a song of gunfire, hydraulic fluid, and burning fuel, and a hundred ways to die.

We crossed the wide, meandering Song Thu Bon, swollen and muddy in runoff, and flew above the low foothills to the mountains beyond, where the clouds formed thick and dark on the peaks.

Near the mountains, the birds began to orbit, then the gunny yelled and pointed for me to look down. Far below, the Hueys were making pass after pass on our LZ. I could see them firing rockets into the side of a hill and wondered if the LZ was hot and whether or not we'd be looking for another one. Just then, Ken's bird dropped and started its approach. We went through a final orbit, and I lost track of the lead bird, the LZ, and all sense of direction as we plunged toward the jungle.

The gunny yelled again, this time to lock and load. With trembling fingers, I slipped a magazine into my rifle. The man next to me cranked a round into the chamber, stood, and rested the muzzle of his rifle in a porthole. I watched him, then did the same.

The ground came up fast, and suddenly a large grassy knoll was before us, and the ramp was dropping. The instant the helicopter set down, we were racing down the ramp and spreading out over the knoll. I searched frantically about for the dreaded rock, and in my hurry to leave the bird discovered I had almost run up one side of it. There it was, large, looming, gray, with me next to it. Expecting the rock to blow up at any minute, I cautiously backed away and put some distance between me and it.

The CH-46s cleared off, and the Hueys made a final pass to check on us. Satisfied we were safely on the ground, they left.

Ken and the gunny were in the middle of the LZ, orienting their maps with the ground. Having prided myself on the map work I'd done in Basic School, I pulled mine out to run my own check.

I couldn't find a single reference point. The tall trees around us cut off all view of the surrounding mountains, leaving nothing to take a compass reading from. I stuck the map back inside my fatigue jacket and decided to find out where we were by asking.

Keeping low, I crossed the LZ and joined the CP group, made up of Ken, the gunny, and the primary tac radio operator.

"We're going up that hill," Ken whispered and pointed to a forest of towering trees.

"What hill?" I asked, unable to make out where one lump in the jungle left off and another began.

He ignored me and told the gunny to get the men in line and moving.

As I fell in, the gunny passed me, grinning, and said, "Looks like the rock wasn't booby-trapped after all, Lieutenant."

I tried to muster a knowing smile.

We moved off the LZ and into the jungle, where the trees rose to one hundred and more feet, and the triple canopy cut the light by half.

Our pace was slow and steady, and we maintained intervals of twelve to fifteen feet between each man.

The men around me methodically and systematically scanned the jungle, while taking care where they put their feet down. Where they seemed to blend and flow, I groped and stumbled awkwardly. Where they saw an abandoned harbor site or the hint of a trail, I saw only a tangle of bamboo or fallen branches. And since communications were kept to a minimum, I was completely baffled by what we were doing and where we were going. Finally, I gave up trying and just concentrated on putting my feet down where the man in front of me put his.

Unused to the stifling heat and humidity and the claustrophobic closeness of the jungle, I was having trouble breathing. My legs soon turned to rubber, and I wanted to lie down and take a long nap and wake up somewhere else. Fear told me my every move was being watched by an unseen enemy, and I began frantically looking for him. He was out there, waiting for the right moment to put a bullet in me. His instructions were to shoot the officers first, and he instinctively knew the tall redhead was a green, bumbling second lieutenant.

Again and again, I shook the feeling off, only to have it return within seconds, and the search for the unseen foe begin all over again. He was out there. I knew he was. I just couldn't see him!

Soon, the lone enemy grew to squad then platoon size. But the others in the patrol, oblivious to the fact that I was certain we were outnumbered and surrounded, marched on.

An hour went by before we took a break on a rocky outcrop overlooking Antenna Valley. Shaking and dripping with sweat, I eased out of my pack and took several long, nervous pulls on a canteen. My shirt and pack were soaked through, and I thought that at this rate I would dehydrate and die before the enemy lurking in the bushes had a chance to shoot me. Somehow, I had to get it firmly established in my mind that there *couldn't* be a Vietcong behind every tree and bush. Henceforth, I told myself, I would worry only about the likely bushes and trees. The problem was, I couldn't tell the likely ones from the unlikely.

We sat and listened for movement around us, but the only sound I heard came from the never-ending chorus of insects and the pounding of my heart.

Satisfied we weren't being followed, Ken gave the signal to saddle up, and we moved on.

For most of the day, we hiked up one hill and down another. Every few minutes, we stopped to listen and watch, and although one tree in the jungle still didn't look any different from another, my fears began to lessen as I slowly became attuned to my surroundings.

Late in the day, we stopped on a hill where several trees had fallen to form a natural breastwork. Word was passed we'd be spending the night on the hill and to eat before dark. I slipped out of my pack and sat down, my back against a log. I took a can of John Wayne crackers and peanut butter out of my pack and started opening the can, sawing at the metal with my P-38. The gunny reached across the log, took the can, pressed a thumb down against the lid and silently worked the opener around the rim.

"Take your time, Lieutenant. You can't afford the luxury of making any more noise than is absolutely necessary," he whispered. "Charlie just might be behind the next tree."

He handed the can back, and I ate for the first time since breakfast.

Ken sent two men out to make a sweep around our position and look for signs of the enemy. He told them to be back before dark. Then they were gone, swallowed by the jungle. It is a strange feeling to see a man take a few steps and disappear.

Cold and wet with sweat, I took the poncho out of my pack, wrapped up in it, and leaned against the log, trying to get comfortable. An incoming flight of mosquitoes soon had me up and digging through my pack for a bottle of repellent.

Just before dark, the two men returned to report that the hilltop was free of any recent signs of the enemy. The gunny got up and walked the perimeter, whispering last-minute instructions and making sure an every-other-man watch had been established. While the gunny was checking on the men, Ken called the 105 battery and gave them the coordinates of our night defensive fires, then reported our location to Beacon Light. Operating as far out as we were, our messages to battalion had to be relayed through a Marine unit at An Hoa, fifteen kilometers to the northwest. While we waited for a reply, Ken whispered that it was not uncommon to go through one and sometimes two relays before reaching battalion. Adding, that working through relay stations always brought home the reminder of just how far out and alone we were.

Beacon Light called back in a few minutes, acknowledging our situation report.

Then, with scarcely any twilight time at all, it was dark. So dark, I couldn't see my hand in front of my face. Around me, thousands of tiny phosphorescent lights given off by dead and decaying vegetation began to come on. Long eerie strands of them seemed to float in space or crawl over the ground, only to mysteriously go out and later come back on. The lights brought with them all the comforts of a graveyard after dark.

I settled back in my poncho, burrowed a hollow for my shoulders, and tried to relax. But thoughts of where we were and who was out there and what a firefight in absolute dark might be like plagued me, and I couldn't sleep.

Something long, spindly, and silent dropped onto my face and ran down my neck into my fatigue jacket. I sat up in a panic, throwing my poncho from me, and slapping down the front of my jacket. The gunny hissed me into silence. I reached inside my shirt and fished out what must have been a giant daddy longlegs and threw it over the log in the gunny's direction. Then I lay down, buttoned my

jacket tightly around my neck, and crammed my jungle
hat down over my ears.

The luminous dial on my watch read 2100 hours.

The high-pitched whine of a mosquito set up between
my cap and one ear. I slapped myself on the side of the
head, and the whine stopped. Seconds later, it started
again.

A mist that soon turned into a drizzle began, and the mosquitoes left. I pulled my poncho over my head to get out of
the rain, but began to sweat so hard in the rubberized compartment, I had to come up for air and leave my face exposed.

My watch read 2115.

The rain stopped, and something short and furry
dropped onto my face and tried to run up my nose. I
grabbed it and flung it into the dark. The mosquitoes came
back. This time they ignored the repellent and went right
to work on my neck and face. In the distance, something
that sounded like the world's slowest woodpecker began
to beat on a tree.

At 2130, the rain started again.

It didn't stop until 0300. I know, because I checked my
watch every five minutes until it did. By then I was cold,
soaked through, and wishing the sun were up.

When at last it did come up, I rose and stretched. Stiff and
lumpy faced, there was an unrecognizable taste in my mouth.
I popped half a stick of gum in my mouth to kill the taste
and looked around, congratulating myself for having survived my first night in the jungle. In the dim, early morning
light, I discovered that except for those on watch, the people
around me were asleep. It was a trick I needed to master.

The second day was a lot like the first. We kept moving,
looking, and listening, and I was only slightly less confused
than the day before.

Late in the afternoon, we found a crude shelter made
out of bamboo and thatched leaves and large enough to
house four people. Beneath it was a bunker reinforced

with logs and rocks. Signs of recent occupancy were fresh, and Ken and the gunny seemed to think the enemy was not far away.

We spent the night on a trail where the vegetation was low enough to see over when I stood up, and although our surroundings were far less claustrophobic than the previous night's, I did not like the choice of harbor sites. If the enemy were moving down the trail, they would surely stumble on us in the dark.

Again, I spent most of the night checking my watch and did not sleep.

On the morning of the third day, Ken and the gunny spotted a squad of Vietcong, four hundred meters from the observation post we had established. They were in a grassy hollow, cooking breakfast over an open fire. According to the gunny, they looked like Boy Scouts on an outing. I asked for the binoculars to see for myself, but after looking for several minutes could not find either the VC or their campfire. The gunny had me sight along his arm and look again.

Nothing.

Ken called arty to shoot but was told there would be a delay due to a priority fire mission.

We waited.

In a little while the 105 battery threw a few rounds our way, but the shots were so far off, the gunny, who was observing through the glasses, said the VC didn't even look up from their breakfast. He made some adjustments and called for another round. After a long delay, it freight-trained down the mountain and exploded in the valley below.

I asked if I could call in the next shot. The radio operator gave me the handset, and the gunny gave me the corrections.

"Red Rover One, this is . . ."

The gunny and the radio operator reached out and yanked the handset away from me.

"Goddamn it, Lieutenant, whisper!" the gunny whispered, returning the handset.

I cupped my hand over my mouth and tried again. A few seconds later I got an "On the way."

The shot crashed into the far side of the mountain.

"Nowhere near," whispered the gunny.

Red Rover called to say another priority fire mission had come up and they would not be available to shoot for an hour or more.

Ken and the gunny held a brief discussion and decided to go after the VC in the hollow.

We saddled up and moved out.

Between us and the VC lay a steep, brush-choked ravine. We started down one side, clinging to the brush to keep from falling. The sun was out, and I was feeling the effects of the heat, humidity, and apprehension. There was no canopy to keep the temperatures down, and halfway into the ravine, my head felt like it was about to explode. I stopped, removed my Jeff's-Sporting-Goods camouflaged special from my head, and tore out the insulated lining before I dropped dead from heatstroke.

We hit the bottom and started up the opposite side.

When we reached the top, we were in a forest of saplings bristling with metal fragments. Everywhere, trees were studded with bits and pieces of shrapnel, the result of some mighty duel between heavy artillery and five acres of new growth. Scattered on the ground were hundreds of propaganda leaflets urging the enemy to abandon the "Forces of Evil" and join the fight for "Truth and Justice." I couldn't resist picking up a few. Most of the leaflets were printed in color and featured a soldier on horseback waving the flag of the Republic of Vietnam. He looked positively heroic. I stuffed him into a pocket.

We left the forest and moved across a grassy saddle to a low ridge, where we deployed on a skirmish line. The corpsman and I were on the extreme left flank. Although I still hadn't seen the enemy, I could now smell their cooking fire and hear them chattering on the other side of the ridge. Bent low, we moved toward the top. My mouth was as dry as a stone, and my breathing was shallow and quick. With trembling hands, I checked to make sure the safety on my rifle was off and the bolt solidly home. Suddenly my drill instructor's voice of years ago started going through my head— "Breathe, relax, aim, squeeze." I kept repeating it over and over as we got into position. "Breathe, relax, aim, squeeze. Breathe, relax . . ." The men on my right were up and shouldering their weapons. I stood, slammed the butt of my rifle into my shoulder and sighted the weapon with both eyes open, looking for a target. Ken yelled to open fire, and a volley crashed out. Everyone seemed to have something to shoot at but me—I still hadn't seen a single Vietcong! Someone yelled out, "Get that guy on the ridge! Get that guy on the ridge!" What ridge, for Christ sake! I searched frantically for the guy on the ridge. Several rounds popped back our way as the enemy got off a few shots on the run, but they had already gone by before I realized we were being shot at and couldn't get too excited about them. Fifty meters away a long wake was racing through the tall grass. I aimed at the head of the wake, fired three rounds, and the wake suddenly stopped. I had no way of knowing whether I hit my target or it just went to ground. The gunny turned and yelled, "Get your ass down, Lieutenant!" Thinking we were about to be overrun by a frontal assault, I hit the deck and assumed the prone position—rifle tucked firmly into shoulder, legs spread, toes dug in, left hand supporting the barrel of the weapon, finger held lightly on the trigger. Then I looked up and discovered the rest of the patrol was still standing and firing.

"Just wanted to make sure I don't have to write any letters to your wife, Lieutenant," the gunny hollered.

Sheepishly, I got back to my feet and looked down into the hollow. Not a soul was in sight, and the shooting had stopped.

Ken opted not to press the attack and gave the order to move back to a nearby hill. We pitched several tear-gas grenades into the hollow to keep the enemy from regrouping and withdrew to the hill. Once there, we waited for a counterattack, but none came, and we set out on a twisting, turning trek that often doubled back on itself, where we set up a hasty ambush to shoot down any who chose to follow. We repeated the procedure for over an hour without results. Ken and the gunny were certain we had killed two of the enemy and wounded three others and believed the sudden violence of the firefight had demoralized them enough to discourage pursuit.

Night found us back in the jungle, where we harbored next to a large pyramid of tightly fitted stones, a surveyor's benchmark, placed long ago by the French.

I managed a few hours sleep that night.

In the morning, we dropped down on the Antenna Valley side of the mountain, looking for an LZ. By noon we had reached the edge of the valley, where we found ourselves in a banana plantation, covering acre after acre of the surrounding foothills. Nearby was a series of terraced rice paddies, now abandoned and dry. We moved onto a tree-lined terrace and set up a perimeter behind the stone-and-mud dikes. Ken checked in with Beacon Light and was told the birds were on the way and would be up on our frequency any minute. We waited in the dry paddy.

About the time the radio operator reported he was in contact with the birds, we heard voices coming from one of the terraces below. Two men worked their way forward to investigate, then returned to report that a small group of Vietnamese were moving along a trail about one hundred meters away. They didn't appear to be armed.

By then, we could hear the helicopters, and Ken radioed in the position of the Vietnamese. A gunship dropped down to look them over. The gunny threw a yellow smoke grenade onto the LZ, and the pilot of the lead bird acknowledged. While the gunships buzzed the Vietnamese and the hills around us, the CH-46s dropped down to pick us up.

Moments before they touched down, we were bent low and running for the open ramps, and the wheels of the first bird were still off the ground when the lead man hit the ramp and disappeared inside. We loaded in a matter of seconds and were still standing when the birds lifted off.

Five hundred feet up, someone down in the jungle began shooting at us, the rounds popping by every few seconds. When we were out of range, the shooting stopped.

The birds swung into a heading for home.

4

Back in the area, we underwent a half-hour debriefing, conducted by the battalion intelligence officer in a room adjacent to the personnel office. Most of the questions asked dealt with enemy strength, location, activity, and type of weapons they carried. We also went over the route we had taken, describing the terrain features and mapping trails and LZs for any future patrols working the same area. Colonel McKeon wanted a detailed account of the ambush we'd sprung and seemed pleased with the action from beginning to end.

It was there in the confines of the debriefing room that I noticed for the first time how badly we smelled. The odor coming from us was a combination of unwashed bodies, decaying vegetation, and fear-induced sweat. If I hadn't been a part of it, I would have probably left the room.

After the debriefing, I was approached by a second lieutenant who had just checked into the battalion. He kept asking me what it felt like to get shot at. I told him it had all happened so fast I didn't have an opinion. Then he asked the same question again. And again. I didn't see any point to it and excused myself to take a shower.

We had less than three days before our next patrol.

My mail hadn't caught up with me, and it was more than two weeks since I'd heard from home. Roberta was living with her parents, and I knew she and Jodi were in good hands, but still I worried about them and needed some written reassurance that all was well. The first night back, I wrote down an account of the patrol, leaving out the contact with

the enemy, and mailed it home along with my love. In the letter, I tried to make it sound as though a recon platoon leader's job was a safe one and not to worry.

After chow the next morning, I spent an hour or more going over the record books of the men in the platoon I would soon be leading. They were due in off patrol that afternoon, and I wanted to learn what I could about them before we met. Reading through the records, I learned that most of them were under the drinking and voting ages of the states they came from. Four were married, six had brothers in the service, and none were the sons of congressmen, senators, or presidents.

Their conduct and proficiency marks were all good, and Captain Dixon spoke well of them and the platoon sergeant, Staff Sergeant Below. I was anxious to meet the men who were to make up my first command, and when the birds carrying them came in that afternoon, I was waiting on the hill above the LZ. Watching them as they climbed the hill, I thought how much older they looked than their record books indicated. When Sergeant Below was through checking weapons, he approached me, saluted, and introduced himself.

"I was told a six-foot-three redhead would be taking over the platoon, sir. You must be him," he said.

I smiled, and we shook hands.

"We've got a debriefing right now, Lieutenant. You're welcome to sit in."

I told him I would, and we headed for the debriefing room attached to the personnel office.

Lean, intense, capable, Sergeant Below impressed me as someone I would be able to work with, which was a relief. A lieutenant in conflict with his platoon sergeant had a real nightmare on his hands, and it was something I wanted to avoid.

The platoon, call sign Dateline, had been in contact the day before while working a section of Charlie Ridge southwest of Da Nang. After the firefight, some of the men had stopped to take pictures of a dead Vietcong, and at the debriefing, Sergeant Below gave vent to his feelings on the matter, making it clear it wasn't to happen again.

When the debriefing was over, I told Sergeant Below I wanted an 0800 formation the next day, which would be followed by a rifle inspection. After that, we parted company.

At the formation, I talked to the men for several minutes, telling them who I was and where I came from and the fact that this was my first command. I also tried to impress on them the fact that we were all in this together and it would take each of us doing his job to make it through the time we had in Vietnam. It was important that I had their confidence and they had mine and that they knew I didn't want my career written in needlessly spilled blood.

Formation over, the men returned to their hooches to stand by for weapons inspection. I had told Sergeant Below to have the men disassemble their weapons and lay the parts out on ponchos spread over their cots. In this manner, each piece of each weapon could be closely inspected. It was a policy I instituted and stuck with after every patrol. For the most part, the men had done a good job cleaning their weapons, but a few had allowed dirt and carbon to build up in the gas chambers and other places difficult to clean. Those who had were told to reclean their weapons and to present them again for inspection.

I next inspected the living quarters, which were crowded, with cots spaced about two and a half feet apart and excess gear stored in the rafters of the hooches, but in good order. When the inspection was over, I left Sergeant Below in charge and went to prepare for my next patrol.

At the briefing, I learned we would be operating on the same ridgeline as our last patrol but would be going in three klicks farther north, on the extreme eastern edge of Antenna Valley. The LZ was a grassy hillside, which the gunny believed was too large to booby trap. Again, our primary support would come from artillery units with a fixed-wing backup. Radio frequencies were assigned, and we left to make a detailed map study of our RAOR. This time, we would be travelling down a large, well-used trail—a place neither Ken nor the gunny liked.

That afternoon, I got my hands on a rifle grenade launcher and fixed it to the barrel of my M-14. With it, I could mark enemy positions by lobbing white phosphorous, or Willie Peter, onto them. The launcher and the grenades would mean more weight to carry, but I felt they were important to have.

In the morning, it was coffee and toast again, and I thought if this keeps up, I'll be down to the size of a ninety-eight-pound weakling before my tour is up.

The weather was clear, and by 0830 we were airborne and headed south, with the turbines singing their haunting song that had already begun to run chills down my spine. When we reached the LZ above Antenna Valley, the gunships dropped down to look it over, making several passes without prepping it. We followed them in, Ken's bird taking the lead, and were soon on the ground.

We moved into the jungle and immediately found the trail we were to follow. It was very wide and very well used.

"Don't be surprised if a Vietcong general drives up in a staff car and wants to know what the hell we're doing on his trail," the gunny quipped.

In spite of the tension, I couldn't help but laugh.

Ken ran out his point men, and we started down the trail, keeping eight- and ten-meter intervals between each man. Again, I was near the tail end of the patrol.

It was hot and humid, and I was soon soaked in sweat, bringing in a swarm of thirsty insects. We moved slowly, carefully checking the sides of the trail and the ground before us. To say I was wound up and sprung tight would have been an understatement. There we were, all fourteen of us, violating *the* cardinal rule for a safe and pleasant trip during our Southeast Asian stay. We were on that trail I'd been hearing about since the beginning of Basic School. The one we were all supposed to stay off of.

We moved on for what seemed like an eternity. Step, stop,

listen, look, step again. We were moving so quietly, birds within a few feet of our passing scarcely gave us a glance before going back to the business of grubbing for worms. The world's slowest woodpecker started a daytime serenade, then someone far off fired a single shot. The sound startled me and set my heart to beating in my throat, but I soon calmed down and figured it was an accidental discharge and made a note to report it to Herman the German. Relieving a Vietcong platoon leader would be a real feather in his cap.

We took a break on a protected rise in the trail, and I emptied half a canteen, trying to quench the dryness in my mouth. It didn't help much.

After thirty minutes of sitting and listening, we got up and went on.

Late in the afternoon, we came to a fork in the trail, took it, and began to drop down the side of a steep mountain. The new trail was only slightly less wide than the one we had been on but bore signs of heavier use. Wooden steps were built in where the going was rough, and the ground was packed hard. I just knew I would be treading on a mine any minute now. Good-bye foot. Good-bye, Pork Rind—which was the name Frank Teague had given to me in Basic School. Frank thought the first two initials I went by, PR, were too bland and wanted something with a little zip to it. Hence, Pork Rind. Frank would soon be wounded, then hit again in the medevac chopper. The second time was more serious than the first, and he was eventually given a medical discharge for a leg that no longer worked like it was supposed to.

We continued down into the Valley of the Cong.

Darkness found us still on the trail. Ken called a halt and signaled for us to get off the trail and move up the side of the mountain to a harbor site. We settled in just before total darkness slammed down. The site was on such a steep slope, I had to brace myself against a tree to keep from sliding downhill. I found a stub of a sapling and hung my rifle on it to keep from losing it, then dug into my pack for something to eat. I found and opened what turned out to be a C-ration pound cake and wolfed it down. Of the ten canteens I carried, I had already emptied three. Most of the water had gone to quench the nervous-induced drying of my throat, and I knew I had better slow down or I would soon be out of water.

It began to rain, and I pulled my poncho over me. Braced against the tree, I tried to sleep.

After an hour of creeping down next to the tree and pushing myself back up with my legs, then repeating the process again and again, I knew it was going to be a long night.

The rain continued.

At first light, we ate and moved out.

Ken and the gunny both thought it was time to leave the trail and find a safer approach to the valley. At one of the switchbacks, we plunged into the thick vegetation and began a long traverse across the face of the mountain before starting down again. On the rain-soaked slopes, we slipped and fell time and again as our feet suddenly shot out from under us in the slippery mud. Quiet movement became next to impossible, and our only hope was that if Charlie was around, he would be making as much noise as we were and wouldn't hear us.

There were no openings in the jungle-covered slopes, and in order to get a fix on our position, Ken called a halt and climbed a tree to take a compass reading. When he came down, he reported that all of the surrounding mountains looked the same and he could not get an accurate reading. He did point to a place on the map where he thought we were. We had moved into jungle so deep that we were several klicks from anything that even looked like an LZ. It was a lonely feeling.

We spent the rest of the day fighting our way through an area so remote, I don't think even God knew it existed. The vegetation was thick, broken, and tangled, and breaking through it was exhausting work. Bamboo and wait-a-minute vines were everywhere, slowing movement to a crawl. The air trapped in the plant life around us was still and lifeless, and we breathed in short, panting gasps. Tired, filthy, sweating, stinking, we were using water at an alarming rate, and

if we weren't careful would be out before the day was over.
But we *had* to have it and kept on drinking. Cuts and scratches
covered every exposed part of our bodies, and the insects
swarmed in to dine on the heady brew of sweat, blood, and
sometimes tears of frustration.

My head was about to explode from the heat. I grew careless and stopped looking in the bushes for Charlie Cong.
Then after a while, I hoped he would show up so I could vent
my anger and frustration by blowing holes in his chest.

We kept going on, looking for an end to our world of
vicious green. But by late afternoon, our situation hadn't
improved any, and when we came to a place where the trees
were huge and the undergrowth not quite so thick, Ken called
a halt and passed the word we would be spending the night
there. Concerned about our water supply, he wanted to use
what little daylight was left to figure out our exact location
and plot a course to the nearest water shown on the map.

I collapsed next to a tree and unscrewed the lid of my
eighth canteen and sincerely hoped that Ken could lead us to
water in the morning.

That evening, I was hungry for the first time since we had
started the patrol. I ate a beans-and-franks heavy and some
John Wayne crackers, then stretched out on top of my poncho
and waited for night to fall. When it did, my hand wasn't
there again, and the long, graveyard strands of phosphorescent decay came out to haunt me. I heard the radio operator
call in a situation report to Beacon Light, then I drifted off
to sleep.

Around midnight, I was suddenly awakened by a bright
flash and an explosion that set my ears ringing. In an instant,
I was on my hands and knees, groping in the dark for my
rifle.

"Grenade! Grenade!" somebody hissed loudly.

"Fuckin' gooks," came another whisper.

Men were moving in the night, grabbing their weapons
and taking them off safe.

Flash, wham! Another grenade went off.

More movement and whispered cursing.

Ken was hissing at the men to lie still and be quiet.

I couldn't find my rifle, even though I had placed it right next to me before going to sleep. In the dark, I had turned around and was searching in the wrong direction. Jesus, I was scared. I kept saying over and over to myself, "How did they find us? How could they possibly have found us?" I began to shake so hard that when my hands finally found my rifle, I scarcely recognized what it was. I grabbed it and hugged it to me and got as low to the deck as I could. By now, the shaking had grown so bad, I began to rattle inside. It was as if my skeleton were trying to tear itself loose from the rest of me. I never wanted to be someplace else so bad in my life! Just when I thought I would self-destruct and fall into a hundred separate pieces, a strange, peaceful calm came over me, and I grew so tired I could not raise my head. My eyes refused to open, but for a while, I fought the urge to sleep, telling myself I had to stay awake. Then I gave in and fell into a deep, dreamless sleep.

When I woke up, it was 0300. I had been out for more than two hours. Clutching my rifle, I crawled over to the radio operator and asked him what happened.

"Monkeys," he whispered. "Some asshole thought we were being probed when a monkey threw a stick at him, so he threw out a couple of grenades. The second one bounced back, and he picked up some metal in one arm. Serves the prick right."

Monkeys, I thought. Goddamn monkeys.

The incident had brought on a fear I never knew existed. A fear that could have destroyed me. If I were going to survive the jungle, if I were going to return home, I could never allow it to take control of me again. I had been consumed by it and unable to function, and deep down inside, I was ashamed of my reaction. I was lucky that time—there were no VC, and I thanked God there hadn't been. If there were, I probably never would have awakened.

I did what I could to put the incident aside, but whether it was innocence, or my sense of immortality, or fair play, or what, something was swept from me that night, and it never returned.

Before dawn, we ate, gathered up our gear, and moved out. The man who threw the grenade was on the gunny's shit list and went about that morning with a sullen look on his face. Several of the men rode him for a while then dropped it. None of them showed any sympathy for the metal fragments stiffening the upper part of his left arm.

The jungle didn't let up.

Sometime after noon, exhausted and out of water, we came onto a small stream of clear running water. Ken put half the men on guard while the other half filled their canteens, dropping a halazone tablet into each one before screwing the lid on. With the tablets in, we were supposed to wait twenty minutes before drinking the water. According to the instructions on the bottle, it took that long for whatever living creatures were present to roll over and die. But after waiting only five minutes, I gave a canteen a shake and drank it down.

An hour later, we broke out of the jungle onto a well-used trail, which we followed for several hundred meters. At that point, we must have been right outside the gates of Cong Land, because we kept hearing distant voices and shots being fired every few minutes.

Ahead, the point man suddenly froze and motioned for Ken to move up. He had found a pair of fresh footprints with groundwater still seeping into them, evidence that someone had passed by only moments before.

Nearby was a water buffalo, so completely flattened into the trail that it looked like a tank had run over it then backed up to see what it hit. As I ducked through the cloud of flies surrounding it and stepped over the dead buffalo, I looked down. Its teeth were in profile grinning up at me. "You're next, fucker," it seemed to say.

Ken moved us off the trail and into an ambush site. We were deployed no more than thirty feet from the trail and had a clear view of it for one hundred feet in either direction. I got down and assumed the prone position, trembling slightly and sweating heavily.

Ken was not the most talkative guy in the world, and for most of the trip, I had been pretty much in the dark about what we were doing and where we were going. However, when we got into position, everything became suddenly quite clear—we were going to kill whoever happened to come down the trail.

We hadn't been there three minutes when I heard something off to my left. I looked up and there on the trail was a man walking briskly toward us. He had on a USMC fatigue jacket, black shorts, sandals, and carried a plastic U.S.-made canteen in one hand. His teeth were so bucked, he looked exactly like Tojo, from another war. Doubts about whether or not I could actually shoot someone from ambush swept over me. I was set to fire, but didn't know if I could when the command came. I had suddenly discovered that it was one thing to shoot at armed people in the open, and entirely another to strike from ambush at close quarters. Sweating and waiting, I noticed the guy wasn't armed. From somewhere inside me, a little voice said, "Hey, you can't shoot this guy. He doesn't have a gun."

On he came. I looked at Ken, who was looking at his watch and hadn't seen Tojo. To my right, I could hear leaves rustling as a couple of men prepared to open fire but wouldn't until Ken gave the command.

The little voice kept hammering away at me, "Don't shoot! Don't Shoot!"

Then one of the men hissed, "Lieutenant!" and Ken looked up. He saw the man on the trail, who also saw him. Ken yelled to open fire, and I dropped my head to the ground, unwilling to witness the slaughter. The world erupted in gunfire. Then it stopped.

The little voice inside me said, "I don't believe this. We just shot a guy armed with a canteen."

One of the squad leaders yelled, "I'll finish him!" and poured out a stream of bullets.

In my mind, I could see the guy writhing in a pool of blood and swore I wasn't going over to look at him.

Then someone cried, "Goddamn it, he got away, Lieutenant! The fucker got away. There's just a little blood here, we only nicked his ass!"

A feeling of unbelievable relief swept over me, and I scrambled to my feet for a look. Sure enough, he had gotten away.

Ken swore and told the gunny to get the patrol moving because all that gunfire was bound to bring on the posse.

We started out at as close to a run as the jungle would allow, crashing and plowing without regard to the noise we made. After a hundred yards, we slowed down and began moving cautiously again. We crossed a stream along the face of a veil of water cascading from high above us. On the opposite side, we set up a defensive perimeter and listened for anyone who might be following. No one was, and we moved on.

Crossing a clearing, the jungle around us exploded with a crashing sound that brought us to our knees, rifles slammed into our shoulders. Seconds later, a huge, female water buffalo and calf charged into the clearing, running straight for us. Just as we were about to open fire, the cow halted in a cloud of dust, snorting and pawing and tossing her heavy horns. The calf stopped with her, frightened, its eyes opened wide. I let out a long sigh of relief but kept watching for the pair's next move. The cow continued to paw and snort, and just when I thought she was about to renew her charge, she suddenly turned and ran back into the jungle, the calf following.

"Damn thing could have killed somebody," the gunny muttered.

We crossed the clearing and entered a series of knolls, where we heard more voices but did not see anyone. We made a slow, silent detour around the knolls and left the voices.

Toward dark, we came to the outskirts of an abandoned village, the thatched houses rotting into the ground, fields overgrown with vines. We found no signs of recent human activity and moved onto a nearby hill for the night. After dropping my gear, I took my rifle and climbed farther up the hill to relieve myself. With my pants around my ankles and the most unbelievable odor coming from my crotch, I looked around and discovered I was in a graveyard filled with small wooden headboards and cement dragons that fought to keep the jungle back. I wondered if I would end up under one of the headboards with no one to know.

It began to rain.

The next day dawned clear and sunny, and we left the valley of the abandoned village and climbed a mountain of waist-high grass, rolling before us like a great, green sea. Although we were in the open and exposed to the enemy, being free of the jungle was like a release from a dungeon. My spirits rose, and I knew if we had to do battle and die, it would be out in the open where God could find us if He chose.

High on top of the mountain, we discovered a large tiger trap with bamboo walls and a deep, steep-sided pit inside. Frank Buck, here I come, I thought.

We were due out, and the birds were on time, and since the area was one vast LZ, we just lay down near the tiger trap and waited.

When the birds broke the horizon, I felt good inside.

On the way out, we were shot at with the same slow fire that bid us good-bye on the first patrol. Somewhere below was a Charlie who hunted helicopters for a living.

5

At the debriefing that afternoon, we outlined the events of the last four days and ended with an estimate of the enemy's strength and control over the area. All of us had come to the conclusion that the Vietcong owned and operated everything in the Hiep Duc quadrangle and cautioned that a patrol set down in any part of the region could expect contact. Ours and previous patrols had repeatedly confirmed that fact, but since division had penciled in large areas of Hiep Duc as being bastions of democracy, recon reports to the contrary were routinely downplayed.

Colonel McKeon was not pleased about the carelessly thrown grenades or the fact that we had missed the man in the ambush. I had not liked that grenade thing either, but as for the man on the trail, he could have been the commandant of the Vietcong Marine Corps, I was still glad he got away.

I slept that night like I'd been drugged, and when I woke up in the morning, felt groggy and listless. I showered and shuffled off to chow, then returned to the hooch to clean my gear. Before noon, I fell asleep again and didn't wake up until the sun was down. I ate and went back to sleep.

The next morning, I found two letters on the mosquito net over my cot. Both were from my wife. I tore them open and eagerly read them then read them again. Jodi wanted to know where her father was and why he wasn't there to tell her stories at night. Roberta reported that after a week of moping around the house feeling sorry for herself, she had decided to put her time to better use and go back to work. So, in spite of the fact that she was four months pregnant, she was now teaching kindergarten at a nearby school. I was glad she had gone back to work, knowing it would help get her mind off my being in Vietnam and make the time go by faster for her.

At a meeting in the company office, Sergeant Below and I learned the platoon was being sent to Chu Lai, where the other half of the battalion operated under the command of the battalion executive officer. We would be leaving in a day or so.

I was not happy about the move. I had yet to work with my platoon, scarcely knew who the men in it were, and didn't know anyone in Chu Lai. Here, I had made several friends I could count on for guidance and help and had begun to get a feel for the territory around Da Nang.

"Why me?" I asked.

"Because somebody has to go," the captain answered. "And you're it."

I told Sergeant Below to start packing the platoon's gear plus anything else he could lay his hands on that looked good. I especially wanted our complement of optics and radios in top working condition—both were vital to our mission and our survival. Before we left, Sergeant Below was able to exchange one of our spotting scopes for a new one and to get the communications people to perform maintenance and repairs on all of our radios. Together, we made sure that each man had a complete issue of 782 gear plus a serviceable flak jacket and helmet, held a weapons and clothing inspection, and replaced what broken and worn-out items we could.

The day before we were to leave, the supply sergeant presented me with my first-ever pair of jungle boots and lightweight fatigues. Battalion was in short supply of both, and even though the boots and fatigues came from a sergeant who had recently been killed, I accepted them gratefully.

On the morning of February 7, we were trucked to the runway at Da Nang, with orders to wait for the arrival of a C-130 that was coming from somewhere at sometime to fly us to Chu Lai, weather permitting.

Da Nang was one noisy place, with prop-driven planes keeping up a never-ending din as they came and went, one

after another. But the sound they made was nothing compared to the Phantoms taking off and hitting their afterburn-
ers. Whenever a Phantom cracked off, buildings rattled, the
ground trembled, and all conversation stopped. A year later,
when I was hollow-eyed and shell-shocked, my last night in
country, those same blistering takeoffs would send me time
and again to the floor of a transient tent, clawing at the wood,
trying to get down to mother earth and safety. But that day
on the runway, the sound was still power in its purest form,
and I loved it.

Our plane arrived at 1300, we loaded and were soon off
for the short flight to Chu Lai, south of Da Nang.

When we landed at the large, sprawling base, a pair of
six-bys from recon picked us up and drove us to the battalion
area.

Two companies, Alpha and Delta, made up the second
half of the battalion, which was located on a quiet stretch of
beach. Our nearest neighbor was 1st Amphibious Tractors.
The battalion was laid out roughly in a square, with the company offices, supply, and the enlisted quarters forming a
neatly aligned L on two sides, one fronting the beach. The
officers' and staff NCOs' hooches, identical to the ones at
Reasoner, were on sand dunes a hundred meters inland from
the company offices. Closing the square was the S-3 shop,
motor transport, a staff club shared with Amtracs, and the
executive officer's quarters. Within was an outdoor theater,
a tented shower facility, and the mess hall.

We were attached to Alpha Company, assigned quarters,
and before chow were settling in.

My new hooch was on a dune near the battalion LZ. My
roommate was a tall lieutenant with a bushy mustache and
reddish hair, who, when off patrol, spent most of his time
sitting in a beach chair reading gun magazines, chewing to-
bacco, and sipping whiskey out of a bottle. His name was
Sam Williams. He was short in country and convinced he
was going to die before his rotation date came up. Prior to
being a recon patrol leader, Sam had served six months with
the grunts, where he had been awarded a Navy Cross. But

with only a few weeks left, his nerves were about shot, and he spent his off hours trying to teletransport himself to another world; one that presumably excluded the grimness of violence and death waiting. Trying to get our minds to refuse the reality of our futures in Vietnam was not an uncommon practice. Personally, I worked hard at it.

I introduced myself and asked which cots were taken.

Without looking up from his magazine, Sam kicked a cot with one foot and said, "This one's mine, take any of the others. Nobody else lives here."

I settled for one in a corner near a door and started unpacking.

The next morning, I reported to Major Johnston, the battalion executive officer. I was given a rundown on recon activities around Chu Lai and told that my company commander, Captain Connelly, was in the bush and due back within the hour. When the captain came in, he would take Sergeant Below and me on an overflight of the area being considered for our first patrol. The major then showed me around the battalion area.

Our first stop was the S-3 shop. There I met the captain in charge and his assistant, a lieutenant named Grover Murray, who had recently rotated out of the bush. I took an instant liking to Grover, a Korean War veteran, who was both patient and helpful. The captain was another matter, and we clashed from the beginning. I was told that except for a place called Duc Pho, enemy activity around Chu Lai was slow at the moment, but not to be lulled into a false sense of security by the lack of sightings and contact. Duc Pho, the S-3 captain said, was hot, and when it came my turn to go, I'd better be ready.

6

I met Captain Connelly as he was coming up the hill from LZ Quail. Strapped to his pack was a large piece of twisted aluminum, a souvenir from a napalm strike the patrol had called in close to its position.

"It landed just outside our perimeter," the captain said, indicating the piece of metal. "The VC were right next to us."

I saluted and introduced myself. We talked briefly, and then Captain Connelly left for his debriefing. He was the first person I'd met above the rank of lieutenant who went to the bush.

That afternoon, the captain took Sergeant Below and myself on an overflight of the mountains we were scheduled to work the following day. Intelligence reported an increase in enemy activity in the area, and we were to go in and confirm or deny the reports. We went out in a pair of ancient CH-34s, designated as the workhorses of the Marine Corps. They were noisy and shook like crazy when they flew but were considered to be highly reliable aircraft.

One of the mountains we flew over was Hill 488, Howard's Hill, named after Jimmie Howard, who had been with recon seven months earlier. It was on Howard's Hill that an eighteen-man recon platoon fought an NVA battalion to a standstill, bringing down a devastating amount of firepower within a few meters of its own position and inflicting heavy casualties on the enemy. The fight lasted for two days, and during that time several of the men in the platoon were killed and nearly everyone else wounded, including Howard, who continued to fight in spite of having lost the use of his legs. At times, Howard, who was a staff sergeant, even got his men to laugh at the enemy to let them know the Marines on the hill were far from being beaten. When their grenades ran out, the men threw rocks at the enemy to keep them at bay. On the second day of fighting, with the survivors down to a handful of bullets, a rescue forced arrived, and the NVA broke contact and fled. For his actions, Jimmie Howard was later awarded the Medal of Honor.

When Captain Connelly pointed out the hill and said it was where we were going in, I immediately offered a prayer to the gods that ward off the return of NVA battalions.

Back in the battalion area, Sergeant Below and I briefed the platoon and saw to it that the men got ready that afternoon. Then I went back to my hooch to pack my gear, a process that usually took about an hour. Every item going into the pack or onto the web belt had to be inspected for rust, wear, rot, and serviceability. I also inspected the pins in each grenade to make sure that none were working their way out or were about to break, and that the spoons were securely held down with black electrician's tape. A grenade accidently going off on your belt is in a league of its own, and I took every possible precaution to prevent such an occurrence.

At 2100, our orders were changed from an area reconnaissance to manning an observation post (OP) on top of a hill called 707. I got the impression Captain Connelly was behind the change. I don't think he wanted to send so green a lieutenant as me into a hot area.

Secretly, I was thankful.

We were in the air by 0800 the next morning, headed for Hill 707 west of Chu Lai. The hill hadn't been used in several months, and there was some concern that the VC might have moved in and booby-trapped the site. We were to approach the mountaintop with extreme caution.

From several miles out, I was able to pick up the bald top of 707. Stripped of all vegetation, the exposed red laterite crest stood out like a beacon.

We orbited while the gunships dropped down for a look, then the lead bird followed them in. We landed, filed off the bird, and began a careful search of the hilltop. However, as soon as I saw a dozen or more unopened C-ration cans and a few hundred rounds of ammunition scattered near the fighting holes and bunkers, I was certain that no VC had been on the hill and called in the second bird. If the enemy had been around, nothing of use would have been left. I told the men to make a thorough search of the area and to clean up the place.

The birds left, and we were on our own.

The top of 707 was narrow and about one hundred and fifty feet long. I set up observation posts at both ends of the mountain and assigned sectors to observe to each post. Then I put the rest of the men to work cleaning out the bunkers and improving the fighting holes. Any trash we found was thrown over the side, adding to the tons of accumulated debris around us. Between the hilltop and the rusted, tangled barbed wire ringing our position were thousands of rounds of spent brass, a sea of tin cans and bottles, broken packing crates, and empty C-ration boxes. It was a regular "Made in the U.S.A." dump site, the crowning piece being a wrecked CH-34 helicopter, used now for target practice.

Once we were settled in and fields of fire were established for each position, I plotted and called in our defensive fires so they could quickly be shot if needed.

The sun was out, and the heat was intense, and there was nothing to do but sit, watch, and endure.

Late in the afternoon, a swarm of two-inch-long flying insects descended on the hill, and we swatted and fought them for over an hour as they crawled over us and into our clothing and everything we'd brought with us. When the sun went down, they left to wherever it is insects go, and things on the hill returned to normal.

After dark, a heavy fog rolled in, and it started to drizzle. At 2200, I called arty and registered illumination over our position. As the rounds popped high above us and turned the night to white, ghosts began crawling out of the mist. In the light, I stared long and hard at the wire and saw nothing. I moved the illumination in closer, and when the next round went off, the canister whistled past and crashed close by in the jungle, and I thought how a guy could get killed. More ghosts drifted out of the mist. I told myself Charlie couldn't get through all those tin cans without us hearing him and knows it and wouldn't climb such a god-awful steep mountain on a cold rainy night to try it, anyway. Still, I had heard all those stories about sappers moving through defensive positions like they weren't there and kept looking and listening as the trees around us danced slowly in the oscillating light. Then the lights were out, and the hill was shrouded in black fog.

Around midnight, I checked the watch, rolled up in my poncho and fell asleep.

An hour or so later, I woke up, ran my hand over my face, and felt something soft and wet clinging to my cheek just below my left eye. There was another soft, wet thing on my neck. Leeches. I shuddered and told my radio operator, Private First Class Nimmo, to get out a flashlight. We pulled a poncho over our heads and turned the light on. Out of the corner of one eye, I could see a fat, swollen leech squirming from side to side, pumping himself full on my blood. We had been warned not to pull them off because the mouth parts easily tore away from the body and stayed in the victim, setting up an infection in the area of the bite.

"There are just the two," Nimmo said. "I'll have them off in a second." He grabbed a bottle of mosquito repellent and squirted some on each leech. Within seconds, they dropped onto the dirt floor of the bunker, where I ground them under foot. Nimmo cleaned the wounds with a disinfectant, but they bled steadily for several minutes before stopping.

For the next four days we watched over the Song Trau Valley and plains beyond and saw nothing we could report as being enemy activity. The days were hot and the nights wet and cold. The monotony of sitting and watching was

broken only by the spectacular sunrises and sunsets that came
with each day. Then the clouds around us changed from white
to hues of billowing reds and oranges. Silently I watched
each change, lost in thought. In the faces of the clouds, I saw
myself soaring above our mountain to stride through the long
halls of the castles above me and leave Vietnam forever. For
quiet moments, I would be free of the place I had already
come to fear. But then the colors would fade, and I would
find myself sitting on a muddy hilltop, wondering how in the
name of Christ I was supposed to survive thirteen months of
playing hide-and-go-seek with bullets.

On the fourth day, we were extended due to bad weather
and spent the day and night in a rain that didn't show any
signs of letting up. When it did, and a hole opened in the
sky the next morning, the birds came down, and we returned
to camp.

At the debriefing, the S-3 captain climbed on me for taking
an old .30-caliber machine gun with us to Hill 707. Sergeant
Below had suggested we familiarize the men with the weapon
just in case it was ever needed. Unlike the newer M-60 machine guns, the .30 caliber had to be fired from a tripod. It
was a good gun to have in a fixed position, but none of the
men had ever worked with one, so we took it along to train
a crew in its use.

What with our two M-60s and the .30 caliber, the S-3
captain thought we had too many machine guns with us on
the mountain. "What if the gooks overran your position and
got their hands on all those guns," he snapped at me.

"At that point, I don't think it would have mattered to any
of *us*!" I snapped back, unable to follow his idiotic line of
reasoning.

After a few more remarks, the captain said he was going
to report the excess number of guns to Captain Connelly,
and we were dismissed.

Three days later, we went out again.

We inserted in a paddy of waist-deep mud that took us
fully thirty minutes to extricate ourselves from. As we fought,
slipped, and fell in the sucking quagmire, I couldn't get my

thoughts off the hills surrounding us, knowing that if the enemy were in them, we could all get killed before we reached the safety of the jungle. Headlines kept flashing through my mind: "Recon Patrol Wiped Out In Paddy. Herman Says Marines Are Here To Play Hardball And Expect To Lose A Few." Playing hardball I understood. Being set down in an LZ chosen by some guy in the rear playing pin-the-tail-on-the-donkey with a map, I didn't. People were getting killed because of the movers and shakers who never set foot in the bush, and I didn't want to be one of the dead.

It was then I made the decision never to land in an LZ I had bad feelings about—regardless of what had been penciled on a map.

We hit dry ground and quickly moved under the canopy and set up a hasty defense while scraping at the mud on our clothes and equipment. After I cleaned most of the mud off me, I took out my map to get oriented. Ahead lay a hill I wanted to be on before dark. Once I knew where we were and Sergeant Below and I had discussed the route to our objective, I ran out the two point men, fell in behind them, and signaled for the others to follow. Sergeant Below trailed with the second squad.

We moved at a slow, steady pace, stopping every few minutes to watch and listen. The trees around us rose to seventy feet and grew close together. Again, I had the feeling that a dozen pairs of eyes were watching my every move. It took us five hours to reach our objective, and by the time we got to the top of the hill, I was wrung out by the climb and the strain of being constantly on the alert. Along the way, we had not seen any signs of recent enemy activity, but it was the rainy season, and what signs there might have been had been washed out the night before.

On the hill, Sergeant Below got the men into their positions, while Private First Class Nimmo and I set up an OP in a tall tree. I went up first and made myself comfortable on a branch forty feet above the ground. Nimmo stayed a few branches below, within easy whispering distance. By taking a fix on two nearby mountains and shooting a pair back azimuths, I was able to pinpoint our location in the jungle. After that, I plotted our defensive fires and told Nimmo to call them in. Done fixing our position and preparing our defenses, I focused my binoculars on the villages below us, Tay My (1) and Tay My (2), and looked for the enemy.

Nothing.

Two hours later with darkness coming on and still nothing.

Nimmo and I climbed down from the tree, radioed in a situation report, and ate.

That night, what sounded like a bobcat hissing and growling prowled back and forth to our front. One of the men wanted to throw out an illumination grenade, but I whispered the word there would be no illumination unless we were under attack.

At first light, I was back in the tree staring into Tay My (1) and (2). I immediately picked up a squad of VC doing close-order drill down the middle of Tay My (1). I was so surprised over the sighting, I lost my balance and nearly fell out of the tree. I read the coordinates and azimuth to the village to Nimmo, who called them in to arty. In a few minutes we got word that arty would have to get clearance to shoot into the vil and to stand by. For thirty minutes I watched the squad of VC march out of step while trying to learn the manual of arms, the squad leader running alongside, yelling and flapping his arms. It reminded me of my first day in boot camp.

Finally, arty called back and said they were sorry, but could not shoot into the vil. When the squad disappeared into a large hut, I switched my attention to the network of trails leading from the village to the mountains around it.

A round suddenly popped through the tree. It was followed by another, and Nimmo and I beat a quick retreat to the ground.

"We'd better move," I told Sergeant Below.

My voice trembled and my hands were shaking. Getting shot at was going to take some getting used to, I thought.

We saddled up and headed for the next hill. If I had been tense moving up from the rice paddy the day before, it was nothing compared to what I felt now. Knowing the enemy had found us and was close by was not a comforting feeling.

An hour into our climb to the hill, Private First Class McNaughton, the artillery net radio operator, passed out from the heat and went face forward into the ground. I went back down the line to check on him. It was then I discovered McNaughton was loaded down with not just his rifle and radio, but he also had the M-79 grenade launcher and twenty rounds of 40-mm ammunition. I asked Sergeant Below what the hell was going on, and he said he was the only man in the platoon qualified to shoot the M-79. While the corpsman, Doc Shannon, worked on McNaughton, I stripped off the launcher and rounds and told Sergeant Below to find someone else to carry them and retook my place at the head of the line.

When Doc Shannon sent word that it was okay to move, I got the men on their feet, and we continued up the hill.

On top of our objective, I found a tree that hung out over the side of the mountain and climbed it to establish a second OP. Along with me came Nimmo, and again I went through the procedure of fixing our position and calling in the coordinates of our defensive fires. Then I settled in to check on life in Phuoc Lams (1), (2), and (3) and the nearby plain carved out by the wide, meandering Song Tra Bong. Below, people were going about the business of living out their lives in familiar routine. Children splashed and played in a small stream. Smoke from a dozen cooking fires curled lazily in the still air. Old men in conical hats squatted in the sun. As often as the village had been torn at by war, life at the moment was serene and peaceful.

About then, the shooter found us. I was way out on a limb when the first round popped by overhead. I turned and started scrambling for the trunk. With my backside exposed to the enemy, I felt ridiculous scooting along the limb. A second round sailed through the branches as I grabbed the trunk and slid down as fast as I could.

On the ground, I took stock of our situation and decided that, since we really didn't have any other place to go and still be able to observe the valley, we would stay where we were. I moved the platoon to another part of the hill, and we set in. Our new position was well protected by large boulders and fallen trees, enabling us to defend ourselves from just about anything that came our way.

Sergeant Below set up the watch, and we ate before dark.

Having been shot at twice in the same day made me more than a little jumpy, and I convinced myself the local VC would come looking for us that night. To make sure I was awake when they did, I took an amphetamine. A small bottle of them had been issued to both the doc and me to be used in the event we were overcome by exhaustion and had to keep going. I just wanted to be ready and, after taking the first one, soon took a second. If one can do the job, two can do it better, right?

Rain came with the night, and I wrapped up in my poncho. As the amphetamines took hold, my nerves, already tight, began to ride the edge of a razor. Every falling leaf, every cracking branch, every movement the men made in their sleep set my mind racing and my eyes darting from one side of my head to the other. I held my rifle close to me, checking it to make sure the bolt was home, the safety was on, and that a round was in the chamber. Then I checked my grenades and the illumination flare next to me and the K-bar on my belt and the magazine of twenty rounds I kept tucked inside my jacket. Then I checked them again. And again. Time crept by at an agonizingly slow pace. Large, fat rain drops fell from the trees and plopped noisily onto my poncho, drowning out the sounds of the jungle. I stuck my head out to listen and was soon soaked and had water running down my neck and inside my jacket. Head back under poncho. *Plop, plop, plop.* Head out. Charlie Cong had to come that night. It was too good a night to pass up. Nearby, someone started to snore. I kicked Nimmo and snapped at him in a whisper to shut the man up. He crawled over and clamped a hand over the snoring man's mouth, and he woke up sputtering. The luminous hands on my watch were stopped at 2330 and refused to move. Then a long time later, they were stopped at 2345. I held the watch up to one ear to make sure it was still ticking. Outside the perimeter, something began snorting and thrashing in the bushes. I eased the safety off my rifle and waited. The sound drew nearer, then there was a loud grunt, and whatever was out there turned and ran back the way it had come. I put the safety back on, my heart hammering in my throat. The rain just kept coming down.

At 0400, a grenade went off, the explosion coming from the position we had left the day before. There was a long silence then another explosion. Charlie had come to probe in the night, but we weren't home.

In the morning, I got up exhausted, swearing off amphetamines forever.

Checking the perimeter, I discovered that Private First Class Sparks and his partner had set out a grenade on a trip wire about fifteen feet from their position. I had them take it in, then had a serious talk about the killing radius of a fragmentation grenade and that if some gook had tripped it, they'd have gone up in smoke with him.

I ate, found a suitable tree, and climbed it. This time, I carried up a green net hammock belonging to the machine gunner and stuck leaves in it to camouflage my position. Nimmo stayed unseen in some thick foliage below me. I dried off my binoculars and looked into Phuoc Lams (1), (2), and (3). Not much was going on.

Around noon, Sergeant Below came up to relieve me, and I went down to eat. Later, one of the squad leaders went up and relieved Below, who reported all was quiet. Later, I went up and stayed until dark, but if there was a war going on down below, I couldn't tell it from where I sat.

The next day was the same.

On the fourth night, battalion called and told us to move to an LZ in the morning and be ready for an extraction by 1000.

At first light, we started down the mountain toward an abandoned rice paddy carved into the top of a knoll. We waited there, exposed and naked all day, but the birds didn't come. To say I was nervous about being left in the open was an understatement. While battalion kept changing the arrival time of the birds, we sweated and gawked at the hills around us, wondering when Charlie would open up.

At 1600, word came there wouldn't be an extraction, and we moved back into the jungle for the night.

By noon the next day, the birds were up, and we had them on the radio. They had a team to insert first and took fire going in, and I thought we'd be stuck out in the woods another day. But luck was with us and they were soon overhead.

Sergeant Below set off a charge wrapped around a tree in the LZ, felling it down the side of the hill, and the birds came in. We boarded quickly and were soon in the air, headed for Chu Lai and the beach.

7

Our turn for Duc Pho came in March.

Duc Pho was the southernmost district of Quang Ngai Province, an area that had been under Communist control for years. Large Vietcong units operated freely throughout the heavily populated coastal region, levying taxes, recruiting party members, and developing a network of fortified villages and underground hospitals. There were so few ARVN and civilian officials in Duc Pho that most of the people living there had never seen nor dealt with a representative of the South Vietnamese government. For them, the Vietcong was the government.

In late January, 3d Battalion, 7th Marines moved into Duc Pho to begin Operation Desoto, designated originally as a mission to relieve an ARVN battalion from its hilltop position at Nui Dang and free it for use in a pacification program elsewhere. However, the operation quickly spilled over into the surrounding countryside as 3/7 found itself in daily contact with the enemy. Operation Desoto soon expanded to become Deckhouse/Desoto, and 1st Battalion, 5th Marines, plus two ARVN battalions and Foxtrot 2/7 (Co. F, 2d Bn., 7th Marines) entered the fray.

By early February, recon had established a liaison group at Nui Dang to work in direct support with 3/7, and on any given day, seldom had fewer than four teams in the field. We soon discovered that once a team was inserted in the hills outside 3/7's perimeter, contact with the enemy was a foregone conclusion. Casualties began to mount, and few of the patrols operating in the Duc Pho TAOR went unscathed.

Then, toward the end of February, Duckbill suffered what was probably the worst experience recon had at Duc Pho. It serves as an example of what we were all up against in the region.

Duckbill, under Lt. Ron Benoit, was the call sign for 1st Platoon, Delta Company. Early in the day on February 23d, the platoon was inserted on a hill south of Nui Dang. The birds took fire on the way in and at the same time flushed four VC from the top of the hill. Once on the ground, the patrol set up an OP and immediately spotted some VC firing at a helicopter from the base of the hill. While Ron was calling in an air strike on the VC below, his platoon sergeant discovered thirty or more of the enemy closing on Duckbill's position. The platoon took them under fire, killing one and wounding six. With the enemy breathing down their necks, Ron shifted the air strike to within 150 meters of his position, inflicting heavy casualties on the VC and driving them off. Their reconnaissance mission compromised and their position known to the enemy, the team was extracted.

The next day, Duckbill walked out of the CP with Foxtrot 2/7 as the company set out on a mission of its own. After covering some six thousand meters, the patrol veered off from Foxtrot to spend the night in an ambush/OP site. No VC were encountered, and the patrol was extracted on the morning of the 25th.

Back at Nui Dang, Ron was briefed and told he would be going out that same morning.

At 0930, Duckbill flew out, headed for Nui Cu, Hill 163, east of 3/7's CP. The first bird had landed, and the men were on the ground before the VC opened up. They had zeroed in on the LZ and were pouring out a heavy volume of machine-gun fire from two positions above the zone. As the patrol ran for cover, the primary tac radio operator, Cpl. Mike Holmes, was wounded and knocked unconscious by a booby-trapped 155 round, which seriously injured another man closer to the explosion. His radio operator temporarily out of the picture, Ron ran into the open and waved off the second bird. He then got to the radio and called in an air strike to silence the machine guns.

With the area for the moment quiet and his radio operator recovering, Ron called for the second bird to bring in the rest of the patrol and at the same time medevac the wounded man. As soon as the second half landed, more booby traps started going off. It was then a 250-pound bomb was detonated, and the platoon sergeant, Sergeant Joe Barnes, virtually disappeared. Before being extracted, the patrol did find one of Sergeant Barnes's legs and returned with it, and some weeks later a grunt unit found what was believed to be his jawbone, but after the smoke and dust had cleared, the platoon sergeant was no longer there.

When the bomb went off, several men were wounded, including Ron, who was knocked flat by the explosion, and his eardrums burst. Deaf and disoriented, he continued to lead his platoon but found himself being slammed to the ground by a now-recovered Corporal Holmes every time he tried to get to his feet. Not realizing their position was once again under machine-gun fire and that rounds were popping all around them, Ron fought to free himself from his radio operator's grip, yelling at him to let go so he could get on with doing his job. After struggling for several minutes, Holmes was finally able to get the message across that to stand up meant to die, and Ron stayed down.

Hospitalman Brodie, the corpsman, was then seriously wounded by another booby-trapped 155 round, the explosion adding to the confusion on the hill and striking fear into the men over who would be the next to trigger a booby trap.

Ron continued to call down air strikes and artillery on the enemy, while at the same time requesting a medevac and extraction.

Heavy fighting continued.

When the birds arrived and the enemy fire had been suppressed, Duckbill, taking all of its wounded and Sergeant Barnes's leg, came out. The platoon had been on the ground for forty-five minutes and had taken one KIA and nine wounded.

For his actions, Ron Benoit was later awarded the Navy Cross, our nation's second-highest award.

The next day, Foxtrot 2/7 swept Hill 163 and found fifty fresh graves around Duckbill's position and nearby picked up several seriously wounded VC. They also discovered that the enemy had liberally sewn the hill with explosives and had laid over a quarter of a mile of comm wire to command detonate them. The recon Marines had not triggered a single booby trap. The enemy had merely waited until the men were on or near a buried piece of ordnance before setting it off, inflicting a great deal of damage on the platoon.

The wounded were eventually flown to the hospital ship *Repose*. Among them was Ron, who, deaf and thinking no one could hear him, went about shouting at everyone around him. Within a few weeks, his hearing returned to near normal, but the ordeal his platoon had undergone was slow healing, and its effects spread beyond the platoon itself. All of us were afraid we would soon be faced with a similar experience. What happened to Sergeant Barnes could happen to any of us at any time.

Within days of Duckbill's fight at Nui Cu, Dateline was on its way to Duc Pho. During the thirty-minute flight, a lot went through my mind as I listened to the song of the turbines. For me, Vietnam was fast becoming a nightmare. Ghosting through a terrain we neither conquered nor held, surrounded by people trying to kill us, I felt like we were being cruelly fed into some monstrous machine with an insatiable appetite for blood, and I wondered whether the people responsible for our being in Vietnam had any idea what they were doing.

Before we left Chu Lai, I had written a long, rambling letter to Roberta. In it, I told her how I missed Sunday afternoon drives, walks in the park, and that I loved her and Jodi so very much. Nothing earthshaking, but I wanted her to know how I felt about things and to leave her with something in case the letter was the only thing to make it home. Shit, I was scared.

As we approached Nui Dang, we flew over a large,

triangular-shaped fort built long ago by the French—a landmark to bitterness and failure. There was a message in that fort, but we were Americans and wouldn't hear it if it jumped up screaming. So now the fort was ours, part of 3/7's growing perimeter, where artillery fired, helicopters came and went, and Marines on foot moved everywhere. It was a regular city down there.

We landed in a cloud of red dust and filed off the birds to be met by a sergeant from the liaison section. He led us to a dried-up, dusty paddy not far from the landing zone and told us to make ourselves comfortable. Sergeant Below and I left the men in the paddy and followed the sergeant to the battalion CP, where we were told we would be going out later in the day and shown where on the map our insertion would be. We sat on a stack of 105 ammo crates and began outlining the assigned grid squares on our maps, writing down radio frequencies and reading current situation reports. We would be changing places with a patrol already in the area, which was not good. I worried about the patrol in place attracting a following and the possibility of stepping into an ambush intended for them. Other Marines would be operating in the vicinity, but none close enough to lend a hand if we got into trouble. Our insertion was scheduled for late afternoon.

Sergeant Below and I returned to the paddy and briefed the men. Then there wasn't anything to do but sit and wait.

At about 1600, the birds came for us. We boarded and lifted off, flying west toward the mountains. Our LZ was down low in the foothills, not far from a large village. The insertion would go about as unnoticed as a setdown at Hollywood and Vine. We went in without incident, and the outgoing patrol leader pointed to the hill he'd been on for the last two days and said it was a great spot to set up an OP. I wanted no part of it and headed the platoon in the direction of a more distant hill. Along the way, we twisted, turned, and doubled back to throw off or kill anyone who might be following. The vegetation was tall and thick enough so we could travel most of the distance to the hill without being seen. Within an hour, we were on the side of the hill, establishing an OP among some boulders screened by trees and heavy brush. I got out my binoculars and climbed a tree to look for Charlie Cong and his cousins from the north.

The area was loaded with them.

A thousand meters away, uniformed bearers moved up and down a trail, carrying weapons and supplies like a regular conveyor belt. Most of the bearers kept to disciplined intervals of one hundred feet or more, but a few of the careless ones tended to bunch up along the steep places in the trail.

Sergeant Below joined me in the tree and kept count while I reported our sightings to 3/7, then read off the coordinates and azimuth of the target to the 105 battery at Nui Dang and called for a shot.

The first two rounds were off, but after calling in the adjustments, they were soon on the trail. One black-pajama-clad oaf, ignoring the previous rounds, walked right into an exploding HE, which spread bits and pieces of him over a wide area. The others took note and went to ground. We stopped shooting and waited. After fifteen minutes, the bearers got up to continue the march. This time, I waited until three or four of them were bunched up on a steep incline before calling in the next shot. It landed about fifty feet from them and they went down like tenpins. After that, nobody moved for a long time, so I began scanning areas farther out. Under a tree, I found six VC squatting around a cooking fire and tried to drop a Willie Peter round on them. But it was off and served only to break up dinner and send the squatters running into the bushes.

Back on the trail, the bearers were moving again, this time at a much livelier pace. I called shots until dark, killing four more and for the time being playing havoc with the supply line. But soon after dark, they were moving by lantern light, and it was difficult to keep the rounds on target. Finally, I told arty to blast the trail every hour or so in the hopes of hitting something and climbed down from the tree.

The next day, it was back to the routine of the day before. We'd call in a few shots, and the enemy would go to ground. We'd wait, and they would start down the trail again, and again we would shoot. Neither of us seemed to tire of the game, and it would have gone on all day if 3/7 hadn't called and told us to move to an LZ and get ready for an extraction.

We saddled up and moved out. On the way, we took a few sniper rounds that were so far off I knew the shooter was guessing at our location and hadn't seen us. I reported it to 3/7, and before the choppers would come in, the pilots insisted that fixed wing make a pass at the area we thought the shots were coming from. A single Phantom roared in and dropped a pair of 250-pound fragmentation bombs on God knows what, then stayed on station while the extraction took place.

At Nui Dang, our next move was outlined for us and within an hour we were back in the air. This time, a first lieutenant, new in country, was assigned to bird-dog the patrol. He didn't seem to like the fact that he would be taking orders from me, a second lieutenant, and scarcely said a word to any of us. With the attitude the lieutenant had, I didn't want him along any more than he wanted to be there but was determined to make the best of it and would do what I could to keep him from getting hurt. As it turned out, he was a very senior first lieutenant about to make captain, and recon had sent him out to have at least one patrol under his belt before taking a job at the company level. His being assigned to the battalion meant that some patrol leader would have to stay in the bush a while longer because a new guy had come along to bump him out of a job in the rear—a practice all of us in the field resented.

We went in southwest of Nui Dang on top of an endless expanse of rolling hills. There was scarcely a tree in sight. Fortunately, there were a number of large granite boulders that offered excellent protection, and we made a beeline for them to set up an OP. Along the way, one of the men spotted a pair of VC moving along a trail below us. Both were armed, but before we could take them under fire, they disappeared into the brush. We weren't sure if they had seen us or not.

After securing our rock fortress, I split the patrol into two

groups and established OPs about one hundred meters apart
to observe as much terrain as possible.

In the OP looking to the east, I set up a spotting scope
mounted on a tripod and focused on a road two thousand
meters away. A squad-size unit was digging holes alongside
the road. I sent a SALUTE message to battalion and was told
the diggers must be ARVN. I called back and said they looked
like NVA. Battalion said they'd check on it. Meanwhile, I
watched them dig in the hot, noonday sun, convinced they
weren't ARVN. When battalion called again, they said they
didn't know who was down there, but I was not to shoot.

The day wore on. Sergeant Below was having more luck
from his OP and called in several fire missions on small
groups of VC moving from a village to the mountains.

Night came. For once, the monsoons had shut off, and the
night sky was clear and filled with stars. A warm, steady
breeze kept the mosquitoes away. Under the light of a full
moon, we watched the hills around us. It would have been
difficult for the enemy to sneak unobserved into our harbor
site, but still I worried about being probed and checked on
the men every hour or so. Around midnight, I woke the bird-
dogging lieutenant to make sure he was all right. I also
wanted him to know we weren't out here on a camping trip.
He sat up and snapped at me, wanting to know why I had
disturbed his sleep. I set my jaw and looked at him without
saying a word. Obviously, there wasn't anything I could teach
the guy, and I let him go back to sleep.

Before first light, I had everyone awake and in position to
fight should the need arise. One didn't. We ate and moved
back into our separate OPs.

Sightings were few and far between.

The day grew hotter and hotter, and toward noon we were
seeking shade wherever we could find it. But there was little
to be had in the scrub growth covering our hill. We lay panting, with our heads in small patches of shade and our bodies
roasting under a merciless sun. Down in the valley, heat
waves rose and quivered to distort the images in the scopes
so badly we couldn't tell what we were looking at. I passed

the word to secure until later in the afternoon when the valley cooled down, and we returned to the rocks to chase what shadows we could find there.

While monitoring the radio, I picked up a call from Sam Williams, who was surrounded by VC. Unaware the patrol was in their midst, the VC were within a few meters of Sam's position, chatting and carrying on like a day at the beach. Few officers had spent as much time in the field as Sam had, and now, due to rotate home any day, he wanted out badly. Over the radio, I heard his whispered pleas for an extraction, only to be told again and again he would have to wait. Later in the day, the patrol came out under fire, but without taking any casualties. I was glad he made it.

At 1600, we remanned the OPs, but our sightings had dried up.

Late that night, without warning, the army fired a "time on target" about one thousand meters from us and sent us scurrying for cover, wondering if we were next. A TOT is designed to have a maximum number of rounds from several widely scattered batteries slam onto a target simultaneously. Delivering such a heavy concentration of fire gives the enemy little opportunity to escape or even seek cover. TOTs were not commonplace, but were always impressive—whether they killed anyone or not. For ten minutes, we watched as 105 and 155 rounds impacted on an adjacent ridgeline. In the morning, more helicopters than I had ever seen in the air at one time pounded over the horizon and began unloading troops on the ridge. Battalion called and told us the army was kicking off a large-scale operation in the area and we would be coming out that day.

I gathered up the men and we headed for an LZ. On the way, we found a 250-pound bomb stuck in the ground. Some VC had discovered it earlier and had been trying to dig it up to use as a booby trap. I decided to blow it before going on to the LZ.

Most of our explosives were in the form of grenades and claymore mines, with a stick of C-4 for knocking down trees. We weren't carrying any time fuses or detonating cord, so

Sergeant Below suggested we rig the bomb with the C-4 and use a claymore to set it off. He packed the explosives into the hole near the nose of the bomb, screwed a blasting cap into the claymore, and unrolled the wire used to detonate it. With the wire unrolled, we were less than fifty feet from the bomb. I attached a second wire and ran it out. One hundred feet looked like a pretty safe distance, and a nearby rock would provide protection from the blast. I sent the rest of the platoon off behind a hill, and Sergeant Below and I got down behind the rock. I attached the claymore line to a small hand-held generator, took it off safe, and squeezed the handle, generating a low electrical current. The bomb went off with a roar. The concussion was enough to rearrange the fillings in my teeth. Worse, the sky was filled with rocks and large chunks of earth that were coming down all around us. We squeezed in tight against the rock, arms wrapped around our heads as rocks and clods of dirt rained down.

"Next time, we use a longer wire," I said after a large boulder thudded to earth not ten feet from us.

Where the bomb had been there was now a large smoking crater. I dug down into the bottom of the crater and pulled out a chunk of twisted metal weighing over a pound. Its edges were razor sharp, and I couldn't help thinking about the damage it would have done had it hit someone.

The birds were late, and we had to sit on the LZ, which was not my favorite thing to do. In the afternoon, they came for us, and we went out without taking any fire.

Back in 3/7's area, we were told we would be going out the next morning and until then we were to sit tight.

We made ourselves as comfortable as we could in our dry paddy, hooched up under ponchos to escape the sun, and devoured a case of C rations Corporal Brown, one of the squad leaders, had scrounged up.

With the night came the snipers. Just before dark, they started shooting from the cane fields surrounding the battalion. The shooting wasn't anything to write home about, it was just there. Two, three shots, then quiet. A while later, two or three more. It took a lot of guts to crawl up close to the edge of a Marine battalion and take up a firing position, and I couldn't help but admire the people out there. If the Marines got a fix on them, they'd be obliterated by artillery fire.

In the morning, our patrol was canceled, and word came we would be returning to Chu Lai. Our first trip to Duc Pho had gone well, and I was glad to be leaving without taking any casualties. Another team, Bennington, under Lieutenant Dick Johnson, would not fare as well. Within two days of our departure from Duc Pho, Bennington was shot out of three LZs. Forced to walk out with an infantry company, they dropped off to man an OP, only to run into VC and have to be extracted. The next day, the patrol went out again. On a hilltop, one of the men triggered a booby trap and was killed. Two other men were wounded.

I didn't even want to think about losing one of my men.

At Chu Lai, I was told I would be taking over the third platoon of Alpha Company and Sergeant Below would be in command of Dateline.

Switching platoons is not like moving to another part of an assembly line. I had been with Dateline long enough for a sense of trust and confidence to develop between us, and it was hard to have to suddenly abandon the men I had worked with for the past six weeks. But I had no say in the matter and was now in charge of Basketball, a platoon that had recently lost its leader.

The platoon sergeant, Sergeant Watkins, was new and inexperienced, and the company commander did not want him to take over the platoon. A second sergeant, one of the squad leaders, was awaiting a court-martial for abandoning an M-60 machine gun to the enemy during a firefight. The primary tac radio operator, a blowhard who turned hysterical when things heated up, could not be replaced due to a manpower shortage. Other than Sergeant Watkins and the sergeant awaiting court, who would soon be removed from the roster, the platoon was made up entirely of lance corporals and privates first class. There were no sergeants or experienced corporals to give the platoon needed depth. They were, however, a closely knit group of men. At the time, they numbered twenty, including the corpsman, Hospitalman Holthaus.

My introduction to the platoon was via a formation, followed by a weapons inspection and a run along the beach. The men were squared away, their weapons clean, and they seemed eager to prove themselves.

Our first patrol was notable in only two respects; elephant grass and a short round.

Two days after I took command, we went in near a mountain named Nui Dong Tranh and got dumped in a sea of elephant grass. Both birds went in at the same time, only I didn't know it because the pilots hadn't said a word about putting the entire platoon down at once. For several minutes I waited in the ten-foot-high grass, wondering what had gone wrong and why the second half hadn't come in. Finally, my radio operator said they were on the ground, only neither of us knew where the other was.

I called Sergeant Watkins on the radio, and he said he thought he was to our west and a little north. We began moving toward each other, but it was like groping for needles in the dark. I thought about calling the helicopters back so they could find us and we could find each other, but they were long gone over the mountains. Twenty minutes later, I heard a crashing off to our right. It sounded like elephants.

I told Sergeant Watkins to hold up his half of the patrol while we talked ourselves together. There began a loud hissing exchange as we tried to get a fix on each other. More crashing followed by cursing. Then the point man for the second squad fell into our clearing, and we linked up.

Sergeant Watkins and I got the patrol in line, and the sixteen of us set off toward a distant hill.

Elephant grass is a world entirely of its own.

Ten to twelve feet tall, the blades cut your skin like a knife and are so tightly interwoven they slow movement to a crawl. Six feet away, the man behind or in front of you disappears and panic sets in because you just *know* you are alone and lost. The grass will not part as you move through it. There is no pushing it aside to step gracefully into a sylvan glade.

It has to be chopped and beaten and crushed to get through it. From the middle of a field of grass, there is no discernible end or beginning; it is just there, everywhere. Down in it, the air doesn't move, and when you breathe it's like inhaling through a bag over your head. The heat is intense. Sweat soon soaks through your pack and runs in rivulets down your neck and back. You quickly grow light-headed, and your feet become so heavy it is all you can do to lift them. You want to give up and lie down to die, but you plod on.

I always walked third man back in the patrol, keeping a point man and backup in front of me. Some days, we would travel for hours like that without changing positions.

Ten minutes of moving through the grass, and the point man, Lance Corporal Morgan, was on the verge of passing out. I sent him back down the line, and the backup took his place. Then it was my turn. I handed my rifle to the radio operator and began throwing myself at the grass. The machetes had proven to be next to useless, and the only effective means of getting through was to break the grass down by throwing ourselves at the wall in front of us, gaining three or four feet at a time. This I did until my skin was cut to ribbons, I was covered with dirt, my tongue was hanging out, my head was spinning, and insects clouded around me. Then it was the next man's turn. Ten minutes was about all any one of us could take, and the moment I noticed a man groping to get to his feet, then swaying back and forth to stay there, I replaced him. During the next two and a half or three hours, I rotated the entire platoon through the job of breaking trail. When we reached the edge of the jungle, the grass was suddenly no longer there, and we had miraculously arrived. We were shaking from exhaustion, had gone through half of our water supply, and were cursing the world in general, the Marine Corps in specifics.

We moved onto the side of a hill and took a break. We had been resting for only a few minutes, when one of the men reported that something was moving toward us. I got the men down behind some rocks and fallen trees and we waited, rifles in position to open fire on whoever it was below us.

The sound grew louder, but still we couldn't see anything. By now, I pictured two or three gooks coming up after us and was set to take them out.

After what seemed like an eternity, one of the men whispered, "Chickens!"

"What do you mean, 'chickens'?" I hissed back.

"Right there, chickens!" the man repeated, pointing downhill.

I crept forward and looked. Sure enough, a flock of wild chickens was pecking and scratching its way toward us. I let out a long sigh of relief and got the men moving again.

On top of the hill, we established an OP. We were in a good defensive position, and what with just taking command of Basketball and the fact that half our water was gone, I decided to stay put.

We had limited enemy sightings and called in only one fire mission that day. At night, the world's slowest woodpecker went at it for hours.

The second day, we moved onto an overhang to watch the valley, saw nothing and went back to our original OP.

That night, I decided to register the night defensive fires I had previously called in to arty. We were on the extreme edge of the 155 fan, and although I was aware of the fact that the rounds might be a little wobbly, I didn't give it much thought.

When arty called, "Shot out!" I told the men to keep their heads down, but wasn't worried because I'd plotted the shot on a hill over three hundred meters away.

Suddenly, there was a sharp crack and an ear-shattering explosion, and the air around us was filled with metal. Shaken, I quickly called for a cease fire, then checked on the men. No one had been hit, but if we hadn't been down in the rocks, half the patrol would have been medevaced out, and one careless second lieutenant would have had a lot of explaining to do.

That 155 round gave me a lot of thinking to do over the next two days.

No rain, no probes, no voices in the dark.

We came out at the end of the fourth day.

8

Back at Chu Lai, it was a return to the routine—hold inspections, eat, sleep, get drunk, and go to the PX and blow dust off the labels of the canned Spam and Vienna sausages and ask yourself if you really wanted to buy this shit and eat it.

It was a dull, sometimes stifling way to live, but it lent the only normalcy I knew to life and beat the hell out of being in the bush. Dull and stifling meant a chance to survive. The bush only offered the opportunity not to.

Three times I managed to escape the confines of Chu Lai on missions other than military ones. Each time it was with two other officers to take our laundry by jeep to see Anne of An Tan. Anne was a willowy, pretty Vietnamese girl, who spoke English, sold souvenirs, and took in laundry. Her shop next to Highway 1, was surrounded by mud and smelled of diesel fumes and wood smoke, but was always neat and tidy. A dog out back growled a lot, but never bit anyone I knew. Anne was soft and friendly and the only female we had to talk to. Whenever we went there, the subject of politics and war never entered the conversation because none of us cared which side she was on, and it didn't matter anyway. The important thing was to joke and kid with her and have a beer and pretend we were somewhere else. And as much as we wished she'd take in more than just laundry, laundry was all we got. But even at Anne's, we couldn't escape the Marine Corps for long. The MPs would soon come by and tell us to move on then wait us out.

* * *

Two days after the elephant-grass patrol, I received my second operations order for Duc Pho. It was mid-March, and Operation Deckhouse/Desoto was still hammering away, and a lot of Marines were getting killed.

We lifted off on a clear, cloudless morning and made the long flight to Nui Dang, which had been beefed up even more since my last trip. It was now a place where people never stopped moving, and artillery fired around the clock into so many forgotten battles.

At 3/7's CP, I was told the patrol would be inserted within a few hours. I briefed the men, ate sparingly, and waited. Across the way from our dry paddy, platoon after platoon of infantry was being lifted into the maw beyond the wire. We knew whatever was going on was big and that we were now a part of it. When I heard Foxtrot 2/7 was going out, I made a trip to the LZ and tried to find Charlie Sudholt, a close friend from Basic School, and wish him luck or some damn thing. But Charlie had already gone.

When our turn came, we were flown out about five kilometers southwest from the battalion perimeter and inserted in the low, rolling hills there. The grass was waist high, and there was no cover, no place to hide, no place to go.

I moved the platoon to a nose offering some protection, instructed Sergeant Watkins to deploy the men so they covered our most vulnerable approaches, and set up an OP. Then I took out my binoculars and looked down on the plains. Below I found VC paradise—armed Munchkins everywhere. Just looking at them two thousand meters away brought on a dry mouth and nervous trembling.

The grunts were stalled outside a village, where air and artillery were trying to hammer an opening. The sounds of automatic weapons and exploding ordnance never let up.

Behind the village, the VC were bringing up reinforcements and carrying away what I guessed were their dead and wounded. I called artillery and tried to get them to shift some of their fire to the rear of the village, but got a negative reply—the grunts had priority. We had to satisfy ourselves by watching and calling in SALUTE messages.

I was very nervous about the position we were in. Sitting in the open on a bald nose that could easily be assaulted from three sides and offered only one escape route was not my idea of having a good time. It wasn't long before Sergeant Watkins cried out that a group of VC was headed our way. I gave the order to saddle up, and in an effort to elude the enemy, led the platoon down into a grassy ravine. Staying low, we worked our way around the nose of the next hill without exposing ourselves to the enemy. On the far side of the nose, we set up another OP. Sergeant Watkins took part of the second squad and crawled to the top of the hill to keep an eye on the VC behind us.

The new OP gave us a view of the plains and the face of a ridge seven hundred meters from the one we were on. On the far ridge, VC in groups of two and three moved steadily along a trail leading to the mountains south of us. This time, I was able to get a pair of 105s to shoot, and for fifteen minutes brought down a steady concentration of fire on the enemy, killing five or six and driving the rest to ground.

Sergeant Watkins came down off the hill and reported that the VC behind us were now approaching our old position. I decided to move again, and we began a stop-go, twisting, turning, deadly form of hide-and-go-seek that took us farther up the ridge we were on and closer to the adjoining one, which remained a beehive of activity.

Late in the day, as the sun was about to touch the horizon, we were taken under small-arms fire from a distance of six or seven hundred meters. The shooting was inaccurate, and none of the rounds hit near us, but the fact that someone knew where we were was not good. I called arty, told them it was urgent, and requested a fire mission. Within minutes, rounds were slamming into the enemy position. The distance from the guns to the target was so short and the fire so accurate, the gunners must have been boresighting their weapons. The enemy fire stopped soon after the first rounds hit, and we were not bothered by it again.

After the fire mission was secured, I began to think about our situation and felt that with such a large number of VC in the area, we would be in serious trouble if we had to spend the night on the ridge.

When the feeling wouldn't go away, I asked for an extraction, something I had not done before. I was told the extraction would have to wait until all of the medevacs the grunts had called for were completed, then battalion would see what could be done.

We held our position until dark, then set out on a march I hoped would keep the enemy from getting a fix on us. We moved to an adjoining hill, established a perimeter, waited fifteen minutes and moved to another hill. We waited, then moved on to the next hill. We kept on moving until about 2100, when we dropped down the side of the ridge and hid in a grove of banana trees not far from a hut, the outline of which could be seen in the dark. I wasn't sure if the enemy was near or not but felt confident we had lost them if they were. We probably could have spent the night unharmed in the grove, but there was something about the place that unnerved me, and I did not call off the extraction.

We waited for an hour before being notified that the birds were on the way. I passed the word to move out, and we climbed back to the top of the ridge. Once on top, we spread out in a wide fan and searched for any VC who might be near our LZ but found no one. Maybe they'd gone home for the night, or we'd lost them, or they were just behind the next hill getting drunk on sake and whipping themselves into a frenzy for a banzai charge. I didn't know, I didn't care. I just wanted to get us safely out.

A flare ship came on station, and the night around us suddenly turned to day as the flares began to drop. A pair of gunships made a pass over the LZ, then were followed by the first of two CH-46s, homing on my strobe light. It came in under tight gunship protection and took out Sergeant Watkins and the second squad. Then the trailing ship came in and picked up the rest of us. We came out without a shot being fired.

Later, I felt guilty about the extraction because we had successfully eluded the enemy and could have stayed on the

ridge. But at the time, I could not shake the feeling I had
about spending the night in a place that afforded the enemy
countless opportunities to do serious damage to the platoon.
There was no place to go on the ridge—something the infantry, which tends to flop down and dig in wherever the setting
sun finds them, never understood about recon. Our survival
depended on our ability to escape detection, which is next to
impossible in open, rolling terrain occupied by the enemy.

In the morning, we were assigned a new RAOR and told
we were going in to locate a VC battalion operating in the
mountains ten kilometers south of Nui Dang. Christ, locate
a VC battalion. I couldn't help but wonder what we were
supposed to do with it once we found it—tell the CO to report
to Nui Dang at once?

I returned to the platoon and briefed the men. We were
going in on the only feasible LZ in the area—a bald mountaintop surrounded by jungle. Our mission was to search an
area of some four square kilometers to determine exactly
where the enemy battalion was. What we were to do after
that was never made clear.

An area of four square kilometers doesn't look like much
on a map, but on the ground it is huge. Unfortunately, this
one lacked LZs, which was my biggest concern. We would
more than likely have to come out using the same one we
would use going in. Since Charlie wasn't exactly stupid, and
LZs attract gooks like a barnyard attracts flies, I knew that
if we did get in, there was a strong possibility we would have
trouble getting out.

Not only was the area difficult to get into and exit, but the
steep, mountainous terrain would restrict our movement and
keep us confined to the ridges and hillsides; places where
Charlie, who tended to occupy the valleys, would expect to
find us.

I did not like our newly assigned RAOR; it was the perfect
place to disappear and never be heard from again.

Sergeant Watkins and I went through the platoon, checking equipment and making sure everyone had filled their canteens. We then moved to the battalion LZ, where a pair of

CH-46s waited. We boarded and lifted off, two gunships rising with us.

As we flew out, I took a long, hard look at the rapidly diminishing Nui Dang and wondered if I'd ever see it again. Funny how you can suddenly feel homesick and lonely for a place overrun with flies that looks and smells like a hobo camp.

Within minutes, we were approaching the LZ. The gunships were already making dry runs on it, holding their fire as I requested. If they shot up the LZ, Charlie would know for sure we were going in and head straight for it; not good. I had also asked the pilots to make a false insertion on a mountain five hundred meters to the east after we went in. Had there been more places to land, I would have asked for half a dozen false insertions. Any confusion we could create in the mind of the enemy would work to our advantage, but here there weren't enough LZs to fool anyone for very long.

We went in clean and were quickly on the ground. Once we got our bearings, we carefully picked our way through the grass and down off the mountain top. We hit a screen of thick vegetation, broke through, and found ourselves under the jungle canopy. I deployed the men in a hasty defense and passed the word to keep quiet and listen for any movement around us. Once I was satisfied we weren't about to be attacked, I checked my map and compass, then got the patrol up and moving.

We were on a wide ridge running north from the LZ. The canopy rose to a height of sixty and seventy feet and the growth beneath was thin enough to move through without having to break it down.

It was hot, humid, and stifling. Not a leaf moved or a vine trembled in the still air.

The ridge was covered with trails, all of which seemed to have been used only minutes before. I passed the word to keep three- and four-meter intervals between each man and to stay absolutely quiet.

Then time seemed to stand still as we crept along the ridge. At each tree he came to, the point man stopped to search the ground to our front and the foliage above and check for trip wires. Once he was satisfied it was safe to go on, he moved silently to the next tree and began searching once again. Each of us in turn followed, first looking ahead, to the sides, and rear. Sixteen of us, strung out over one-hundred eighty feet, performing a ballet of life and death through the forest. Glide forward. Stop. Turn the head slowly from right to left and back. Look up. Listen to the jungle through the beating of your heart. Glide forward. Stop . . .

An hour went by, and we hadn't gone more than two hundred meters down the ridge. All of us could sense the enemy's presence, and the farther down the trail we went, the more tense and jumpy we grew. I moved in a crouch and was sweating heavily from the exertion of holding the bent-over position. My head ached, grease paint and mosquito repellent stung my eyes. My mouth was so dry I had to stop time and again to drink from a canteen to keep from gagging on the cotton in my throat. I wanted to urinate badly, but didn't dare to for fear of an ambush being sprung while I was holding my dick in my hand. The muscles of my arms spasmed constantly from carrying my rifle in a ready position—right hand at the small of the stock, index finger resting lightly on the trigger, left hand supporting the barrel. Maybe someday they'll issue us plastic guns with suction-cup darts, and we can play this fucking game all day long without getting hurt, I thought.

Our defensive fires were already plotted and in place, ready for instant use. But the fact they were there, capable of blowing gaping holes in the jungle, didn't give me much comfort. If we walked into an ambush, we would be so close to the enemy we probably couldn't use them anyway. I kept on taking sips from my canteen.

The tension grew until we could have cut it out of the air with a knife and served it up in large chunks. Finally, I decided I'd had enough of the ridge and its countless trails and moved the platoon off and down the side to some rocks beneath the trees. For some reason, I didn't deploy the men in a perimeter, but left them strung out in a line. Thinking we were well off the trail above us, I passed the word to take a break.

Less than two hours on the ground, and I felt like I'd been in the bush for a week.

I finished off one of my canteens and ate some C-ration pound cake. A small green snake slithered over a nearby rock, and I watched, fascinated by its rippling colors. Odd how your mind sometimes tries to free itself from its surroundings. I didn't know whether the snake was poisonous or not, but I found myself obsessed by its color and movement, and for a moment it carried me from that place.

Then the jungle exploded.

Automatic rifle fire poured over us so heavily, the leaves above rained down in chopped bits and pieces and kept on raining. In an instant, we were on the ground and facing uphill. Shouts and curses coming from above added to the confusion around me. In a state of near panic, I yelled at the men to get on line and began shoving and pushing those nearest me into the positions I wanted them in. Bullets were hitting everywhere in the trees and ricocheting off the rocks as the men scrambled on hands and knees to form a line. The shooting was high, and the rounds were passing two or more feet over our heads. No one near me was hit, but I couldn't see more than twenty or thirty feet uphill and didn't know if anyone farther up had been or not.

The initial burst of fire had been so heavy it was impossible to tell if any of it was ours, but now I could hear the trailing element firing steadily at the enemy. The position we were in prevented half the platoon from shooting back without hitting our own men, and our volume of fire was not what it should have been.

Word came down that Private First Class Lucas, the last man in the column, was pinned down in the rocks above us, and the gooks were trying to close on his position. Voice shaking, but with a mind that was amazingly clear, I yelled for those around him to provide covering fire while Lucas withdrew. Lucas, who was very cool about the whole thing, not only got himself down, but continued firing at the gooks as he came.

My radio operator kept asking over and over what he was supposed to do, and I finally snapped at him to tell battalion we needed a gunship and to get it up now.

Our return fire picked up gradually as the men came on line, rose to their knees and pumped round after round back uphill. Lucas scrambled into our midst unhurt, but minus his pack. We were spread out, and, in spite of the enemy being above us and still shooting, seemed to have taken control of the situation. Still, I wasn't about to order a charge up a hill no one wanted in the first place.

Then the firing stopped, and all we could hear were the groans and babblings of three or four dying gooks. Not forty feet away, one kept repeating the same plea for help over and over. His cries were so pitiful, I couldn't help feeling sorry for him.

Sergeant Watkins reported that none of the men had been injured during the firefight. The only casualty was Lucas's pack, which had been shot off his back. The straps and frame were there, but the pack was gone.

We stayed on line and backed a hundred feet downhill as I talked to arty and got them to put a few rounds on top of the ridge. When I heard, "Shot out," I got the men down. The first round was on target, and I called for a fire for effect. As rounds pounded up and down the ridge line, we moved farther downhill. Within a few minutes, the gunships were over us, and I gave them the enemy's position and told them to make a run from north to south along the top of the ridge. Arty ceased firing, and the gunships made several passes, raking the target with machine-gun and rocket fire.

Battalion had already told us to move to the nearest LZ for an extraction, but by now I wasn't sure of our position and didn't know in which direction our alternate lay. I asked the pilot of the lead gunship to fly toward us and look for a colored flare. When he saw one, he was to give me our location and a heading to our zone, a rice paddy in a high valley. Then I began firing pencil flares up through the canopy, the flares trailing blue and yellow streamers two and three hundred feet into the air. The pilot spotted one of the streamers and radioed down our coordinates and the heading I needed to get to the LZ, which was over five hundred meters away. I radioed back that it would take two hours or more to get there, thanked him for his help, and asked if he would continue buzzing the ridge while we cleared out of the area. He Rogered my request, and the gunships went back to shooting up the ridgeline.

I could have kissed those guys.

Then, after I found out what had happened on the ridge, I could have kissed Private First Class Lucas.

I passed the word we were heading for an LZ and to be alert because every VC in the neighborhood would be looking for us. However, at that moment, the men couldn't have been more alert than they were.

We moved quickly through the forest, pausing every few minutes to see if we were being followed. For a while, we were, then whoever it was behind us changed their minds and broke off the chase. Signs of the enemy were everywhere around us, and we fully expected to make contact before reaching the LZ. Several times the point man balked at the narrow defiles in front of us and motioned for us to pull back and work our way around them, convinced they were ambush sites.

There was no doubt a large VC unit was in the area, but the gods were smiling on us that day, and we only bumped up against a patrol rather than a larger force. Thus blessed, we found the zone without further incident, and I called battalion asking for an extraction. Within minutes, the birds were overhead.

We were going out of a paddy, thigh-deep in mud and water. When the first bird came in, the pilot failed to tell me how many men to board. As the men struggled through the mud to reach the bird, I ran slipping across a dike and up the ramp, yelling at the crew chief for a number. But as I approached him, he turned and went back to his gun at a forward porthole. I grabbed his shoulder, spun him around and

yelled again, and he held up eight fingers. I turned to exit
the bird and discovered that, with the exception of one
man, the entire platoon had boarded. I began shoving men
toward the rear in an effort to get them off the overloaded
helicopter. Just then, the ramp closed, and we were airborne.
I pushed my way forward again, yelling at the crew chief,
trying to tell him I had a man on the ground. He couldn't
understand a word I was saying, so I grabbed his head and
turned it in the direction I was pointing and yelled, "You
asshole, one of my men is still on the ground!"

Below, Lance Corporal Carr, alias The Grunt, stood in
the middle of the paddy, growing smaller by the second, a
look of complete dismay on his face.

After much arguing and yelling, the crew chief got the
message across that a second bird was already going down
for Carr. I stuck my head out a porthole and watched until
he was picked up and in the air. Then, when the sickening
feeling of having left a man on the ground passed, I sat down
on the floor of the helicopter, put my head between my knees,
and shook.

At Nui Dang, I found out what had happened to Lucas on
the ridge.

When we moved down the side of the mountain and
stopped in a position I thought was well off the top of the
ridge, Private First Class Lucas and another man were still
up near the trail. About the time I was eating my pound cake
and watching the green snake, Lucas heard something coming toward him and grabbed his rifle. When a pajama-clad
Vietcong parted the bushes in front of him, Lucas shot him
in the chest, killing him instantly. Two other VC ran firing at
Lucas, only to be shot down. When a fourth appeared, Lucas
shot him, too. The man next to him opened up, and two
more of the enemy went down. During this time, the VC
patrol was putting out a heavy volume of fire, and it sounded
like a one-sided engagement in their favor, which it wasn't.

Hurt, the Vietcong, whose number was about twenty,
backed away from the edge of the ridge, and the fighting
subsided.

Later, I wrote up Private First Class Lucas for a Silver Star, accrediting him with saving our lives. During a battalion ceremony a few months later, he received the award.

We were told by 3/7 to stand down for the rest of the day. In the dry paddy we ate and turned to cleaning our weapons.

That night, I spent a long time looking at the stars and wondering about the future.

In the morning, I was told we were going in six hundred meters east of the same low hills we had been on two days prior.

Two new men and a first lieutenant, bird-dogging his second patrol, were assigned to the platoon, bringing Basketball's strength up to nineteen. I put Sergeant Watkins in charge of the lieutenant and assigned one new man to each squad.

We lifted off early in the afternoon and were inserted without any problem. Once we were organized on the ground, we moved out along the face of a hill that seemed to go on forever. There wasn't a cloud in the sky, and the air in the waist-high grass was dead calm. The temperature hovered in the midnineties.

Forty-five minutes into the patrol, one of the new men passed out and fell heavily to the ground. Between the heat and the fear of being on his first patrol with a dirty, ragged group of Marines, who bore no resemblance whatsoever to the clean-cut, all-American superhero depicted on your local recruiting poster, he caved in. The corpsman, Hospitalman Holthaus, went to work immediately, trying to revive him. When the unconscious man failed to respond, I called for a medevac, which was in the air within minutes. When the bird came in, we loaded the heat casualty, and he was flown back to the tent hospital at Nui Dang. We were close enough so that I was able to follow the flight all the way to the battalion LZ without using binoculars.

We saddled up and moved out.

Less than an hour later, the second new man, who was near me, turned pale, and his eyes started to roll in his head. I decided it was time for a break and led the platoon to the top of a nearby hill. Just as we reached the top, the man's eyes rolled all the way back, and he pitched to the ground. I called for a second medevac.

Three minutes after I made the call, Sergeant Watkins yelled, ''Gooks on the hill!''

I looked up and saw several VC peering down at us from no more than one-hundred fifty feet away. They seemed just as surprised to see us as we were to see them.

Hollering, ''Shoot the fuckers!'' I grabbed my rifle and opened up, emptying a magazine in one long burst. The men, still keyed up from the day before, opened up at the same instant with a solid wall of fire that knocked down two VC before they had a chance to take cover.

We were on open ground, with the enemy above us, and would have been in trouble if it weren't for the volume of fire we were putting out. Because of it and the aggressive action of the men, the enemy's fire never got any better than unaimed and sporadic throughout the duration of the fire-fight. Some of the incoming rounds dug into the ground around us, but most of them passed harmlessly overhead. Still, we were in a dangerous position.

Separated from my radio operator, who had flattened himself on the ground thirty feet away, I shouted at him to contact battalion and get a pair of gunships over us. Then I turned back to directing the platoon's fire, which had tapered off from its original explosive volume to shorter, more disciplined bursts, punctuated by the *thump crack* of the M-79 as the 40-mm grenades impacted on the gooks' part of the hill. The smell of cordite was strong, and the noise was deafening as we fired, cursed, and maneuvered to improve our situation on the hill.

Then, in the middle of the firefight, the medevac suddenly appeared overhead. It was escorted by two gunships. I yelled at the radio operator to tell the medevac to move off and to bring in the gunships to start a run from west to east and begin firing on the hill as soon as they crossed the red smoke we had thrown toward the enemy. However, a breeze came up and the smoke began to curl back toward us, and things got a little out of hand.

Instead of talking the gunships in, the radio operator, close to panic, began screaming at them to get us out of there. Just then, a gunship came in from the north, making a run on our position, its sights fixed on the red smoke.

I stopped firing at the enemy and watched dumbstruck as the ship came in, rockets streaming out of their pods to impact moments later. They were walking directly toward us, throwing clods of dirt and grass into the air and leaving a chain of smoking holes in their wake. On they came. *Crump! Crump! Crump!* I was mesmerized by their twisting deadliness and speed. Then in a cloud of swirling smoke, one left its pod headed straight at me, and the world stopped. There was no noise, no shooting, no cursing, no Vietnam. Only quiet and a strange sense of peace, and it seemed only natural when my daughter's face appeared, filling the sky. She smiled down at me, and I felt myself reaching out to touch the curls of her hair and feel their softness. Nothing else was there, just her face haloed by the blue sky. It stayed there for the longest time.

Then she was gone, and the rocket sizzled by so close I could have grabbed it. It impacted behind me, and I whipped around in time to see The Grunt flying over backwards through the air and think, Jesus, he's dead.

I yelled at the radio operator to get the birds off us and jumped to my feet and began waving my arms and screaming in an effort to divert the next gunship. Just as he started his run, the pilot saw me and peeled off.

I ran over to the radio operator, yelling at him to get the pilots to hit the top of the hill. This time, the message got through, and the gunships began working over the ground above us.

The fire coming from the hill diminished gradually, but several gooks tried to hit us from the flanks by moving down a ravine filled with thick brush. They got in close enough to throw five or six Chicom grenades and wound the machine gunner, who was slightly forward of our perimeter and about one hundred feet from me. When he cried out that he couldn't see, I yelled for someone to go get him and bring him to a safer part of the hill. About then, I caught sight of The Grunt streaking over the top of our hill and thought that for a dead man he runs pretty well. With him went the corpsman, and together they brought the machine gunner and his weapon safely back.

At some point in there, riding an adrenaline high I had never before or since experienced, I knew I was bulletproof. Rounds popping around us, grenades going off, I stayed on my feet, yelling words of encouragement to the men, directing fire, and throwing grenade after grenade into the ravine.

Unable to stand up to the volume of fire we were putting out, the gooks broke contact and fled, and the fight was over as quickly as it had begun. Later, the S-3 captain at Chu Lai climbed my frame over the ammunition we expended, taking me to task for not being more conservative and thinking in terms of a prolonged engagement, rather than a twenty-minute firefight. Then he got on me about leaving Private First Class Lucas's pack on the ridge, accusing me of resupplying the gooks with food and ammunition and insisting that we should have gone back for the pack. Very slowly, very carefully, I explained the events as they happened and how I felt about sacrificing lives for a pack containing one hundred rounds of ammunition, a bouncing betty, and six cans of C rations, plus assorted other items, when the gooks had an abundance of their own. But the captain was not satisfied and remained unhappy with my performance. I was upset by his attitude, but there wasn't much I could do about it. After all, how do you explain to someone who never went to the field just what it's like when a firefight erupts?

After the gooks scattered into the hills around us, the medevac came in and took out our heat casualty, who was still unconscious, and the men who were wounded: The Grunt with a piece of metal in his chest, the machine gunner with a head wound, and a third man with shrapnel in one hand. None of the wounds were serious. The rest of us came out in a single CH-46, and we flew back to Nui Dang. From there, we went on to Chu Lai, where I wrote up The Grunt (Lance Corporal Carr) and Hospitalman Holthaus for Silver Stars. Carr received his, but some magician at division reduced the Silver Star for Holthaus to a Bronze.

Private First Class Lucas, Lance Corporal Carr, and Hospitalman Holthaus represented the spirit of the platoon, and I was sorry I couldn't have written up each man for an award. After our trip to Duc Pho, I could not have been more proud of the men under me, and that pride exists to this day. As for the radio operator, I made it clear to him that in future emergencies he was to glue himself to my ass and stay there or he would find himself reduced in rank and out of a job.

9

In my hooch at night I found myself deeply troubled by the picture of my daughter's face in the sky. It had been so real and indelible that in the dark when I closed my eyes I could still see it. She had been there with me, smiling, serene, and confident, somehow knowing her daddy was going to be all right. But how had she come so far and why?

During a long, leech-infested patrol when the monsoons were still on, I had seen someone else, and her image was also etched in my mind.

We were harbored for the night in a tangle of fallen trees, having moved there shortly after Private First Class Henderson, the machine gunner for Dateline, had a VC stand up in front of him just before dark. Henderson didn't kill him because he had almost opened up on me the day before while I was going over the ground outside our perimeter—an incident that left us both shaken. Before Henderson was sure of what he was looking at, the VC was gone. He reported the incident to me, and we moved in the dark to a new harbor site. When we got there, the rear element reported hearing movement around our old site. Nervous, I sat up most of the night, monitoring the radio and listening to the jungle. A slow, steady rain began to fall, and it wasn't until 0200 that I went to sleep. Shortly afterwards, Margie Hansen came to me.

I had known Margie since the fourth grade. One winter day when we lined up after lunch to go back to class, she was just there, a new kid. In class, I couldn't keep my eyes off of her and had to be reminded several times by the teacher to go back to work. Margie was far from being beautiful or well dressed, and she was outshown in both respects by many of the other girls in class. She was skinny, her mouth was too wide for her face, and her hair was a plain, dishwater blonde. Her clothes were also plain, and everyday she wore the same green, threadbare coat to school. Her mother worked in a restaurant and barely made enough to get by on. And unlike any of the other kids in class, her father had abandoned the family. Margie had all the ingredients for a troubled life, but that wasn't her style. Instead, she was kind, quick to help, and radiated an inner strength and confidence none of the rest of us had at that age.

I fell instantly and completely in love with her.

I wanted to be her protector, but she never seemed to need protecting. I wanted to kiss her, but didn't have the nerve. Instead, I asked her for help with my school work, help she readily gave.

We attended the same church, went to school dances together, and in the years to come were often in the same class. In high school, I was still in love with her but was too shy to tell her. Then in our junior year, Margie died of cancer. I didn't understand why and was a long time getting over it. In the years after high school, I still thought about her.

Then in the heavy mist falling in the forest above a valley deep in the mountains of South Vietnam, she appeared, framed in a bright shimmering light. She wore a long white gown and moved toward me through the trees without touching them or stirring the leaves beneath her feet. As she approached, she kept calling my name, softly repeating it over and over. Her hands and face were clearly defined, but the gown she wore was so white it was hard to look at. Then, standing before me, she called to me for the last time, and I woke with a start and jumped to my feet, searching for her.

But Margie was gone, and only the mist and the blackness and the sounds of the jungle were there. Her image was so clearly etched in my mind, I carried it with me for days, convinced she had been with me in the forest.

Now, after seeing my daughter's face in the sky, I began to wonder if something was wrong with me.

Coupled with seeing people who weren't there and nightmares that began to plague me was a chronic fatigue I could not shake. Often after getting up and dressing in the morning, I had to sit down and rest. The trudge through the sand from the company office to my hooch left me listless and breathing hard. I am sure we were all affected by fatigue to one degree or another, but no one ever seemed to complain, and we just carried on as though it were normal. Which, in a sense, it was.

The fatigue was especially bad whenever we picked up a bug from the jungle water we often had to drink. The weekly malaria pills had us all crapping loads the consistency of mush, but with a waterborne bug in the system, the mush turned to soup. There were times when my bowels moved with such liquid fury they doubled me over in pain and left me faint and shaking with my pants around my ankles.

On patrol, my nerves took over and blocked out most of the fatigue, but the moment we were extracted and safely in the air, it returned, and I felt limp and helpless. I began to worry that the feeling would come on me while we were in the bush and cause me to become careless.

After Duc Pho, we were sent up to Hill 707 to lay around and do battle with the insects for a week. There was no sign of enemy activity around us or in the valleys below.

When we returned to Chu Lai, I learned that Dick Johnson had been killed. During a firefight in the mountains north of the Song Tra Dong, he was hit in the chest and bled to death in the medevac chopper. I had known Dick in Basic School, where he had graduated at the top of the class. We had become friends at Chu Lai, where he was well liked by both officers and enlisted. His death hit all of us hard. When Grover Murray and I went out to pick up our laundry from Anne, she asked where Dick was. After a long pause, Grover told her he was dead. Then skinny little Anne with the wide smile said, "He's asleep now," with such kindness and heartfelt belief, her words reached inside and touched us both.

Before our next trip to the bush, Basketball was split into two patrols. But due to illness, casualties, R & R, and beefing up the second squad for Sergeant Watkins' first time out as patrol leader, I ended up going to the field with just seven men. Two of those were new in country. One of the new men was an out-of-shape gunnery sergeant on his second tour. His first tour had been with a rifle company, and his assignment to recon was not his choosing, and he was nervous about going out.

We went in on a sandbar in a stream at the base of 410 South and immediately lost radio contact with everything but the birds. The mountains around us blocked out our signals so effectively that the radio operator was forced to use the long antenna. We made contact with an artillery battery that relayed our messages to battalion, but even with the long antenna up, the signal was broken and weak. Once we had checked in, we took down the antenna and moved out to find an OP.

To say I was riddled with anxiety over the facts that our communications was poor, there were only eight of us in the patrol, and the ground around us was covered with trails showing signs of recent enemy activity, was an understatement.

We crept through the jungle in silence, with Lance Corporal Morgan running point. We didn't hear anything, we didn't see anything, but the tension grew. When Morgan got tired breaking down the heavy brush we were in, I rotated the other men through the point. I was soon down to one of the new men, a private first class. I had never stuck a new man on point before, but this time I didn't have a choice. He was badly frightened and kept looking back to me for reassurance, which wasn't something I had a whole lot of to give at the moment. It wasn't long before he was turning pale and staggering. I sent him back behind me, and Morgan again took point.

We set up an ambush near the junction of several trails. The gunny was showing all the signs of heat exhaustion, and as we waited for some unsuspecting soul to wander past and get shot full of holes, I kept pouring water over him and made sure he was drinking. No one walked into the ambush and after an hour, I passed the word to move out. We started up the side of a mountain, but by now the gunny was really getting sick, and we were soon forced to rest, then head back downhill. The heat and humidity in the low river bottom was fast approaching brutal, and each time we moved, the gunny got sicker. Heat and fear had also gotten to the new private first class, who had become as pale and clammy as the gunny.

Contact with the enemy at that point would have been a disaster.

We stayed hidden until dark, then moved into a thick tangle of brush and vines that, once cut, dripped water on us all night long. We were tightly bunched up in our hiding place, but I didn't think anyone would find us in the dark.

I didn't sleep.

By morning, the gunny and the private first class were only slightly better, so I called for an extraction. The message was relayed to battalion, and an approval was given. Our next move was to get to an LZ, and we spent the next three hours backtracking, while carrying the gunny's pack and rifle and pouring water over him. As the morning grew hotter, the gunny got worse. At times, he was so bad off he wandered at a tangent to our line of march and had to be grabbed and set back on course.

The birds came up early, but I couldn't find an LZ in the thick vegetation around us. I fired off my pencil flare, and one of the pilots saw the brightly colored streamers rise above the canopy and gave me the heading to a small clearing he said he would set down in. We pushed on, but still I could not find the LZ. Finally, the pilot marked the LZ by landing in it, trimming branches and leaves off the trees as he came in; the zone so tight there was scarcely room for the big CH-46. The guy had balls.

Fifty feet from the LZ, we hit a wall of brush so thick we

couldn't break through to the bird. I was up front, dragging the gunny by the suspender straps, when we ran up against the brush. I threw him into it as hard as I could, then picked him up and threw him again. He was almost dead weight, but he served beautifully to break down the bushes keeping us from the helicopter. After the fourth throw, the gunny fell through to the LZ. We were right behind him and dragged him onto the chopper. I was exhausted but eternally grateful to the pilot who had the guts to set down where he did and wait for us.

Cutting our way back up through the branches overhanging the LZ, we lifted off and headed for Chu Lai.

We hadn't seen or heard any VC, but the patrol had been a nightmare. Being so far out with so few men had gotten to me, and I wondered how many more recon patrols I could take. I was at the point where I was afraid all the time.

At Chu Lai, we left the gunny and the private first class at the medical battalion and flew back to LZ Quail. The gunny was transferred to a line company, and I never saw him again. I believe he was a good man and capable of doing his job well. Recon just wasn't for him.

When we returned to the battalion area, I was told I would be taking over my old platoon, Dateline. Lieutenant Ridgeway, recently arrived from the grunts, would now be leading Basketball.

Dateline had been hit hard at Duc Pho. It had happened during an extraction from the same low hills we had fought over a few days before. On the way out, the bird came under heavy fire and several of the men inside were hit. An incoming tracer struck Private First Class Spark's pack, which immediately began to burn. Sergeant Below tore the pack off Spark's back and threw it out of the helicopter moments before a claymore and a stick of C-4 exploded with enough force that would have blown the bird out of the air. For his actions, Sergeant Below was written up for a Silver Star, which he later received. However, he and three other men had been wounded and were in the hospital. Private First

Class McNaughton, the primary tac radio operator, had been shot in the head and was not expected to live.

A total of fifteen mustered for the next patrol, and we were inserted in country of unbelievable beauty. Black granite monoliths towered above us as we wandered through a valley of scattered trees and waving grass. Our OPs overlooked clear streams and cloud-capped mountains that reached into Laos. Truly, we had found paradise. However, I had no idea where we were.

On the way in, the pilot and I both agreed that the LZ looked like the one plotted on my map and down we went. I called in sitreps on the hour and kept battalion posted as to our location, but something wasn't right with the terrain. No matter how many times I tried to orient the map with the ground, things didn't line up like they should have. They were close, but not right.

By the afternoon of the second day, I knew we were in the wrong place. Corporal Brown, the assistant patrol leader, and I sat down and tried to figure out where we were. After a great deal of trial and error, we got a pretty good fix on our location, but weren't sure. In an attempt to confirm it, I called up arty and asked them to shoot a Willie Peter round at a distant hill. If the round hit anywhere near the hill, we would know exactly where we were.

Arty called back and said they wouldn't shoot.

"Why not? Over."

"Because you don't have a legitimate target," came the reply. "Over."

"What do you mean, it's not legitimate? It's a hill. It's in Vietnam. And right now nobody's on it, and I need a marking round to fix our location. Over."

"Are there any friendly troops in the area? Over."

"How do I know? I'm not even sure where we are. That's why I want you to shoot. Over."

Long pause.

"Dateline, be advised, your request is denied. Over."

"Grand Canyon, how in the fuck am I supposed to find out where I am if you won't shoot? Over!"

"Dateline, be advised to use proper language over the air. Over."

"Bullshit! Out!" I swore, signed off, and threw the handset to my radio operator.

We moved and kept moving, and the day before we were to come out, we ran out of food. Then we got extended for forty-eight hours. After we went through a bottle of Vitamin Es the corpsman had, we chewed grass and waited. Luckily, there was no shortage of water, and we did not want for something to drink.

When we came out late on the sixth day, I discovered something peculiar had begun to happen to me. I had started to lose track of time. I came off patrol thinking it was Monday, and it was Wednesday. Then I came off another patrol thinking it was Friday, and it was Sunday. I knew the dates but not the days. As time went on, the offsetting became worse, until the largest number of days I was ever off was six. Try as I did, I could not explain why the days were lost, but since the offset always worked to my advantage, I stopped questioning it. I never gained days, I always lost them, which did seem to make the time go by faster.

Five patrols went by after Duc Pho, and we had not seen hide nor hair of the enemy.

Then at the beginning of April, I got word to pack up and get ready for a move up north. Dateline and a platoon from Delta Company were being attached to the 3d Marine Division, operating from the DMZ to south of Phu Bai. Casualties were heavy throughout that area, and the news we were going north was not good.

Two days after I received the order, we were flown out by C-130 to Phu Bai, headquarters of the 3d Marine Division. After we landed and off-loaded, we had to wait on the runway next to another C-130 being loaded with bodies in large green bags. The stench in the air around us was close to overwhelming. Watching the bodies being transferred from the deuce-and-a-halfs that brought them, did nothing to boost my morale.

Eventually, we were picked up by 3d Recon and driven to our new quarters in the division compound.

The camp at Phu Bai was laid out in neat orderly rows, much like Chu Lai, but in a more confined area. It was about fifteen kilometers south of Hue, just off Highway 1. The surrounding hills were low, rolling, and covered with a tough, low-growing brush. Farther to the west were the mountains.

We were shown to our hooches, briefed, given a welcome-aboard talk and promptly had one hundred magazines for our newly issued M-16s stolen. The magazines were eventually returned and an apology given. It was the rifles that should have been stolen, and I could have cared less if they were returned.

When the M-16s were first issued to us at Chu Lai, we thought we really had something. Lightweight, shorter than the M-14, the M-16 could be fired on full or semiautomatic. The ammunition was smaller and lighter, and we could easily carry more of it. And, it looked like a space-age weapon—complete with carrying handle, a pistol grip, and a front handguard streamlined enough to do Buck Rogers proud. There was, however, a minor problem. The M-16 didn't work. After firing three or four rounds, it would fail to eject. With a spent round still in the chamber, the next one would jam in the receiver. Immediate action involved prying out the round in the receiver, then running a cleaning rod down the bore to knock out the cartridge stuck in the chamber. Instead of carrying a weapon we were able to drag through the mud and know would unfailingly hammer out round after round, we now had something akin to a muzzle-loader—a real comfort to the foot soldier.

All of the words of wisdom dictated by all of the senior officers in the Marine Corps, and all of the denials that the M-16 malfunctioned repeatedly, did not make it work. Not even after every man in the battalion was required to listen to a taped message from the commandant of the Marine Corps explaining to the press that reports of the M-16 malfunctioning were exaggerated and false, did it work.

The fault, it was said, was because the troops weren't

cleaning their weapons properly. We didn't keep the dust cover over the receiver closed. We let carbon build up in the gas chamber. We were filling the magazines to capacity, rather than leaving two rounds out as prescribed.

We followed every set of directions published about the M-16 and cleaned until we were blue in the face, and it still didn't work.

Finally, I ordered my men to tape their cleaning rods alongside their weapons, ready for immediate use. It was the only insurance we had against a jam. M-16s that ran through a full magazine without malfunctioning, were looked upon with no small degree of awe. "Hey, that one works!" we would exclaim and point excitedly.

For my part, I hung onto my trusty M-14, arguing that we had nothing else to fire rifle grenades with. It was an argument that kept me from having to draw an M-16 for two months after the troops got theirs.

After the incident of the stolen magazines, Sergeant Browning, who was now my platoon sergeant, put up a sign on the troops' hooch. The sign bore the skull and crossed paddles of our battalion emblem, but in place of "Swift, Silent, and Deadly," Sergeant Browning had substituted the words, "1st Recon, Second to None." When I told him I liked the sound of it, he said, "I just want these assholes in 3d Recon to know who we are, Lieutenant."

Our first week with 3d Recon was spent going through a training program that involved map and compass reading, radio procedure, artillery and mortar fire direction, and a chance to zero our weapons on a firing range. We were grateful for the break, and it proved to be a good opportunity to train all of the men in the platoon at one time.

Just outside the 3d Marine Division compound there was a large ARVN recruit training facility that we passed every day on our way to our classes. It was the first time I had seen the South Vietnamese Army up close, and I noticed that they seemed to sit around a lot. Also, when they were doing close-order drill or in outdoor classrooms, they were easily distracted by every passing truck, motorbike, and stray chicken.

They were adept at giving us hard looks and their version of the finger, which was to hold the middle and index fingers aloft while rubbing the former up and down against the latter. Either hand can be used to give the sign, but the right was the hand of preference.

My overall impression was that enthusiasm was lacking.

Third Recon had paid its dues in the north, and their numbers were down. They were short of patrol leaders above the rank of corporal, and, in fact, many corporals were leading patrols. However, morale was good.

The first week we were there, a recon company arrived from Okinawa to build up the roster. All of the officers and men were new in country, and only a few of them had any combat experience. The company commander was an overweight, energetic captain about my age, who strutted about officiously with a pipe clenched between his teeth. His entire demeanor stated, "*I* have arrived." And indeed he had.

When it came time to go out, the platoon was split into two patrols, and mine was the first to go.

On a hot, overcast day, we were inserted in the hills due east of Hue city, near the Song Bo. The vegetation was low and offered very little in the way of concealment. We moved for several hours before finding a protected hilltop offering a good view of the Song Bo and surrounding countryside.

We set up an OP and spent the rest of the day looking for a platoon of NVA reported to be in the area. We didn't see a thing. That night, we moved to another hill, and I sat with the radio until midnight, calling in our hourly sitreps. Every time I called, someone out there in the surrounding vastness monitoring our frequency would mimic the messages I sent. When I sent out, "Flaky Snow, this is Dateline, over," I got back, "Fraky Snow, this is-a Date-er-rine. Ha, ha, ha!" It was either an ARVN playing with himself over the airwaves or a NVA radio operator trying to learn English.

The next day went about the same, nothing unusual to report.

On the morning of the third day, I broke the big toe on my left foot when it got wedged between two rocks and I fell.

Great, I thought. Maybe I can get put on light duty for a few weeks. The break was painful, and after a while, I couldn't put any weight on the injured foot. I told battalion about it, and they said they would pull us out in the next few hours.

When the birds came in, Sergeant Browning and the second half of the platoon were on board, and we flip-flopped in place. There was no one in my half of the platoon who had enough experience to take charge, so out we came.

At the Phu Bai med battalion, a doctor X-rayed my toe, gave me some pain killers and a pair of crutches, and put me on light duty for three weeks. I was overjoyed.

The first thing I did was to write Roberta and tell her the good news. She was due to deliver in early May, and I didn't want her to worry about whether or not I would come back from my next patrol. Three weeks would give us both some needed breathing space.

Two nights later, we were heavily mortared. It was Ho Chi Minh's birthday, and the NVA were out celebrating.

The first round dropped about 0100. It was my first time on the wrong end of a mortar, but the instant the round went off, I knew what it was and began heel-and-toeing it as fast as I could for the door nearest my end of the hooch. Some of the others didn't bother with the doors and went straight through the screens to the open bunker between our hooch and the next one. I hit the door, tripped on the top step, and landed on all fours in the dirt, just as a round went off across the street, filling the air above me with metal. Then I was up and running for the bunker. I threw myself over the top and made myself as small as possible against a wall of sandbags.

Then the rounds started raining down. They came so close and so fast that, while my teeth were rattling in my head, I lost count. There was a lot of yelling going on, but at the time, I was too busy trying to protect my head with my arms and wondering if my skivvy shorts would be enough to stop shrapnel to add my voice to the confusion. The rounds were dropping about twenty feet short of our bunker, detonating on and around some buildings the Seabees had just finished constructing. I was close to the point of impact, but due to the arced flight of the exploding metal, the fragments were passing over me and hitting some of the men farther back, and none of us up front were hurt.

The NVA gunners then started walking the rounds up the street toward the motor pool, and within a few minutes after it started, we were out of danger. Had they added instead of walked, the rounds would have been in among the bunkers and hooches, and we would have been in deep trouble.

Within minutes, arty was firing a counterbattery, and the men on the line opened up. A key figure on the line was an army Duster, a tracked vehicle with twin 40-mm cannons mounted on it. Its rhythmic *pom pom pom*, brought a cheer from our bunker as morale suddenly lifted.

As the incoming shifted toward the motor pool, I peered over the top of the bunker. The sky was alive with tracers, flares, and exploding ordnance. Impressive, I thought. The counterbattery quickly got on target, and the incoming first slowed then stopped completely. When the excitement died down, the wounded were taken to a nearby medical facility. The rest of us got dressed, lay down on our cots, and tried to get some sleep.

The next morning, the captain fresh in with his troops from Okinawa had lost his strut. His pipe drooped, and there was definitely a serious look in his eyes. He had every man in the company out filling sandbags and improving the network of bunkers between hooches.

Hey, a guy could get killed.

With nothing to do, I often went to the airfield to meet incoming patrols and sometimes flew out on insertions. It was at the airfield that I ran into Bruce Eaton, a close friend from my home town. Bruce and I had gone to the same high school, worked together in the village market, and he had, on occasion, dated my wife's sister. In Vietnam, Bruce was flying CH-46s and had made several recon insertions. When we were together, we caught each other up on news from home and reaffirmed the fact that there really was life outside Vietnam. Intelligent, motivated, liked by everyone who came in contact with him, Bruce was without question your all-American Kid.

Three weeks later he was killed when his helicopter was shot out of the sky.

Early in May, we were told to pack our gear and catch a flight to Da Nang, where we would rejoin the battalion at Camp Reasoner. The news was a great boost to our morale. Being detached from your parent unit and assigned to another may sound good in theory, but it has its drawbacks, and you usually end up like the ugly stepsister who forever gets the short end of the stick.

We were glad to be leaving.

10

FIRST RECON — SECOND TO NONE

On the 10th of May, Dateline took over Chickie Pie OP, relieving a patrol that had been up there for a week. On the map, Chickie Pie was officially designated as Cua Tan—hill 452. Eight klicks south of An Hoa and the Arizona, an area of intensive rice cultivation controlled by the Vietcong. The OP, although surrounded by hostile territory, was considered by recon to be an R & R trip to the bush.

Narrow on top, with a sheer drop-off on two sides and a steep climb on the third, the only way Chickie Pie could be assaulted was up its north slope, which was steep, barren, and covered with claymores. The fighting holes on top were built around rock outcrops and improved with sandbags. The hill was not an impregnable fortress, but any unit trying to take it would have to be willing to suffer heavy casualties.

With Antenna Valley to the northeast, and two heavily populated valleys along the Song Thu Bon to the west and south, Chickie Pie looked right into the heart of Cong land. Because of the OP, Charlie was forced to do most of his moving through the area at night. If he moved during the day, he would be under constant surveillance and subject to repeated attacks by both air and artillery.

The top of Chickie Pie was too steep and narrow for helicopters to land, so we relieved the outgoing patrol in a saddle two hundred feet below the summit. From there, we humped the food, water, and ammunition needed to sustain us for the next seven days. After three weeks with a broken toe and no exercise, the steep climb had me blowing hard by the time I reached the top. Once there, we spent an hour getting settled in, then set up OPs at both ends of the mountain. Sergeant Browning took charge of one, and I took the other.

We watched until midday, when it turned blistering hot, and we were forced to hooch-up under our ponchos to escape the sun. I brought the spotting scope in with me, and with a set of tent poles we had to support the roof of our hooch, made an extension for the tripod. Thus, I was able to sit comfortably behind the scope, rather than curl awkwardly in a ball alongside it, while trying to steady the scope and see through it at the same time, which was normally the case. However, the heat waves rising off the plains cut the viewing distance by half, and anything beyond five klicks wove and jumped so badly it made my eyes water.

At 1400, I turned the OP over to Lance Corporal Wimer, an acting squad leader, and went out to look over the holes we had taken over and were now calling home.

Most of the holes weren't really holes, but depressions scraped in the thin layer of dirt covering the hard rock outcrop called Hill 452. Rocks and sandbags filled with more rocks had been built up around the edges of the depressions to form protective walls. None of the positions had overhead protection against shrapnel or small-arms fire. Also, the downslope perimeter was not strung with barbed wire, an oversight that could prove to be costly. The position was a readily defendable one but needed improvements. However, we didn't have the tools or equipment to make them. Had some of the senior officers in the battalion been more aggressive about inspecting our OPs, I am sure the positions would have been made far more defendable than they were. Instead, most of them chose to sit out the war in the rear and never saw Chickie Pie, Ba Na, or Hill 707, or went on a long-range patrol.

The machine gun was set up near Sergeant Browning's end of the hill in some boulders and kept hidden under a poncho. It covered the main avenue of approach to the top of 452. The M-79 gunner stayed with me on my end of the hill; the weapon to be used in direct fire or as a mortar against any enemy in defilade. Each fighting hole had its flares, smoke grenades, CS gas, hand grenades, extra ammo, and LAAW rocket. The LAAW was a light-weight, shoulder-fired weapon that was originally designed to kill tanks but was used against everything from bunkers to individual Cong. They were light, handy, went off with a *whoosh*, which was followed by a loud *bang*, and were disposable. So we shot them whenever we had a target, or even thought we had a target.

On the cliff side, near the center of the hilltop, was an ammo bunker with extra of everything, including an E-8 gas launcher, which could blanket the slopes below with tear gas. Handy, during an attack—providing the wind's in the right direction.

Claymore lines were strung out everywhere, and I took three men with me to trace down each line and check out the small directional mines. Since your average VC tended to be just as warped and hard up for entertainment as we were, we had to check the claymores daily to make sure someone hadn't crawled up during the night and turned them around—it wouldn't do to have one go off in your face.

Overall, the original positions had been well placed. We filled a few more sandbags and thickened some of the bunker walls, but without wire and picks, there wasn't much else we could do to make Chickie Pie a safer place. Late in the afternoon, clouds rolled in, and a small storm developed, bringing with it a light shower and a brief but welcome relief from the heat. When the storm passed, I went back to looking for the enemy.

Below us was the village of Ninh Binh (3).

Viewing life through a spotting scope is not quite as good as having a ringside seat to a glass house, but it's close. Very little of what went on in the village escaped our attention. Since the villagers spent most of their day outdoors, they were easy to keep track of. With the exception of the kids, who made a game out of everything they did, everyone in the village worked from dawn to dusk. Around noon, they would all disappear for a couple of hours to escape the heat, but would soon reappear and go back to working in the fields, tending to their animals, and processing the harvest. Large, orange pumpkins and a grain other than rice were being harvested and set out to dry on brick-surfaced work areas scattered throughout the village. The brightly colored pumpkins lent a festive touch to the otherwise drab colors of the village. There was nothing more sinister or evil looking about the people of the village than there is about an Oklahoma farmer driving a combine through a wheat field. They were just plain, hardworking people concerned with growing enough to eat.

So how, I thought, am I supposed to separate the good guys from the bad?

Fascinated by life in the village, I spent most of the afternoon watching the people work and neglected the rest of our RAOR.

That first evening, there was a sudden flurry of activity along the river flowing past Ninh Binh (3), and I thought we were onto something. A dozen or more boats had been launched and were headed for midstream, when a waterspout suddenly erupted and rose twenty feet in the air, then collapsed in a huge ring that rippled across the water to the banks. Moments later, the sound of an explosion clapped over us. The boats quickly converged on the spot where the waterspout had risen, and the men in them began scooping up fish with long-handled nets. What I thought at first was a VC amphibious assault, turned out to be a fishing expedition. Not much sport in fishing with explosives, but I don't think the villagers looked on the harvesting of food as a sporting activity.

At night, our hilltop cooled down, and we sat outside our shelters to take advantage of the drop in temperature and talk. Most of the talk was about home and what we were going to do when we got back. Lance Corporal Wimer had been a member of a motorcycle gang, whose main purpose in life had been to drink beer and terrorize whatever bar they happened to be in. He expressed a strong desire to pick up where he left off as soon as he got home. Some of the men had jobs waiting for them, others wanted to continue their education, and a few were going to make a career out of the Marine Corps, which prior to Vietnam, had been my intention. Now, I wasn't so sure.

Around midnight, I checked the watch and turned in.

At first light, I was up and prowling the top of our hill. Down below, the valley was blanketed with a thick covering of snowy white clouds, and the surrounding mountains rose like islands out of the silent, winterlike scene. Struck by the beauty around me, I couldn't help but think that somehow we had been transported overnight to a newer, more peaceful world.

Cold, I put on my field jacket and stood alone on the edge of our mountain fortress and watched until the sun broke the horizon and began to burn away the clouds and slowly reveal the land beneath. Wet from a gentle rain, it spread before me like some vast, well-tended garden.

I have never been to a more fascinating, beautiful, or deadly place as Vietnam.

The moment the clouds were gone, we started picking up small groups of VC. Some were far out across the river, and a few were on the hill trails above the village. We called arty and began to adjust, but as soon as the first rounds came in, the VC were off and running. At that point, all I could do was estimate where they would be in the next few seconds and call down a round in front of them. It worked a couple of times, and as a result, three VC were either killed or wounded. Then they went to ground, and we lost them. We watched until noon when the heat waves began to dance so badly we couldn't tell if someone had a pack and rifle on his back or a water buffalo.

I passed the word to secure, and we crawled into our hooches to escape the sun.

At midafternoon, a thunderstorm rolled over us with such violence I thought that, if the lightning didn't kill us, the cracking concussion of the thunder would. The radio operator, Private First Class Smoger, quickly tore down his antenna, and we all divorced ourselves from any nearby metal objects. Then, while the lightning crashed around us, we stayed curled up in the rocks and hoped like hell we were low enough to avoid being hit and that the lightning didn't set off any of the claymores, which happened occasionally. Fortunately not to us.

When the thunder and lightning passed, we stripped down and bathed in the torrential downpour that followed. I had brought along a bar of soap and used it to scrub off the sweat and grime that had already accumulated on my body, delighting in the chance to be clean again. However, the moment I rinsed off, I was cold and shivering and racing for the protection of my hooch and the dirty but dry clothes therein.

The same storm blew in every afternoon, and every afternoon we cowered in the rocks, then raced out to bathe. I've never had a more exciting shower.

Toward evening, an air force forward air controller buzzed our position. On his second pass, he dropped a rolled-up paper that turned out to be the current edition of the *Stars and Stripes*. We waved and hollered our appreciation. Then on his third pass, the pilot came in about ten feet over our heads, cut his engine, and dove straight down the face of the cliff. We stood on the edge whooping in delight at the madman in the Piper Cub as he swooped on the valley like a giant bird. Far below us, he started his engine and leveled off just above the village, then turned and followed the river toward An Hoa. Every afternoon, he returned to deliver a paper and entertain us with his aerobatics. I never found out who he was, but the guy was a real showman.

And so the time went.

Enemy sightings were few and far away. Adjusting artillery on them was difficult, and the results were usually disappointing. But we manned the OP for as many hours out of each day as we could and sent in SALUTE messages whenever we had something to send. Nights we treated like any other night on patrol and maintained a heavily manned watch, knowing it was the time the enemy was most likely to strike.

But we skated, and after a week another patrol came in to take our place.

On the 17th of May, my son Dan was born. I got the news that night when I called home via a radio patch made through the battalion to a ham operator in California, who placed a collect call to my mother-in-law. Roberta had delivered just a few hours earlier, and both she and Dan were doing fine. He was a ten-pound monster, but the delivery had been an easy one. Feeling melancholy after making the call, I went off by myself and told God that if He promised never to stick my son in a place like Vietnam, He could point me out to some gook and let the asshole blow me away as a trade-off. Then I scrounged up a bottle and got drunk.

Two days later, we were roaming the hills between Nui Go Hoa and Nui Go Gac, forty klicks south of Da Nang. The vegetation on those hills was about head-high, and the heat was grim. Each of us carried from fifteen to twenty canteens of water, and still we ran short. Humping through the hot, stale air and fighting the thick brush, we were each consuming upwards of a canteen an hour. Our fatigue jackets, packs, and web gear were soaked through with sweat, and regardless of how much water we drank, we were all staggering from the heat. But there was no escaping it.

By nightfall of the first day, most of us were down to five canteens of water. If we were going to last out the four days, we would have to find more. From reading previous patrol reports about the area, I knew there was a stream about three hundred meters away, but since fresh signs of Charlie were everywhere, the stream would have to be approached with caution. In the morning, we would head for it.

Our harbor site was a rock outcrop, completely covered with vines and low-growing trees. I could not have picked a more defendable position. Exhausted from tension and the grinding hump we'd made that day, I fell into a deep sleep soon after dark. About 0200, I woke up in the middle of a wet dream. It was the first sex I'd had in months and felt great.

We found the stream the next morning and filled our canteens without running into Charlie. From there, we moved onto a hill overlooking the bombed-out, pockmarked, desolate villages of An Thanh (1) and (2), where the only feet to ply the trails belonged to Charlie. The entire valley looked like the aftermath of World War III. The fields were so full of bomb craters that nothing but weeds grew in them. Most of the houses had been burned to the ground, and the people who owned them long gone.

An artillery lieutenant by the name of Jones had been sent with us to call in a special beehive round that was supposed to devastate any and all found within its bursting radius. No one in recon had ever used it before, and all of us in the patrol could hardly wait for a subject to try it out on. I felt like a kid with a new toy.

We didn't have long to wait.

Eight hundred meters away, I spotted two VC with packs and rifles as they started up a long steep trail on the ridge opposite ours. Their trip from the valley floor would take them twenty or thirty minutes, so I turned the radio over to Lieutenant Jones and told him to shoot the beehive round. He called in the coordinates, azimuth, and nature of the target, and asked for the special round in code.

Meanwhile, the two men across the way had started a regular Laurel-and-Hardy routine as they climbed the trail to the top of the ridge. One of them was obviously less motivated than the other and kept falling back and sitting down on every rock he came to. When he did, his partner would angrily wave his arms over his head, go back down the trail, and drag him off the rock. Five minutes later, the one we were soon calling Stan would be perched on another rock, and his buddy, Ollie, would be waving his arms in the air again.

Word came back from arty that the round we wanted was in effect a secret weapon and how come we knew about it, anyway?

"Because I am out here specifically to call it in," Lieutenant Jones radioed back.

Long pause.

Over on the trail, Ollie had Stan by the pack straps and was pulling him up the hill. The rest of the men in the patrol had broken out a second pair of binoculars and the spotting scope and were laughing in whispers as they took turns watching the two.

Arty called back. "Be advised, we cannot fire that round without authorization from division."

"Well, call up and get it!" snapped Jones.

Another long pause.

By now, we all agreed that Stan was the most reluctant VC we had ever seen and was sure to wind up in a shitbird platoon if he didn't change his ways.

Arty called back. "That's a negative on your request to fire."

Jones and I looked at each other and shook our heads. "Only in Vietnam," he muttered, disgusted.

The exchange between Jones and his unit for the request to fire the beehive round went on for some time, so I went back to watching the two across the valley. Ollie was now walking behind Stan giving him swift kicks to the seat of the pants whenever he showed signs of slowing down. Entertaining as it was, they were approaching the top of the ridge, and if we didn't shoot something soon, they would be lost from sight.

Finally, Jones replotted their position and said, "Screw it. Give me an HE air burst."

Then came the best-called shot I ever saw in Vietnam. It burst directly over the heads of Stan and Ollie and made them permanent parts of the trail.

I turned to Jones, who had been watching through his binoculars, and said, "You realize you just killed a great comedy team, and the world will never forgive you for it."

At night, I would lie back in the bushes and watch out over the valley, where every passing helicopter was shot at by every yahoo with a weapon. The long, brightly colored streams of tracers arcing up to find the birds were fascinating to watch.

We had a number of sightings over the next few days, but were never able to get the battery to fire the fabled beehive round. We were all disappointed because we wanted to see just what it would do for a Vietcong.

On our last day in the bush, I managed to put a forty-five degree lean on the last remaining house in the valley by landing an HE round just outside the door after three VC entered seeking shelter. I never did see them come out.

11

Late in May, Dateline was assigned the mission of doing an Arc Light assessment in an area southeast of Antenna Valley.

The name Arc Light came from the glow a B-52 strike puts on the horizon at night as hundreds of 250- and 500-pound bombs detonate in a rolling chain that lasts thirty or more seconds. I had seen several Arc Lights in the mountains west of Phu Bai and would later see them near the DMZ and around Dong Ha in even greater numbers, and they were always impressive. The ground shakes, the heavens roar, and the horizon burns with a low, flickering rainbowlike light, minus the colors, that arcs from one end of the strike to the other.

The strike area assigned to us was one suspected of harboring a VC battalion. There was that word *battalion* again.

Ten of us would be going in.

It is one thing to drop bombs while cruising at an altitude of thirty thousand feet ("Would you like a few doughnuts with your coffee? No coffee. Tea, then?") and fly back to a base in Thailand, the R & R capital of the world, and get laid, and another to walk the ground where the strike took place. From a B-52's point of view, it must look like total destruction on the ground, and the crews no doubt run around issuing crafty little statements of self-congratulation like, "Hey, baby, don't nobody survive in our wake, cause we is *bad* motherfuckers."

But survive they did, and during the insertion, the second bird took fire on the approach to the zone. It was hit in several places, but no one was hurt, and the minute the men were

On LZ Quail, Chu Lai, February 1967.

Hospitalman (corpsman) Holthaus (left) and Lance Corporal. Lucas after awards ceremony at Camp Reasoner, May 1967.

CH-46 that took nearly forty hits while going into LZ above Antenna Valley in June 1967.

Looking at "The Arizona" as we lift out of An Hoa, June 1967.

Camp Reasoner, Da Nang, July 1967.

Lt. Paul Young, Ba Na, Vietnam, October 1967.

Patrol with Capt. Bill Warren, above Mortar Valley,
October 1967.

Lance Corporal Legally being prepared for medevac out
of Mortar Valley, Da Nang area, October 1967.

First Platoon, D Company, 1st Reconnaissance Battalion, on rubber boat training, China Beach, November 1967.

Observation post Chickie Pie, Hill 452, out of An Hoa. May 1967.

Privates First Class Soechtig, Smoger, and Bruch on Hill 452.

Members of Dateline, waiting to go back out. Duc Pho, March 1967.

First Force Recon team Killer Kane, lead by Andy Finlayson, after ambushing the 402d Sapper Battalion, June 1967.

Gran Hotel de Tourane, Ba Na, Vietnam, October 1967.

Operation Badger Catch, north of the Cua Viet River,
February 1968. (Left to right) Cpl. Quintin Evans, Lt. Paul
Young, Cpl. Dan Hostetler, Doc Stomp.

With Battalion Landing Team 3/1, north of the Cua Viet
River, February 1968.

on the ground, I had them moving quickly toward a low hill. Once under the canopy on top, we set up an ambush and waited. But after two hours and no gooks, I got the patrol up, and we faded off to another hill.

That night, a thick fog rolled in, and it wasn't until 0900 that it burned off and we could see the area of the strike. It trailed down from a mountain opposite ours and into a village named Ap Hai (3), of which there wasn't much left. The Arc Light had been dropped two days before, and Ap Hai (3) appeared now to be abandoned. Not a soul tread the village paths, and no smoke rose from the few remaining thatched houses.

Shortly after noon, I started the patrol toward the mountain where the strike had begun. Corporal Brown took the point, and we slowly made our way down a deep ravine and up onto the mountain. When we reached the top, we found ourselves in a strange moonscaped land, where craters the size of swimming pools had been blasted in the ground. Where two or three craters overlapped, three-bedroom houses could have been dropped in and covered up with just the roof-tops showing. The jungle around the craters was stripped and plowed to bare earth, and the vines and trees that hadn't been vaporized were thrown in impenetrable, weblike mats against the surrounding forest. The place had all the warmth and cheer of a mortuary.

As we moved in and around the craters, I took pictures with a camera division had provided to record the destruction. Somebody, somewhere, wanted tangible evidence that the bombs had actually gone off and that the American tax-payers were getting their money's worth in their fight against worldwide Communist aggression. But since we hadn't found any destroyed bunkers or body parts draped in the trees, I couldn't help but wonder just how successful the strike had been. Most of the pictures I took were of torn up jungle and gaping holes in the ground.

Farther down the mountain, we came in close to the village. I called Beacon Light and asked if we were to actually enter it to continue our assessment, then crossed my fingers, said a quick prayer, gritted my teeth, and waited. I did not want to go into that village and look at three-day-old bodies; two, bloated and close to splitting open, we could already see near a destroyed hut.

At Chu Lai, Sam Williams had once described in detail his experience on an Arc Light assessment, and I figured it was something I could do without. He said seeing so many dead and dying people was bad enough, but when he walked into the hooch and saw the rocking woman, he nearly went over the edge.

Sam had been with the grunts then, and was assigned the mission of checking out a village where an Arc Light had hit. I never got it straight whether the strike was by design or an accident, but Sam said it didn't matter; the damage had already been done. All of the victims were women, children, and old men, and the patrol found no hard evidence of either VC or NVA having been in the village when the bombs hit. But then the war was like that. A report of VC in a village might be a week old before an air strike was laid on, and by the time it hit, the VC were long gone. At that point, the powers that be would declare the entire village to be the focal point of a hard-core Vietcong infrastructure and a real thorn in the side of democracy, so what's the loss?

In this particular vil, bodies were everywhere and most had been ripening in the sun for days.

When Sam entered one of the few remaining hooches, he found a woman squatting on the floor, rocking back and forth, not making a sound. On a table was a body under a piece of wood. Sam pushed the wood aside and discovered a dead eight-year-old boy, with a chain of ants going in one nostril and out the other, carrying away parts of his brain.

Sam said he couldn't get out of there fast enough.

So when Beacon Light called back and told me to stay out of the village, I uncrossed my fingers and ungritted my teeth and told God what a great guy He was for not making us look at brain parts being carried away by ants.

We turned around and headed back up the mountain.

So far, we hadn't seen anything of the enemy, but we had

heard them shooting rifles and yelling in the distance, which was not uncommon for the VC to do when they thought they were the only ones in the forest. In spite of having taken fire on the way in, I was certain that we had slipped in among them and they had no idea we were there.

We dropped down into a gardenlike valley and waited in ambush behind a stone wall next to a trail. An hour went by, and nothing came our way, so I passed the word to saddle up, and we moved silently on.

Under an overhanging rock, we found a platform shelter and a cooking pot with a few spent AK-47 rounds, but no VC.

The only exit from the valley was a trail leading up the side of a granite wall, which we took, using every rock and bush along the way to mask our movement. The trail was open and exposed and gave me the feeling of complete nakedness and vulnerability.

At the top, we found several trail markers and fresh footprints on the ground around them. I called a halt to examine the area and the markers—which were pieces of rattan twisted into designs none of us knew the meaning to—and tried to determine just how many Cong had passed this way. A lot, was all I could come up with. When I was through, Corporal Brown, who had been looking over the ground with me, squinted and whispered, ''Just when are we getting off this fucking trail, Lieutenant?''

I couldn't have agreed more. We went back into the jungle.

That night, we harbored in a rock pile under the canopy. It was warm enough not to use my sleeping bag cover, which I carried now instead of the heavier poncho because the rains were over. The sleeping bag cover was lighter and didn't sweat or make loud rustling noises like the poncho and was generally the preferred item to bundle up in. However, the weather determined its use, as the sleeping bag cover would not keep out the rain.

All the next day, we moved through the jungle, but saw nothing of the enemy. We did continue to hear them yell out or fire their weapons. But since shots were always being fired in the jungle, I usually put it down to the kid-with-a-new-toy phenomenon.

Late on the third night, Beacon Light told us to find an LZ by 1000 the next day and be ready for an extraction.

Other than the bomb damage to the village and several acres of forest being ripped out, we didn't have a lot to report. Either division was happy with what information we had sent or had decided the Arc Light was a bust. I never found out. The only thing that really mattered was that we were coming out a few hours earlier than planned.

On the way to the LZ in the morning, we passed through a few hundred acres of ground we hadn't covered, and it was there we found a tunnel blown open during the Arc Light. After searching for an entrance and not finding one, I radioed Beacon Light and said I was sending two men inside by way of the crater to check out the tunnel.

"Negative, Dateline. Birds are on the way," came the reply.

It was our only significant find, but we didn't have time to explore it. I plotted the location of the opening to the tunnel on my map, and we headed for an LZ.

We had not seen or heard any gooks that morning, yet the minute the birds came in, they started taking fire. I hustled half the patrol onto the first bird, and it went out. Then I tried to direct the gunships onto the enemy as the second one came in, but I didn't have a fix on their position. The gunships made several runs on the jungle around us and for a while silenced the incoming. But the minute my half of the patrol lifted off, the gooks opened up again. This time, we were able to see their muzzle flashes, and while the men returned fire through the portholes, I threw out a red smoke to mark their position. The gunships dove on it, but bullets continued to come our way.

Then I threw another smoke. And another. The higher we rose, the longer they took to reach the ground. After a while, the shooting stopped, but I kept throwing out smoke grenades, fascinated by their long, trailing streamers. At two thousand feet, I threw out a blue and watched it go. The blue was followed by a bright yellow, the colors dropping forever down to the dark jungle below us.

It was the most colorful extraction I ever had.

We were in for two days then bounced back down to Nui Go Gac, where the vegetation is low, and the sun hangs in the sky a whole lot longer than it should.

On the third day, we ran out of water, and I sent Sergeant Browning and four men down to a stream to fill our canteens, while the rest of us stayed in the OP.

An hour went by before Sergeant Browning called to say the canteens were filled, but he had gooks around him and couldn't move.

We waited.

Most of us were so thirsty, we were gagging on our tongues. I tried an old Indian trick of putting a smooth pebble in my mouth to stimulate the flow of saliva. Didn't work.

Just when I was thinking seriously of drinking a bottle of mosquito repellent, Sergeant Browning showed up with the water. I was never so grateful to see someone.

We were extended a day, had limited sightings, and called in only two fire missions.

12

My physical-fitness program was suffering badly. I was lucky to get the platoon out for a run more than once between patrols. What with men being stuck on guard duty, mess duty, cleanup details, and the platoon split into two patrols (the second half was now Bulrush, under Sergeant John Witmer), it was difficult to muster more than a handful of men for PT.

However, the main reason for the failing program was the permanent state of fatigue that had settled over most of us—the price we paid for going to the bush. In the relaxed atmosphere of the rear, we tended to let down so hard we moved like zombies. For my own part, I often found myself starting out in one direction only to discover I had forgotten where I was going and what I was supposed to do when I got there. Eventually, I would end up back in my hooch, rethinking what it was I had set out to do in the first place.

When I did have the energy to run, it was usually late in the day after I'd taken a nap. By then, the men were either somewhere on duty or relaxing in their hooches, from where I didn't have the heart to drag them just because I felt the urge to exercise. So I would set off by myself and run until recon and the inevitable next patrol were pushed from my mind, and the only thing I could think about was my next breath.

At the end of each run, I would hammer up and down the hill above the LZ until my legs felt like rubber, my lungs ached, and sweat poured from me. Then, and only then, did I have some perspective on who I was and what I was doing.

I already knew I was afraid, but more important, I did not like what I was doing. Deep inside, I felt that something was terribly wrong with killing people and that some day I would have to answer for it and knew that nothing I had to say would atone for it. Yet I couldn't stop. When I was in the field, my whole attitude changed, and a gook at ten meters or two thousand meters was a threat to our survival and had to be eliminated like some contagious disease. Sometimes I found humor in the killing, sometimes it was like pulling weeds, sometimes it was a desperate struggle to live. But how do you explain it all away so you can live with yourself? And who was I supposed to explain it to? And who gave a fuck, anyway!

I did know that if I could make it through the next two months, I would be out of the bush and able to skate the last seven months, then home. And that mattered.

It wasn't often we were able to look over the area we would be patrolling, but due to the fact that multiple insertions out of An Hoa had been scheduled over the next three days, a pair of CH-34s were laid on and several of us were sent out to overfly our assigned areas.

The idea behind an overflight is to fly past your RAOR and continue on as though you were out for a morning jaunt above the countryside. However, since most of our insertions took place far from any beaten helicopter flight paths, the VC knew what was up the moment we putted by. Consequently, I was none too keen on overflights. But when the S-3 shop said an overflight had been laid on, we went.

So, with maps, compasses, and weapons in hand, six of us boarded the birds and flew out from the battalion LZ.

It never failed. Every time I went airborne on an overflight, I forgot to take a jacket or sweatshirt along. The minute we got above five hundred feet, I started to freeze. The higher we climbed, the more I froze, until I ended up hugging myself for the entire trip. You'd think I'd learn.

Larry Stone was along for the flight. I had known Larry since 1960, when we were in recon together at Camp Pendleton. During the summer of 1965, we had gone through

Platoon Leader Class at Quantico. A year later, we were in Basic School together. And now Reasoner, where Larry had joined the battalion about two months after I had. Quiet, athletic, dedicated, Larry was one of the finest Marines I ever met. He led from the front, trained his men well, and the entire time I knew him, I never heard him complain about any assignment that came his way. Larry was so quiet, efficient, and indifferent to hardship, we called him the Stone Man.

We flew over Larry's area first, which was in the mountains thirty klicks south of An Hoa, west of the Song Thu Bon. Artillery support for his patrol would be from an ARVN battery working near Hiep Duc. It was a long way out.

From there, we headed north past Geo Coc, where it was my turn in the door to check the terrain against my map and quickly plot LZs in the jungle-covered mountains. We then flew on to the other areas while the remaining patrol leaders checked their RAORs.

Finished, we swung around and headed for home.

As we reached the southern edge of the Dai Loc plain, the bird Larry and I were in was fragged for a medevac mission. Below, a grunt platoon had taken a casualty and the man needed to come out.

We reached the area and began a slow, circling descent.

A shot popped by the door. Then another. I quietly slipped my hands under the cheeks of my ass and squeezed them shut as tight as they would go.

Another round popped past. Life as a shooting gallery duck, I thought.

Whoever it was down there was sending a round our way about every ten seconds. The door gunner, with his armored vest and seat, looked on, unconcerned. Almost bulletproof, he could afford to be unconcerned. I kept right on squeezing, and the rounds kept right on coming. A black sergeant, deciding to put an end to all this nonsense, went to the door and emptied his M-16 at where he thought the shots were coming from. It did absolutely no good.

Finally, we spiraled in for a landing, and the grunts rushed the wounded man over to our machine and loaded him. Within a minute, we were back in the air. The guy with the rifle started up again. *Pop. Pop. Pop.* Now I had my eyes *and* my cheeks squeezed shut and was trying to make myself as small as possible. This time, the shooter only got off four or five rounds before we cleared the area, the pilot taking a more beelined route to the sky.

On the floor, the wounded grunt was stretched out on his back. A bullet had gone through the middle of his right thigh, breaking the femur and swelling the thigh to the size of a basketball. I hated the guy. He had my wound. It was a bonafide, guaranteed, Look, ma, no hands, Stateside, all-American beauty. It was the wound I had been dreaming about for months—the one that had YOU GOT IT MADE! stamped on it.

My first urge was to throw the grunt out of the helicopter, shoot myself in the leg, and take his place.

Instead, I got up, fished a cigarette out of his jacket pocket, lit it, and stuck it between his lips. Sedated and feeling no pain, he smiled, nodded thanks, and took a long, slow drag off the cigarette. I returned to my seat and sat down.

We flew him to Charlie Med and left him with a stretcher crew with *my* wound.

The gooks were waiting for us on the LZ the next day. We were on the final approach when they opened up from a dozen different places, and rounds started popping through the sides of the helicopter like buckshot through a beer can. I had already given the order to lock and load and stand when it happened, and that may have saved us. We instantly turned toward the portholes and began firing back in three- and four-round bursts, the hot casings rattling off the bulkheads and clattering over the floor. Down below, muzzle flashes winked at us from every part of the forest, and from one position, big glowing tennis balls rose at terrifying speeds to meet us. The bird kept taking hit after hit, but we stayed in the air, and none of the men went down. It was all yelling and shoot-

ing and cursing, trapped inside that aluminum monster, but
nobody flinched, and every gun on the ship was in action.

Then the pilot got hit in the legs and the bird plunged into
a steep, turning dive toward a narrow valley, and we were
suddenly away from the incoming fire. The copilot quickly
brought the ship back under control, and we leveled off a
hundred or more feet above the valley.

Breathing hard from the adrenaline rush, I looked back as
the gunships descended on the gooks like angry hornets,
raking them with rockets and machine-gun fire. A forward
air controller would soon be on station to bring in napalm
and high-explosive bombs, and I knew the gooks were in for
a long day. But that was their problem, and at the moment I
couldn't wish enough shit their way.

The bird was leaking hydraulic fluid badly, and we had
slowed to a speed that was just enough to keep us airborne.
The copilot relayed a message back that he was going to try
for An Hoa, so there wasn't much to do but say a few prayers
regarding the safe passage of machines that fly through the
air and grit my teeth as we shook and vibrated along.

While the crew chief tried to stop the leaks in our ship, I
went down the length of the bird checking on the men; one
of whom exclaimed, wide-eyed, "Goddamn, Lieutenant, we
were looking right down the muzzles of those guns!" As I
passed each man, I gripped him by the shoulder and told him
how well he'd done. If we hadn't returned the volume of fire
we had, I am certain things would have gone worse than they
did, and we would have been that flaming wreck on the LZ
the gunny warned me about so long ago.

Much to my relief, none of the men had been hit, which,
considering all the holes in our vehicle, was a minor miracle.

The entire incident had happened so fast there hadn't been
time to be scared. But before we reached An Hoa, a delayed
reaction set in, and I spent several minutes shaking and running my hand back and forth over my head to make sure it
was still there.

On the airstrip, we discovered the bird had taken close to
forty hits and that one of the large glowing tennis balls had

gone through the shaft of a blade where it narrowed and was bolted to the forward turbine.

After he had inspected the ship, an air-wing gunny walked by, muttering to himself.

"What's the problem, Gunny?" I asked.

"Somebody must like you people, Lieutenant. That blade should have snapped off long before you reached the air-strip."

I looked at him with a sickly grin on my face and couldn't think of anything to say.

Late in the day, we were flown back to battalion where we were greeted by the S-3 with, "What the hell are you doing back here? Didn't you get the word you'd been assigned an alternate LZ and were to go in just before dark?"

My statement that I hadn't was met with a "Shit!" as the major turned and stomped back up the hill.

Guy puts in a hard day at the office and gets his ass chewed out.

I headed for the shower and spent a long time under the wing tank, letting the hot water work out the kinks.

Sergeant Browning had been pulled out of my platoon to take over Chargesheet, another Bravo Company patrol. My assistant patrol leader was now Sgt. William Brandt, an experienced recon NCO who had once had to carry a dead Marine around for three days before the weather broke and a medevac could come in. The Marine had been killed taking in one of the patrol's booby traps, and Brandt went to great lengths to impress upon me the necessity of not setting out booby traps at night. I assured him that other than stringing out claymores, I normally didn't booby-trap the areas we worked in.

The day after being shot out of our LZ, we were back down on Finch, waiting for a ride. The patrol had been moved over a couple of klicks, and our new LZ was a vast expanse of grass. Too large to ambush, I hoped.

For most of the morning, we sat and listened to Brandt's

exploits as a temporary MP assigned to chase Marines out
of the whore houses in Dog Patch.

"At one house," Brandt said, "I went in the front door
and kicked out a bunch of guys lined up to screw your basic
sixteen-year-old, telling them that if I caught them coming
back, I'd run them in. After they left, I got to thinking just
how long it had been since the last time I got laid, and before
you know it, there I was in the saddle. It didn't take long,
and when I got off, my dick was smokin'! Even an MP's got
needs, ya know."

Late in the morning, a couple of Vietnamese kids came
by, begging for handouts. Both of them were regulars, and
neither was regarded high on anyone's popularity list. When
we didn't give them anything, they ran off a ways, stopped,
and turned around. Then one of them dropped his pants and
began to masturbate, hollering, "You numba fucking ten,
Marine!" I picked up my rifle and sighted in on the kid with
his dick out and came very close to shooting him. Then they
ran away.

"You should have shot him, Lieutenant," one of the men
said.

I lay back on my pack and thought, "What the fuck is this
place doing to me."

During the insertion, a gunship made a run over our heads,
firing into a tree line. I hit the deck thinking we were in
contact, my heart pounding in my throat. When I got back
to my feet, I grabbed the handset from Private First Class
Smoger and yelled, "What the fuck was that all about?"

"Thought you wanted the LZ prepped," came a reply.

"Not while we're in it!" I snapped and threw the handset
to Smoger, who laughed.

Once inside the tree line, we came onto a wide trail, followed it for a short distance, then dropped over the side of
the mountain to set up an ambush and wait for anyone who
might be following.

After an hour of waiting and listening, we moved on.

We were working under a canopy that reached up eighty

to one-hundred twenty feet, and the ground beneath it was relatively free of the thick, tangled growth found in regions where the trees are shorter. Our progress was steady, tense, silent.

That night, we harbored at the base of some ancient, fungus-covered giants that rose to the stars and gave off a greenish glow in the dark.

In the morning, we climbed one and established an OP so far off the ground we had to communicate by a pair of PX walkie-talkies we'd brought along.

For some time, my primary tac radio operator, Private First Class Smoger, had been after me to let him call in a fire mission. So when I came down, I sent him up the tree with a map and a pair of binoculars and told him to let me know if he saw anything.

Smoger was kind of an odd duck by Marine Corps standards. His long hair, dark glasses, and laid-back manner rubbed many First Sergeants and officers the wrong way. But for some reason I liked him and kept him on as my radio operator. He was cool under fire, I could always count on him to be there when I needed him, and he never got creative with the messages I sent.

About an hour after he'd gone up the tree, Smoger sent word down that a large enemy force was moving in a valley about three klicks away. He used the walkie-talkie to relay the message, and the set hissed and cracked so badly we were almost yelling to communicate with each other.

About then, Sergeant Brandt came down from the ridge above us and said, "Lieutenant, you are going to have every gook in the neighborhood on our ass if you keep it up. We can hear you way up on the ridge."

With that, we gave up on the walkie-talkies, and I sent the artillery net radio up to Smoger, who tied it to a branch next to him.

I monitored the net, while he called arty and gave them the coordinates and azimuth of the target he had. When the first round came in, the enemy spread out some but kept right on coming, Smoger reported. After a while, he started getting some hits; several of the enemy went down, and Smoger got so excited over his successes I thought he was going to fall out of the tree.

I climbed up for a look.

There must have been at least a company of NVA in the valley.

A FAC soon came on station and started calling in shots of his own. Meanwhile, we kept our battery hammering away, and dead NVA started piling up in little clumps everywhere. Then a pair of Phantoms swooped in from the wild blue yonder and laid on a little napalm—the friend of the working Marine.

Finally, the NVA went to ground, and we lost them.

An hour went by and all was quiet. Then someone wearing a white smock, who we took to be a medic, appeared and began making the rounds from one pile of dead and wounded to another.

Smoger called in a preregistered concentration that landed right on top of the doc, and he became the lining for a newly made crater.

As I sat in the tree eighty feet above the ground, with my legs dangling, watching the destruction in the valley, a song I had learned in the fifth grade started running through my head, and I began singing it to myself.

Down in the valley, the valley so low
Hang your head over, hear the wind blow.
Hear the wind blow, dear, hear the wind blow
Hang your head over, hear the wind blow.

It was an ill fucking wind that blew in the valley that day. After the doc got it, we didn't have any more sightings.

The next day, the NVA were back, and the shooting started again. One of the rounds hit a grass hut, and it started to burn with a vengeance. People came running from everywhere to put the fire out. Then the house started to explode, and they all ran in the opposite direction. It continued to explode for several minutes, sending large chunks of burning thatch high into the air. This went on for about ten minutes, with people running everywhere, chunks of burning house flying through the air, and artillery rounds impacting in the vil.

"They live pretty exciting lives down there," Smoger commented.

I almost laughed myself out of the tree.

The house we'd hit must have been an ammunition dump because it kept on burning and exploding for a long time. By the time the fire died down, there wasn't anything left of it or the surrounding hooches.

When a FAC showed up, all of our targets moved beyond a tree line, and we lost sight of them. So we sat for the rest of the day and watched the Phantoms make runs on the fleeing NVA, whom we couldn't see but whose progress we could follow by the orange napalm blossoms.

By the fourth day, there wasn't much for us to look at, so we moved back to the LZ and waited for our extraction, which as usual was late.

13

The Stone Man was dead.

For two days I walked around in a catatonic state, feeling numb, alone, hollowed out. I had known Larry too long for him to be dead. But dead is dead, and it didn't make a shit how long I'd known him because there wasn't anything I nor anyone else could do to bring him back.

Mingled with the hurt and the grief was that ever-present sense of self-preservation that said if the Stone Man couldn't make it out of Nam, how in the hell was I going to? Here was a guy I looked up to; a guy who was *supposed* to survive. And now, by dying, he had somehow betrayed me. Larry *knew* recon. He *knew* the bush. While most of us sat on our asses when we were in the battalion area, Larry had his troops out in the rice paddies running ambush drills. Every move he made was good. Yet he was dead. Killed by some gook with a rusty rifle in a no-name forest on the side of a no-name mountain.

It is difficult to absorb the loss of a friend. Sorrow, frustration, anger, injustice, all get mixed together in a strange kaleidoscope of memories and flashbacks that leave you reassessing your beliefs as you keep asking over and over again, why? Why did it have to be this particular person and not someone else? Then you name a dozen assholes who could drop dead any minute and no one would be the worse off. And why now? Why not thirty or forty years from now when death might not be such a terrible thing?

But the questions go unanswered, and out of the grief grows revenge, which is eventually tempered to an even greater sense of the need to survive. Even if it's only to tell someone some day what it was like.

Bravo Company had a new commander, a captain named Bill Warren. He had the habit of riding along on insertions and accompanying patrols to the bush whenever he could get permission to do so. The opportunity had always been there, but few company commanders ever opted to go to the bush in recon. The ones who did stood a cut above the others and were a real boost to morale.

On July 1st, Dateline flew out for an insertion on a hillside overlooking the western end of Antenna Valley—an area that was never pacified and never would be—regardless of how many hearts and minds division said we were winning there. Every unit that entered the valley stepped into a world of shit, and I was glad we wouldn't be stepping very far that day.

Captain Warren flew out with us on the insertion. He had an easy, quiet way that instilled confidence in all of us. Somehow, I felt stronger, more sure of myself when he was around.

We would be inserting in plain view of the inhabitants of the valley, some six hundred meters from the nearest vil. I asked for a prep of the LZ before we went in and got one. While we orbited at two thousand feet, the gunships worked over the LZ with rockets and machine guns for about fifteen minutes. When they didn't take any return fire, we went in.

The rockets had started a large fire on the hill, and as we approached the zone, the smoke masked our view of the valley. I gave the order to lock, load, and stand as the ramp dropped. Captain Warren clapped me on the back and gave me a thumbs-up, and we exited the bird the moment it touched down.

The fire had already burned off an area half the size of a football field and ringed us on three sides. The heat of the flames was so intense it drove us down hill, where we found an opening and began circling back up to get away from it. Adding to the excitement of the fire were the odd bullets dropped long ago by passing soldiers that kept cooking off as the flames reached them. Every few minutes one would go off with a bang, and we would drop to our knees, weapons pointing in the direction of the sound, hearts pounding, only to rise cursing.

The smoke on the open mountainside was thick, and we were all coughing and hacking as we went, but it served to hide us from view from the valley floor. After a half hour of climbing steadily, we broke free of the smoke and fire. I stopped and looked back, as it raced across the mountain, and secretly wished it would keep on burning until all of Vietnam was no more than a pile of ashes. Maybe then we could go home.

Our mission was to establish an OP on top of Hill 284 and watch for enemy activity, calling in fire missions on targets of opportunity. The climb up the mountain had us all sweating and breathing hard, but once on top, we found ourselves under a fifty-foot canopy that cut out most of the sun, and we soon recovered in the cool shade.

We set up a single OP and began watching the villages. Much to my surprise, the people in them were going about their daily routines as though our insertion had never taken place. We immediately spotted several VC carrying rifles and packs on a trail near one of the vils.

I plotted and called in our first fire mission, but the rounds were so far off that my targets didn't even look up! I guess a guy can get used to anything going on in the neighborhood.

I called for an adjustment and was told by the battery we would be shooting into a vil with the next round and the fire mission was canceled, to which I replied, "Horse shit!"

Canceled fire missions were not only frustrating, but there was never any consistency to them. One day we could blow a vil off the map, and the next day we couldn't. Other than the officer in charge of one battery being more concerned about repercussions than killing the enemy than the officer in charge of another battery, I could never figure out why.

For the rest of the day, we had repeated sightings around the vil, but could not get permission to fire. When targets away from the vil presented themselves, they were either too small to entice arty to shoot or didn't hang around long enough for the mission to be plotted and called in.

Time dragged.

Late in the afternoon of the second day, I caught myself puffing on a C-ration cigarette. I had lit it and smoked it down by a third before I realized what I was doing and threw it away in disgust. Old habits are hard to break. It had been four years since I had smoked a cigarette, and I wanted to keep it that way. But between the endless waiting and the pressure of leading patrols for almost six months now, I had reverted to something that used to comfort me. Sort of like playing with yourself; it gives you a friendly feeling and takes your mind off everything else.

The fact that I was due to come out of the field at the end of the month didn't help any. If anything, it made me even more anxious. I was afraid I would either get killed in the short time I had left, or be extended as a patrol leader mere days before I was to be relieved. Either one was bad news.

I was at a point where I needed a break. Lately, I had been visited with some strange, gripping fears that came close to paralyzing my ability to think clearly. During my last patrol, I had spent nearly half a day huddled against a log, scarcely moving, afraid that if I did, I would be shot by the guy who always had me in his sights. Other than an acute awareness of death and a raging paranoia about thrashing through the jungle, there was no real reason for my behavior. But that day with the log, I curled myself into a ball and pretended to be asleep, while I gripped my fatigue jacket and hung on like it was a line thrown to a drowning man. I felt as though I could not stand another week, day, hour of the jungle with its smell of death and decay and its prisonlike confinement. If I had to die, I didn't want it to be under the darkness of the canopy.

Chargesheet was in trouble over on Charlie Ridge. Sergeant Browning was leading the patrol, and they had run into a company of NVA. One man was wounded, but the patrol was holding its own. We listened, huddled next to the radio as the team called for a medevac and fixed wing to hit the area around their position while they tried to break contact. However, three hours went by before they were able to beat the enemy back and get a medevac in. Once they did, fixed wing came in and saturated the area with CS gas. The men in the patrol put on their gas masks and made a break for an LZ. An hour or so after the medevac went out, the patrol was extracted, leaving a number of dead and wounded NVA behind them.

On the morning of the fourth, we spotted several VC entering a village about twelve hundred meters from us. They strolled down the road like assembly-line workers coming home after a hard night on the job. I called arty, gave them a plot well outside the limits of the vil, and called for a shot. It came in right where I'd called it, but I reported it as being way off target and called for an adjustment. The next round dropped right into the vil—arty thought it was in a rice paddy.

While the adjustments for the shot were being made, the enemy kept breaking into smaller groups as the men split off singly and in pairs to go to their respective homes. When one black-pajama-clad VC broke off from the group he was with, I followed him with the binoculars. He entered a house, and through a large unshuttered window, I watched him hang his rifle on the wall. The way he went about it, you'd think it was his lunch pail, or plow, or some damn thing. Just at that moment, the first round came in. It hit one corner of the house, collapsing most of it and blowing the man inside right through a wall and into the yard outside. I couldn't believe I had called such a great shot, then so clearly witnessed the results. Corporal Brown, who had also seen the shot come in, let out a low whistle and whispered, "Lieutenant, that was *good*."

I have never been able to express to a noncombatant what a great sense of accomplishment that shot gave me.

The next two rounds landed squarely on a house at the far end of the village, and it burst into a huge ball of fire. Secondary explosions started going off as the house burned, and flying debris set a neighboring house on fire. What with the fires and the exploding ordnance, it looked and sounded just like a war going on.

I reported to arty that we had a dozen VC running around in the paddy they thought they were shooting into, and they cranked in fifteen more rounds before securing the mission. When the shooting stopped, most of the vil was in ruins. With the fires burning brightly and secondary explosions going off right and left, it put all of us in a festive, 4th-of-July mood.

Later that morning, we were lifted off a ridge between our mountain and one made up of towering granite slabs that reminded me of some lost civilization rising out of the jungle.

I must have seen too many Tarzan movies when I was a kid.

We were in the battalion area for two days, then sent up to Ba Na.

14

For those of us who had never been there, R.C. Ba Na was the fabled city in the sky. Everyone who had been to Ba Na had a story to tell, and the mystery surrounding the place grew with each telling. Some said it was a rest area for French officers and their families during the war with the Vietminh. Others said it was used by wealthy plantation owners to escape the hot, humid summers of the plains below. A few said it was once a brothel for the very rich. Maybe it was all of the above. Two things were certain; nobody believed it was built for the Vietnamese, and whatever it had been, it was abandoned now and slowly being reclaimed by the jungle.

Intrigued by stories of Ba Na, I cut short our stay in the rear so we could be the next patrol to the city in the sky.

Like Chickie Pie, Ba Na was considered to be an R & R trip to the field. Teams sent there acted as radio-relay stations for recon patrols working the far edge of Happy Valley, near the Laotian border.

The flight from Reasoner to the top of the 1467-meter-high mountain took twenty minutes, but due to a cloud cover, we spent most of the morning on the LZ. Waiting, I studied the maps of the area, thinking that during better times the trip from Da Nang by road must have taken half a day or longer. Now the narrow, winding road to the summit only invited an ambush, and no one had used it in years.

When we went in, we flip-flopped with an outgoing patrol on the hotel tennis court, which was still intact, complete with boundary lines.

The roof of the two-story, concrete hotel had been destroyed by fire, and the second floor was cluttered with broken tile, charred beams, and melted glass. Some of the second-story walls were collapsing, but the first floor was sound, with the second-story floor now acting as a roof.

I sent half the patrol off with Corporal Brown to check out the surrounding area. Then while Smoger established radio contact with the team in Happy Valley, I took a couple of men with me to explore the main building. Before we entered the hotel, I told the men to take cover and pulled out a fragmentation grenade. With my back to a wall, I said, "I've always wanted to do this." I pulled the pin and threw the grenade into the main downstairs room, which at one time must have served as a ballroom.

The sound of the explosion was staggering. Ears ringing, I entered the hotel.

"Too many John Wayne movies, Lieutenant," Private First Class Martin remarked dryly.

"Couldn't help myself," I replied.

There were probably fifty rooms in all of the hotel, but since one wing had been bombed into rubble, it was hard to tell the exact number. By American standards, the rooms were small. All were without bathrooms or shower facilities. The toilets and bathhouse must have been in the rubble because we didn't find either. Scavengers and souvenir hunters had picked the place clean—right down to the window frames.

After spending an hour exploring the hotel and the cisterns beneath it, I decided it was too large to defend by such a small group as ours and moved the patrol into a chalet on top of a hill three hundred meters to the west. There we set up our radio-relay station.

Several chalets, connected by road, dotted the surrounding hills. At one time, each had provided seclusion and privacy for the wealthier guests at Ba Na.

Ours was Chalet B, one of the larger and roomier chalets we had to choose from. The roof was still on, and the shutters were in place, making it more livable than those that had been damaged. However, the main reason I chose Chalet B was because it could easily be defended. Three sides of the hill it sat on dropped off sharply, and the main approach was narrow, making it impossible to spread troops out on line for an assault.

Smoger set up his radio in one of the rooms, broke out his long antenna, and wove it among the branches of a nearby tree. Then he ran a cable from the antenna to the radio, plugged it in, and reestablished contact with Beacon Light and the team in the field. Handset hung on the lapel of his field jacket, Smoger then pulled out a deck of cards and started playing poker with the other men in the room, using bullets as chips.

The rooms of our new home were spacious, and the ceiling was ten feet high, designed to minimize the effects of the heat. Some of the doors were still in place, and we even had a bathtub. The only real disappointment was a flush toilet that didn't work. We did stand around admiring it and jiggling the handle for some time.

Corporal Brown set up a radio watch, and once the newness of our surroundings wore off, we settled into a routine of relaying messages and killing time as best we could. While the card game progressed in another room, I stretched out in a room with a view of the jungle, propped a book on my chest, and read until the sun dropped low on the horizon.

With the night came the cold. The temperature dropped quickly, and we were soon putting on sweat shirts and field jackets to stay warm.

Later, wrapped in my sleeping bag cover, I listened to the jungle until midnight before falling asleep.

At 0300, I woke up wet and freezing. A fog had moved in through the open windows, and it was as wet indoors as it was out. Shivering, I sat with my back to a wall and waited out the dawn.

When the sun came up, I gathered up half the patrol, and we set out to search the surrounding area. Mainly we went because I can't stand being cooped up for any length of time, and I was curious about this place in the sky.

No sign of the enemy had been seen in or around Ba Na for months, but I treated our movement like any other patrol.

Moving in wet silence through the forest, we checked out the chalets scattered over the mountaintop. Some were larger than others, but the design was pretty much the same—tile roof, main room with a view, kitchen outdoors. Like the hotel, each was made of concrete blocks, covered with a coat of plaster, and painted white, although very little paint was left on any of the buildings. All of them were being taken back by the jungle, and in one roofless chalet, vines, grass, and a tree grew through the cracked floor. It wouldn't be long before a once cozy home would be just another vegetation-covered lump in the forest.

We continued to prowl the area.

Not finding any signs of the enemy, we got pretty loose, and as we went, we took photos and stopped to rummage through every dump site we came to, looking for a piece of Ba Na to carry away with us.

Near the hotel was a stand of pine trees, the first I had seen in the forests of Vietnam and probably planted by the hotel staff. Listening to the wind whispering through the pines reminded me of the mountains near home.

Rock-lined paths that once offered guests a quiet stroll on an innocent afternoon wound deep into the woods. We stayed off the paths and worked through the trees along the sides, fearful of booby traps.

We stayed out all morning then returned to Chalet B for lunch. When we got back, the card game was still in progress, and Smoger had a corner on the bullet market.

For several weeks, I had been fighting an infection called cellulitis. My corpsman, Doc Shannon, said it was the result of living under unsanitary conditions. The infection was particularly bad on my left forearm and over one eye. Both areas itched constantly, and I couldn't keep from scratching them, which only worsened the condition. At Ba Na, my right eye became so swollen I could hardly see out of it, and my forearm grew to twice its normal size. The skin on my arm got so hard and tight, I kept thinking it was going to split from wrist to elbow. It not only itched, but it ached as well, and scratching it was painful. But it had to be scratched! The infected areas wept a yellowish puslike liquid that dried, crusted over, cracked, and continued to ooze.

By the third day on the mountain, I was running a temperature, and my arm was so painful I didn't leave the chalet. Feverish, I spent most of the time sleeping on the concrete floor, over which I had laid a pile of grass.

Late that same afternoon, clouds moved in and shrouded the mountain in a thick, wet fog. Visibility fell to less than fifty feet, and I grew depressed and edgy in the gloom.

We waited. Fog rolled in through the windows, covering us with a fine mist. Then it started to rain, and the wind began to blow. Cold, miserable, and beyond the point of caring, I gave the men permission to build a fire. Once it was going, spirits rose. Feeling better, I joined the men gathered around the fireplace, and we sat and talked and drank tea until dark.

Difficult to describe my fascination with Ba Na. Maybe it was another one of the lost civilizations I always seem to be dreaming about, or another cloud castle I'm forever building, but I couldn't keep from exploring while we were there. Once the fever was gone, I was back poking through the ruins, wondering what it had once been like and looking for a ghost to explain it all to me. I didn't find a ghost, but I did return with a few doorknobs and a porcelain bowl someone had thrown out with the trash.

I could have stayed up there for the rest of my tour in Nam, daydreaming, but after six days, we lifted out and returned to battalion.

15

On the morning of July 15th, we were back down on LZ Finch, waiting to go out. Two days prior, I had turned twenty-eight. I felt closer to fifty.

This time out was supposed to be my last. When I returned, I would take over the battalion intelligence officer's job and become the new S-2. One last patrol to sweat out before being handed my reprieve.

We were going in on a bald ridge west of the Arizona and five hundred meters south of the Song Vu Gia, and would be working in support of a large grunt operation, the name of which I have forgotten.

The vegetation on the ridge was knee-high and sparse, and the place could easily have been mistaken for the Mojave Desert. I had everyone turn out in helmets and flak jackets. We also carried with us a number of tear gas grenades, one gas mask per man, sandbags, and entrenching tools. This wasn't a recon patrol, it was the occupation of an outpost deep in Indian territory. And since we would be relieving a patrol in place and our arrival wouldn't be a surprise to anyone, I wanted to be prepared.

When we left Finch, we flew down to An Hoa and staged, arriving in the early afternoon. Due to a heavy commitment, the birds would be late making recon insertions, and we were told to make ourselves comfortable in the waiting area—a large tin roof supported by metal poles. There seated on benches and squatting on the ground was as odd a collection of people as could be found so far from anywhere.

147

We gathered in the shade, dropped our gear, and sat down to wait.

Across from me were two Red Cross workers I took to be Danes. They didn't seem to speak English and wouldn't have anything to do with us, wearing a sort of fuck-the-Americans-but-we-will-ride-in-your-airplanes look on their smug, blond faces. Considering all the business we were drumming up for the Red Cross, I couldn't understand the attitude of these two. I mean, shit, without us, there wouldn't be any need for them.

Near the Danes, in their shorts and sandals, was an attractive Vietnamese woman, dressed in a long, flowing *ao dai*, slit to the waist and worn over black pants. The *ao dai* was the hallmark of a city dweller, and what she was doing here on the edge of the Arizona was beyond me. Her face registered a calm, detached look, and she gave me the impression the rest of us weren't there. Not having been so close to a woman in a long time, I had a hard time keeping my eyes off her. Soft, curvaceous, lovely. I wanted to sit next to her and ask if she minded if I played with her tits.

Squatting around on the floor and hanging onto an assortment of kids with no pants on, were your hard-core betel-nut chewers, chicken raisers, and pig farmers. Dressed in black pajamas and carrying their conical hats slung on their backs, they kept up a continuous head-bobbing, black-toothed, grinning chatter, while spitting between their knees and attracting more than their share of the flies. God knows where they were going with their baskets of live chickens, whose heads stuck out between the weave, and tied-up pigs, but they were going by air, compliments of the U.S.A., to get there!

I was a little put out that not one of them came over to shake my hand and say, "Hey, GI Joe, thanks for coming to liberate my country from the Mongol horde! Here, take this bottle of champagne I've been saving just for the occasion. And while you're at it, screw my wife. She'd like to express her appreciation, too."

Never hoppon, GI. You numba fucking ten.

Off by itself was a very sullen group of military-age men who, I was sure, had their loyalties fixed to the North. I kept wondering where *they* were being inserted.

A patrol from Force Recon was also waiting to go out. It numbered eight. There were ten of us.

Force usually worked in smaller numbers than we did and often went out with as few as six men.

The patrol leader, a second lieutenant new in country, had only led two or three trips to the bush. I had seen him around Reasoner, and he sticks in my mind only because he always talked too loud and laughed too hard. He acted no differently there in the shade. He would say something loud enough for it to sound like it was coming over a PA system, then slap his squad leader on the back and laugh outrageously. The whole time we were there together, he talked, slapped, laughed, stood up, sat down, and turned around.

I knew he was scared shitless.

I didn't think too badly of him because I had been there myself. Instead of pounding someone on the back and barking "Hardy-har-har" in his face, I usually fell asleep, sometimes in the damndest places. I guess we all have our own way of reacting to stress.

The lieutenant was lucky, though. He had a father or an uncle who was a Marine general, and within a few days some strings were pulled, and he went from Force Recon to manning a desk at MACV—Military Assistance Command, Vietnam. I had seen that happen only once before. When I was stationed in the Philippines, a private first class who had an uncle who was an admiral didn't like the PI, and unc swung him a transfer to Japan.

Few of us in the bush had any strings to pull, but I think if we had, we'd have pulled them.

We sat and sweated and swatted flies and flinched every time a nearby artillery battery fired.

A cargo plane came in for the Vietnamese and the pigs and chickens, and they left. Then a Red Cross vehicle, filled with more blond Teutons, arrived and carried away the Danes. Force Recon went out, with the lieutenant talking and laughing louder than ever. I stretched out on the concrete and fell asleep.

Shortly after sundown, our birds came. We boarded and lifted off for the short flight to the ridgeline. For once, I was grateful for the coming of darkness. I knew that if we did run into Charlie, we could lose him in the night and just keep humping until we found a place to harbor.

The flip-flop went smoothly, and by the time the second bird came in, I had spotted a granite outcrop on a knoll about three hundred meters away. I got the patrol in line, and we moved without incident to the outcrop, arriving just as the moon broke the night sky. We were in an ideal defensive position, and I told the men to start digging in, because unless Charlie came up and dislodged us, we weren't going anywhere for the next four days.

For the next two hours, we built our defenses, digging holes two and three feet deep and filling sandbags to form walls around them. Then we camouflaged the position by uprooting some nearby bushes and replanting them to screen our presence. When we were done, I was confident the enemy couldn't see us unless they actually came onto our hill.

Corporal Brown established a watch, while I checked on the completed positions and set fields of fire for each man. Earlier, I had plotted and called in our night defensive fires and checked out our communications with Beacon Light. By midnight, there wasn't much left to do but wait for the sun to come up. I stretched out near my hole and watched the stars drift past, wishing I knew their names.

The night was warm, and a gentle breeze blew away what few insects there were. Even though we were exposed on the dry, desertlike ridge, I felt a sense of relief at not being trapped in the claustrophobic atmosphere of the jungle, where clearings became escape hatches to the sky and beyond to the face of God, if He ever chose to look down on me. Often as I looked, I never saw Him. But it was at the clearings I could hear Him, mocking me. ''I see you, Lieutenant, you insignificant sack of shit. You're three klicks from an LZ, and the vegetation between you and it is so thick you'll be a slobbering idiot by the time you get there."

Strange, I thought. My last patrol wasn't a patrol, it was the manning of an outpost on a hill surrounded by the enemy. It wouldn't take a genius to eventually figure out we were on the hill, but I hadn't felt so relaxed in a long time. I was also feeling oddly defiant. I didn't care if Charlie found us.

At 0300, I passed the word to put on gas masks, then threw tear gas into the only approach to our position offering cover and concealment, a narrow ravine. If we were going to be attacked, it would develop out of the ravine and I had decided to throw tear gas into it at regular intervals each night we were on the hill.

As the gas filled the approach, we sat, watching, sweating in our rubber masks. When nothing happened, I passed the word to secure and get on with the night.

Dawn found us manning OPs at the opposite ends of our position. There wasn't much moving in the Arizona, but across the river, a pair of bulldozers were scraping down the road to Thuong Duc, where a Special Forces unit operated. I stayed tuned, wondering when Charlie was going to KIA two dozers. But an ambush never materialized, and the machines slowly scraped their way out of sight.

About an hour after they were gone, a squad of Marines moved down the same road and immediately got into a firefight. It lasted about ten minutes before the enemy broke contact and the Marines moved on. The only reason I could think Charlie let the bulldozers go by was that they wanted the road improved just as much as we did.

As the morning wore on, it got hot, and we were soon stripping off our shirts and stringing up ponchos to make more shade on the hill. Heat waves danced crazily on the Arizona, forcing us to cut down on scope and binocular time to save our eyes. Looking into the writhing, twisting waves quickly brought on eyestrain and throbbing headaches. Our best viewing hours were from first light to about 1000, then from 1600 until dark. Anything in between those hours was often misinterpreted for something other than what it was,

and on particularly hot days, we were plagued by mirages—
villages rising out of lakes, people treading the air above the
ground.

When the heat was on us, we sat with our tongues half
out, shirts off, heads so hot they were about to explode, flies
buzzing with a vengeance.

That first day, like the next three, was unmercifully hot.
We dripped sweat, swatted flies, and discussed the prospects
of taking a dip in the invitingly nearby Song Vu Gia. But
since the trip held all the prospects of being a fatal one, we
stayed where we were.

Sightings didn't pick up until late in the day when we saw
several groups of the enemy moving away from some grunts
pushing from the southwest. The guns were tied up, and
since the groups we saw weren't a threat to anyone, we didn't
connect with a fire mission.

At dusk, I called a 155 battery and asked them to shoot in
our night-defensive fires. They rogered my request and said
they would come back on the air when the shot was ready.
Just then, one of the men jumped up, excited, saying there
were three VC on a trail at the base of our hill. I grabbed a
pair of binoculars and spotted them near the river. We had
brought along a tripod for the machine gun, and Private First
Class Henderson, the gunner, quickly sighted in on the target.
The lead VC carried a rifle and pack, while the second one,
a woman, carried only a rifle. The third person appeared to
be a young teenage boy, who was unarmed. Henderson
opened up with a short burst while I observed the strike of
the bullets through the binoculars. He wasn't far off target. I
gave him the adjustments, and he poured a long stream of
tracers directly onto the trail. The man in the lead never
broke stride as he walked into the bullets and died. The
woman and the teenager turned and ran back down the trail.
While Henderson was adjusting on them, Smoger yelled that
arty had called "shot out." On the trail, the woman and the
kid were pumping along like a pair of Olympic sprinters.
Suddenly, the woman veered off and headed for a clump of
bushes. The kid kept running and was soon out of sight

around a bend in the trail. The woman dove into the bushes, and the instant she did, the 155 round impacted directly on top of her. I had never seen a shot quite like that, someone taking a direct hit from an artillery round. It was about fifty meters off from where I had plotted it but on for her.

"Ruined *her* day," someone remarked.

Darkness was almost on us, and we used what little light we had to finish our nighttime preparations. If Charlie hadn't known we were on the hill before, he sure did now—a stream of tracers leads in two directions, and only the dullest of observers wouldn't have been able to figure out exactly where we were.

About 2200, a loud banging of drums, gongs, and metal pots started up in the village of Minh Tan (1) down near the river. AT&T it wasn't, but it did effectively communicate to villages nearby that a Marine unit was in the area. I suspected a grunt patrol was out and about. Then again, it could have been a call to mount a human-wave attack on our hill. Or, for all I knew, to assemble a quilting bee. From where we sat, there was no telling. But when one has been exposed to outdoor life in Vietnam, one automatically assumes the worst.

I contacted the grunt battalion operating nearest us and told them what was going on in Minh Tan (1) and was told the matter would be looked into.

About twenty minutes went by, and the noise from the village hadn't let up. We were all gathered around the top of the hill, looking down toward the village and speculating on what was going on when we heard a *thunk, thunk, thunk* that went on for several seconds. Moments later, Minh Tan (1) was enveloped in mortar fire. The exploding rounds took us by such surprise, we all leapt to our feet much like fans at a football game during a scoring run.

When the rounds stopped exploding, there wasn't a sound coming from the village.

After several minutes passed and the drumming failed to start up again, one of the men commented, "I guess they lost their sense of rhythm."

That night, I increased the security and left word to be awakened every hour.

Early the next morning, I picked up a long procession of people moving down a road. They were so far away I had difficulty keeping them in focus. The people in the procession were dressed in brightly colored costumes, and several groups carried something resembling royal palanquins, complete with pagodalike structures on top—shades of Hollywood, I thought. Bring on Sabu and the elephants.

The distance between us was extreme—over twelve kilometers. I had no idea what they were up to, but reported it to Beacon Light, then called up arty, described what I was looking at, and sent in the azimuth and coordinates. I did not identify the procession as being enemy or otherwise. It was just a procession.

A few minutes later, arty called back and wanted to know if I could adjust from where I was. I said I probably could, then stated I didn't believe the target was a military one and had called it in only because I had never heard of anyone reporting anything like it before.

But arty wanted to shoot, which was a definite breach of the so-called rules of engagement we cursed and labored under and the higher-ups used to protect their careers with.

Personally, I thought we would be firing into a funeral party or a religious convention, but having been in the bush so long, I really didn't give a shit. At the time, I could have called in a fire mission on an LA freeway during rush hour with equal indifference. Besides, it was a hell of a challenge adjusting on a target so far away.

I replotted the azimuth and location of the procession, noted the direction it was headed in, and radioed everything to arty. Then I mounted my scope on a pile of sandbags, fixed it firmly in place, and curled up in a ball behind it, trying not to move. Staying on a target at that distance is very hard to do. Any movement throws the scope way off, and the target is lost while valuable seconds and sometimes minutes are spent trying to find it again. With the scope's narrow field of vision and the fact that only one eye can be used to observe with, it was not uncommon to lose a target altogether and never find it again.

It was still early, and the heat waves hadn't come up to dance the target all over the Dai Loc quadrangle. I was able to clearly see the bright colors worn by the people in the parade and make out something that looked like a huge dragon's head on one of the palanquins. It was unlikely this was an NVA regiment on the move.

Arty called, "Shot out" and the first round came in on our side of the road the procession was on. The people were obviously startled by it and began milling around. But since I took so long figuring out just what adjustments to make to get the next round on the road, they reorganized and started out again.

I called in my corrections, then muttered to no one in particular that I hoped the people in the parade had a good sense of humor.

The next round was right on target.

I called for a fire for effect and an entire battery of 155s opened up. Life on the road got pretty exciting after that. People began running everywhere as craters opened up around them and whole trees were uprooted and thrown through the air.

Then a battery of 105s came on the air and wanted to shoot. I fed them the coordinates and azimuth and soon found myself adjusting two batteries at the same time.

Far away as the target was, we could clearly hear the thunder of the impacting rounds. It was impressive.

I still didn't know what I was shooting at and had to think that someone higher up knew more about the target than I did—otherwise a clearance to shoot wouldn't have been given. I think, deep down in my little heart, though, I really didn't care.

The shooting went on for about fifteen minutes before I called in a cease fire. By that time, I couldn't see anything left to shoot at.

From where we were, it was impossible to give a damage assessment, so a FAC was called in to fly over the target.

Shortly after he came on station, the action in that part of the Arizona picked up and never seemed to stop. The grunts moved in, and we could hear them blazing away but couldn't see what they were up to. Then Phantoms started hitting the area with napalm, taking fire each time they made a run. A regular war had been kicked off, and the fighting lasted for most of the day, flaring up in different parts of the Arizona, as one grunt unit after another ran up against the enemy. There really wasn't much for us to do but sit and watch.

Night came, and both Spooky and Puff worked over several targets until well past midnight. The planes used to fill the roles of Spooky and Puff were usually twin-engine C-123 cargo planes: the former fitted to drop large, parachute-suspended flares, and the latter fitted with mini-guns that fired 7.62-caliber bullets at such a rapid rate that the sound they made was like a giant piece of cloth being ripped. Often, a single plane would serve in both capacities—the intention being to light up an area then plow it clean with bullets.

The next day, save for a few firefights, the Arizona was quiet.

I never did find out if our target was a funeral procession or an NVA unit in drag.

One more night was all I had to survive. Just one more, and I would be out. Out of the bush and out of the war. So long as it wasn't in the field, I could do the seven months I had left standing on my head.

God, smile on me just a little longer.

When the night came, I couldn't sleep. Nervous, I sat by the radio, monitoring calls to Beacon Light and watching the approach to our hill. About 0200, I caught one of the men on guard sound asleep. I almost snapped. I stuck the muzzle of my rifle up next to his ear and thought seriously about blowing it off just to get his attention. Then I dropped the rifle, grabbed the man by the shirt, and yanked him to me. He came awake in a wild state of fright. "You motherfucker," I hissed. I let him go and went back to my hole.

For the rest of the night, I just sat and waited.

* * *

Late in the afternoon, the birds came for us. As we lifted off, I was going through an unbelievable range of emotions. First, there was the overwhelming relief that I had made it, that I now had a future and would one day return to my family. I had my reprieve, my wife had a husband, my kids had a father. Then on the long flight back to battalion, guilt and depression set in. I was coming out of the bush, but my men had to stay. There weren't any jobs in the rear for them, and their only early escape from the field was through death or severe wounds. The one long shot they had was a next to impossible one. With three Purple Hearts they could come out. But what were the odds of being wounded on three separate occasions and surviving? It would take more luck than any of us cared to admit we didn't have.

After a while, I took my release from the field for what it was and pushed the guilt to the back of my mind.

16

The primary purpose of the battalion S-2 was to brief and debrief patrols and to provide information on assigned RAORs. Normally, a patrol knew where it was going a day prior to its insertion, and most of the patrol leaders and their assistants came to the S-2 shop to learn as much as they could about the areas they would be working. On file in the shop was an extensive collection of situation reports, passed on by division, that provided past and recent enemy activity in areas the grunts operated in. Also on file was information passed on by Vietnamese informants and some intelligence reports completed by the army. But more important were the patrol reports compiled by both Recon Battalion and 1st Force, which included information on the terrain and vegetation of the areas we operated in and map overlays. The overlays were particularly valuable because they showed trails, bunkers, and streams not depicted on our topographic maps and helped to keep the maps accurate and up-to-date. A few high-quality stereographic photos were available, but even these failed to penetrate the canopy and reveal what was on the ground.

Patrol leaders were particularly interested in the kind of terrain and type of vegetation they would be operating in. Some areas were a breeze to pass through, and others were a nightmare of tangled wait-a-minute vines, steep ravines, and mosquito-infested swamps. It was important for a patrol leader to know as much about his RAOR beforehand so he didn't bog his team down in the same mess a previous patrol may have spent a day or more trying to extricate itself from.

Contact with the enemy was also written up in each report

in standard SALUTE form, plus a detailed account of the contact. No matter how old this information was, it always had some value, especially the location and circumstances under which the contact had occurred. Contact initiated by a recon patrol usually resulted in serious casualties inflicted on the enemy. However, when the opposite occurred and the enemy initiated the contact, recon was the one to suffer. Therefore, it was important to a patrol leader to know exactly what led up to a patrol being ambushed, in the hopes of avoiding a similar fate.

My job, as it turned out, had very little to do with the actual placing of a patrol in its RAOR. The S-3 (operations shop), under Major Welzant, assigned most of the areas to be worked. In turn, many of the S-3's decisions were based on the wishes of division, which responded to intelligence reports gathered from throughout the division tactical area of operational responsibility (TAOR).

While the plains region of the division TAOR was left up to the grunts and FAC pilots to cover, recon had the mountains and jungles beyond. There was no question that the jungle was too vast and the mountains too rugged to be controlled or even entirely observed by ten-man recon teams. It was up to division and recon to determine the most likely avenues the enemy might use through the mountains and jungles and when he might be there. Much of the planning was based on guesswork, but it was guesswork with a lot of effort behind it, and more often than not, a patrol would find the enemy within or near its RAOR.

Since the enemy usually worked in small groups, large sightings of them were uncommon. When we did sight them in large groups, the results were often impressive, such as Hateful, under Lt. Bob Drake, having an NVA company pass within feet of its position, then calling down a heavy concentration of artillery. When artillery came down on the NVA, they were routed and turned back into the mountains from which they came.

Had someone not thought to put Hateful where it was, the company of NVA would have slipped through to the villages northwest of Da Nang to an area considered to be under government control. The results would have been both politically and militarily embarrassing to the United States as well as the South Vietnamese.

To be sure, recon couldn't and didn't get every enemy unit moving into the division TAOR, but it did its share of damage to a large number of them and made others think twice about the routes they chose and the frequency of their visits.

Once the RAOR and mission of a patrol were established, the information was passed on to the S-2 shop where the LZs and patrol route were worked out. Normally, leaders were given a wide variety of choices regarding LZs. And while actual patrol routes would be penciled in for them, team leaders had the option of approaching objectives along routes of their own choosing. Although many of the planners in the rear were not enamored with the idea of giving the leaders on the ground as much flexibility as possible to carry out their missions, I firmly believed that it was essential they have it. Often one of those planners would be working with no more than a map when assigning missions, and when he sent a team out to watch a trail that existed only on paper and days were wasted trying to find something that wasn't there, frustration and a lack of credibility set in. Better to provide options than a rigid set of instructions as guidelines.

With options, a patrol leader was able to capitalize on situations as they developed. Offering several LZs instead of just one or two was one key to the success of any mission. It not only caused patrol leaders to think about all the approaches they had to achieving their objectives, but gave them the opportunity to refuse a zone they didn't like and possibly avert disaster before it had a chance to develop.

Prior to a patrol going out, the S-2 was present at each briefing to pass on any recent information about the assigned RAOR and give the latest changes in weather. Major Welzant usually conducted the main body of the briefing, confirming supporting arms available and their locations, assigning radio frequencies, the time and location of insertions and extractions, and so on. Often, the battalion CO or XO was in attendance, but they had little to say other than offer a few words of encouragement to the outgoing team.

When patrols were going out or coming in, I made it a point to be on the helipad. In some cases, I even flew along on insertions and extractions, but it was difficult to get permission to do so. In my own small way, I wanted the men in those patrols to know I cared about them. After all, I was one of those responsible for their fate.

Once a patrol returned to battalion, it was my job to debrief it. The procedure took anywhere from thirty minutes to an hour, and it was a process carried out entirely by the members of the patrol and the debriefing officer. The battalion commander often sat in but in no way tried to influence the debriefing. If he had anything to say, it usually came in the form of a question to clarify some incident. In July, the battalion had changed hands and was under the command of Lieutenant Colonel Steinmetz, who was quick to praise and slow to chastise. Both he and the previous battalion commander, Lieutenant Colonel McKeon, frequently attended the debriefings and always wanted complete details of any enemy contact, especially if we had taken casualties.

When contact with the enemy had taken place, all of the men were encouraged to speak so that a complete description of the action could be developed. By the time the debriefing was through, everyone had a clear picture of what had happened and perhaps knew how to improve their reaction the next time contact with the enemy was made.

Once a patrol was debriefed, the notes were taken back to the S-2 shop, where a clerk would type them into a smooth draft, and a copy was kept in the office. Other copies would go to the battalion commander and up to division.

As a patrol leader, I had normally received second and thirdhand information about what took place on other patrols. Now, I was getting it all firsthand and sometimes within hours of its occurrence. Many times, the patrol members were still shaking from the residual effects of an encounter with the enemy and would repeat over and over again the events that had taken place. When this happened, the men were often close to violence there in the debriefing room, especially so if a member of the patrol had been killed or wounded. Sometimes, when they had killed one of the enemy under unusual circumstances, they would relate the entire event down to the most minute detail, often laughing at the way the victim had died, which was a common reaction.

In one such case, a VC had been following a patrol for several hours when they set up an ambush for him. When he came into the ambush, instead of shooting him, one of the men stood up and motioned for the gook to come to him and surrender. At that point, the VC stuck his hands in his pockets, turned around and tried to stroll away while whistling a tune one might whistle while passing a graveyard at night. Try as he might to pretend the patrol wasn't there, he paid for his refusal to come with his life. When the incident was related at the debriefing, complete with animated movements by the speaker, the laugh was heavily on the dead gook.

To sit and listen through session after session soon began to take its toll on me, and I started coming away from them with the feeling that I should be out there with the teams in the field and not holding down a desk in the rear. Guilt was raising its ugly head.

While I was working in the S-2 shop, we began hearing rumors of a Marine running with the enemy. He had been spotted in several different locations, each time in the company of a group of VC or NVA. The description of him was always the same: Blond, six feet tall, dressed in Marine Corps issue fatigues, and wearing a red sash around his waist. On numerous occasions, he had tried to lure Marines into an ambush by calling to them for help, or exposing himself to view. He had been seen too many times by too many different units to be a figment of someone's imagination, and when a Force Recon patrol reported seeing him, most of us considered the sighting valid.

He was soon given the name, The Marine With the Red Sash. Whoever he was, he seemed to live a charmed life, eluding capture or death for a year or more. Eventually, however, his charmed life ran out. Several months after my return to the States, I ran into a sergeant from Force Recon, who told me one of Force's patrols had killed The Marine With the Red Sash. The Force team had walked head-on into an NVA patrol led by the blond Marine and were at first so surprised they failed to get off a shot. When the shooting did start, the Marine leading the NVA was wounded and went down. When he cried out in English for help, the Force patrol leader called back, "I'll help you!" and shot him several times. Due to the intensity of the firefight, the patrol was unable to approach the body and had to withdraw, but they were certain The Marine With the Red Sash was dead.

He was not the only American to go over to the other side. First Force Recon had its own defector.

In early August, a plan was developed to reach some of the more remote and inaccessible parts of the jungle by rappelling a team in from helicopters. The plan called for a Phantom to first drop a one-thousand-pound, high-explosive bomb to knock down trees and create an opening in the jungle. Then a team would rappel in from a hundred or more feet while helicopters hovered over the newly created zone, which was too littered with splintered trees and too small to take a bird.

Dutch Oven, now under the leadership of Lt. Pete Badger, was chosen for the job. Under the instructions of Lt. Joe Campbell, a long time recon man and graduate of the Mountain Warfare School, Dutch Oven began an intensive training program to learn the fine art of rappelling. The team began on the hill above LZ Finch, learning how to snap into a Swiss seat, walking through a rappel, and unhooking at the bottom. A set of double ropes was used to tie into the Swiss seat, which was a diaperlike harness equipped with a pair of D-shaped carabiners meeting in front at the waist. The ropes were passed through the carabiners, which acted as a braking bar to accelerate or decelerate the rate of descent. Normally, the right hand was used to brake with at the waist, while the left grasped the rope above the head to maintain balance and keep the person rappelling from flipping over backwards. Using the Swiss seat, sudden drops of fifteen and twenty feet can be made before braking. Thus in three or four very quick drops, a man can descend a rope and be on the ground in a matter of seconds.

Once the basics were mastered, the team was soon practicing short rappels off the rear ramp of a CH-46 hovering thirty and forty feet above the paddies surrounding Finch. As the men got better at it, the speed of their descent down the rope increased. So did the distance from the ground, and they began dropping from one-hundred to one-hundred fifty feet, while braking a minimum number of times on the way down.

There are considerable risks involved in rappelling from a helicopter, mainly because flying machines have been known to come down when they weren't supposed to. But other than becoming involved in an occasional downdraft that caused a bird to suddenly drop while disgorging its load and bring on an instant intake of breath among the observers, no injuries were sustained because of helicopter problems. The pilots reacted to a drop so quickly that the birds were immediately stabilized and back in position.

The only accident that happened during the training program was when a rope broke, and one of the men fell one hundred feet to a paddy. Luckily, he was not hurt and, after being checked out by a corpsman, soon rejoined the team.

As they got better, half the team could insert and secure the practice LZ in three or four minutes. Then the second half would be brought in, and Dutch Oven was ready to go to work. The method was a dangerous one, but recon now had access to areas previously denied to it.

The locations for the insertions were chosen for their remoteness, such as Nui Ca Nhong, a one thousand-meter-high spine that ran for ten kilometers through the vast jungles south of Back Ma. It was an area so inaccessible that it had rarely been visited by recon and never by any of the other U. S. forces in Vietnam. Now, with the means to shove the canopy aside and rappel in, we could, for the first time, learn to what extent the enemy was using this remote area.

Their first time out, Dutch Oven went in without mishap. The thousand-pound bomb opened up a large clearing in the trees covering a section of Nui Ca Nhong, and the team dropped onto the ridge. Soon after they were on the ground, they discovered a small Montagnard village, the inhabitants of which having fled only moments before. Due to the area it was in, the village was considered to be under the influence and control of the VC. Approaching it with caution, the team searched the village, found no one, then emptied it of all food and equipment they found. The food and equipment were taken out by helicopter. None of it was of any military value. At the time, it seemed like a real blow to the enemy, and the division CG even came over to personally congratulate the men in Dutch Oven.

Reflecting back on it, I think that following the team's visit, some poor, miserable tribe went without for a long time—bystanders caught up in a conflict they neither understood nor wanted any part of.

But the team did get in, and the method worked. More insertions by rappelling were laid on, and when not in the field, Dutch Oven continued to practice, reducing the time it took to get on the ground.

When a man went down the rope, everything he needed to sustain him in the field was carried on his back, making the descent not only awkward but dangerous. Occasionally, a man got his gear tangled in the rope and became stuck. This had so far happened only in practice, and the situation was quickly remedied by landing the helicopter and untangling the man. In the jungle, there was no place to land and untangle.

When an LZ was blown for an insertion above Elephant Valley for Dutch Oven's third rappel, a tremendous amount of debris was left in the zone, limiting access to it and creating a real obstacle course for the team. Due to prop turbulence and crosswinds, the rope was weighted with a PRC-25 radio to straighten it out and keep it from getting tangled in the debris.

Lt. Pete Badger was the first one out and, when he reached

the ground, found he could not gain a footing in the blown-down trees and broken branches. He also discovered he was stuck fast to the radio at the end of the rope. While trying to keep his balance, he managed to cut himself out of his Swiss seat, but still couldn't free himself from the radio and the rope. A cable was lowered to reel him back into the helicopter, but Pete was unable to hook onto it. In the meantime, the helicopter turbines began to overheat. Through hand signals, the men in the bird got the message across that they had to take off, and Pete gave them a thumbs-up that he understood.

When the bird got underway, Pete, who confesses to a great fear of heights, was dangling beneath it. As he dangled, the rope caught on his cartridge belt, driving it into his diaphram and cutting off his breath. While he flew through the air, one hundred feet below the bird, unable to catch his breath, his men tried to reel him in by hand. It didn't work. Off they soared, two thousand feet above the ground, with Pete turning and twisting in the breeze and turning blue in the face.

Finally, they reached the coast south of Hai Van Pass and set down on the beach long enough to get Pete back on board. Shaken as he was by the ordeal, Pete was still able to marvel over the fact that his much prized bush hat was still firmly in place on his head.

Dutch Oven returned to Reasoner to regroup.

The team continued to make insertions by rappelling, but when the regions being worked proved to be unproductive, the method was dropped. Apparently, the areas were too remote for all save a few primitive wandering tribes, harmful to no one.

17

For some time, two or three platoons in recon and Force had been working with the Stoner weapons system, which involved a machine gun and rifle with interchangeable parts. Both weapons were lightweight, accurate, and highly effective. They fired the same 5.56-mm round as the M-16, were gas-operated, and belt-and-magazine fed. Unlike the M-16, however, the Stoner system was not prone to jamming. The system was highly regarded by those who used it, and the machine gun was a much-sought-after item. Lighter and smaller than the M-60, it was ideal for reconnaissance work. We wanted to see more of the Stoner system in the battalion, but the weapons we had were handed out sparingly. For some reason, the system was never adopted, and we had to stick with our unreliable M-16s. I mention the Stoner only because it was a prime example of a good piece of equipment being shelved for an inferior one. Most of us worried the M-16 would malfunction just when we needed it the most, and we would have felt a lot more comfortable with the Stoner.

Enemy contact and casualties in the battalion steadily increased during the summer of 1967. There was also a steady increase in sightings of NVA units, and our patrols often found themselves in contact with these well-trained soldiers. Not only were more automatic weapons being used against us, but a few of the teams came under fire from RPGs, a shoulder-fired, antitank weapon, employed much like we employed the M-79 grenade launcher. It was an item we had rarely before encountered in the jungle.

When a team near Elephant Valley was hit by an RPG round that knocked out both its radios and wounded two men, we waited in tense speculation for three hours before they came back on the air to let us know they were still alive and operating. During the long interval of silence, we all feared the worse, that a recon team had been wiped out. It was something that hadn't happened while I was with the battalion, but just the thought of it struck most people squarely in the pit of the stomach.

One of the most spectacular results of any reconnaissance team operating in the field occurred early that summer. It serves as an example of what a well-led, hardhitting small unit can do when it has the element of surprise.

Killer Kane, a team from 1st Force Recon under Lt. Andy Finlayson, was working an area in Happy Valley in support of Operation Pecos, when it came upon the 402d Sapper Battalion bivouacked along a stream. After hearing voices below them, the twelve-man team approached the enemy position from a ridge above the stream.

From the ridge, Andy could only see two NVA soldiers near the stream but could hear the voices of others. Not knowing how many enemy troops were in the gully below, he told his point man, Sergeant Pugh, to fire on the two NVA while the rest of the patrol opened up in the direction the sound of the voices was coming from.

After a five-minute firefight, the enemy ceased to return fire, and Andy, Sergeant Pugh, and the assistant patrol leader, GySgt. Walter Webb, went down into the gully to search for bodies and weapons. They found two NVA soldiers killed by Sergeant Pugh, several blood trails, sixty-three packs, two RPD machine guns, two RPG grenade launchers, one AK-47 assault rifle, a Russian pistol, numerous cooking pots, and two hundred pounds of rice. More important, they found numerous documents and codes belonging to the 402d Sapper Battalion, an elite enemy unit.

Due to the suddenness and violence of the encounter, the enemy had abandoned much of its equipment and fled. Killer

Kane had executed a textbook ambush without taking a single casualty.

Hateful, under Lt. Bob Drake, went in to retrieve the captured equipment and documents, and Killer Kane was instructed to continue patrolling. While the captured gear was being carried to an LZ, Gunny Webb spotted two NVA soldiers moving along a stream toward the patrol. He and a corporal named Russell took them under fire, killing both. When they searched the bodies, they found a pair of East German binoculars, a Russian compass, an AK-47 assault rifle, and some Chinese hand grenades—a regular international gathering of equipment.

Three days later, Killer Kane returned from the field, only to discover that much of the equipment they had gathered and the Russian pistol were missing. Souvenirs now in the hands of the undeserving. However, three flags captured by the patrol were safely in the hands of the company. Unfortunately, Major General Robertson, the division CG, had seen one of the flags and mentioned it "would look nice in the division CP." The flag was a large, colorfully embroidered one that had been presented to the 402d Sapper Battalion by the Da Nang Central Committee of the LAO Dong (Communist Workers) Party. It was Andy's hope that the flag remain with 1st Force Recon Company.

The dilemma was finally solved when an enterprising young Marine suggested that a duplicate flag be made by one of the seamstresses in camp and presented at a ceremony in the general's office. The presentation went off without the general ever knowing the flag he received was not the genuine article, and the original flag stayed with the company.

While Killer Kane came away from its encounter unscathed, some of the other teams were not so fortunate.

Lt. Nick Schriber, leading Petrified, lost his assistant patrol leader, Sergeant Rudd, in an ambush above Elephant Valley. A Sparrow Hawk, (a reaction platoon from a nearby infantry unit) had to be sent in to rescue the patrol and bring it safely out. Sergeant Rudd's body came out with the patrol. For his outstanding leadership and bravery under fire during the ambush, Lieutenant Schriber was later awarded the Navy Cross.

Working out of Chu Lai, Lt. Bill Cole was killed while on patrol near Tam Ky. During a battle that lasted most of one night, Bill was shot in the head. The bullet entered by way of an earhole, did not leave a noticeable wound, and for some reason did not cause any external bleeding. Until someone later discovered the entry wound, no one could figure out why he was dead.

In late August, an assistant patrol leader from 1st Force was killed and his body mutilated by the enemy. He was a young sergeant I had come to know well because he spent a lot of time in the S-2 shop, reading patrol reports and studying maps of the RAORs assigned to his team. When he was killed, the rest of the team was forced to retreat under heavy enemy fire and leave his body behind. Two days later, a team went in and recovered it. The enemy had tied the dead sergeant to a tree, cut him up badly, and even burned him.

Some mutilation of bodies was done by both sides, but rarely did I ever hear of a recon Marine mutilating the dead, and at no time did I ever see a body that had been carved on. There was an incident where a recon lieutenant allowed his corpsman to cut the ears off a dead VC, an act explicitly prohibited in a directive handed down from division. The lieutenant in question was given a letter of reprimand for allowing it to happen.

And so it went.

However, not all of our casualties occurred under fire.

While on the LZ, waiting to go out with his team at Chu Lai, Lance Corporal Faulkner had a pin work its way out of a fragmentation grenade hung on his belt. Unable to get rid of the grenade, he pulled it into himself to prevent others near him from being injured. When it exploded, Faulkner was mortally wounded, and one other man, a sergeant, was only slightly hurt. Cpl. Ron Molnar, a friend of Faulkner's rode with him to the hospital and later said that he was awake for the entire trip and kept apologizing for the grenade having gone off. He died a short time after reaching the hospital.

Another Recon Marine walked into a helicopter blade during an extraction. The blade hit him in the head and removed a large portion of his skull, exposing the brain. He never regained consciousness.

On Hill 452, the R & R outpost, lightning struck the ammo bunker, killing two Marines. One was blown over the cliff and the other blown down the sloping approach. One of the Marines killed had only seven days left in country and before going out to the OP told his platoon leader he thought he was going to die. At the time, the platoon leader thought he was crazy to make such a statement.

Lt. Joe Campbell headed up a team to recover the bodies, both of which were thought to be at the bottom of the cliff. Joe and one other man rappelled down the face of the mountain and began a search for the bodies late in the evening. A captain and a major from battalion had attached themselves to the operation and managed to add a sour note to the recovery.

While the two men went over the side and searched for the bodies below, the captain and the major stayed on top of 452. For both of them, it was a first trip to the field—not much of a trip by any stretch of the imagination.

By nightfall, Joe said he could smell one of the bodies, but couldn't find it. He and the other man came up and with the remainder of the team and the two other officers, spent the night on the hill. The next morning, Joe went back down and found one of the bodies, a black Marine who had been sitting on a case of grenades when the lightning struck. The explosion had removed the back of his head, but done very little other damage to the body. The second body could not be found at the base of the cliff, and the search there was abandoned. Later in the day, it was found on the approach.

When all was said and done and the men returned to Reasoner, the good captain and the major wrote each other up for medals. I personally did not see the citations and only heard about them, but they must have been real pieces of artwork. When Colonel Steinmetz got wind of what they had done, he killed the citations. Unfortunately, the two tainted the recovery operation to such an extent that Joe never fully received the recognition he was due for an outstanding performance of duty.

The I'll-write-you-up-if-you'll-write-me-up approach to career development was not uncommon in Vietnam, and unfortunately, recon had its share of those who dabbled in the practice. We even had a lieutenant who created his own guaranteed-to-have-a-medal-pinned-on-him scenario. Shortly after an insertion on his fourth or fifth patrol, the lieutenant fired off a few rounds, yelled "Gook!" at the top of his lungs, and threw himself on a Chicom grenade. A regular John Wayne. The only problem was, it turned out the grenade was a souvenir item that mysteriously went missing from the gear of one of his men a day or so prior to the patrol. It is *believed* that the lieutenant lifted the grenade from the man and took it along on patrol so he could have a little something to play hero with.

I don't know what words the battalion commander whispered in the lieutenant's ear, but he promptly quit telling the story of his heroic deed and no mention was made of medals.

Months later, after I climbed down off the DMZ, I ran into the lieutenant, whose personality conflicted strongly with mine. He had been creased in the skull by a bullet and was proudly showing his wound to any and everyone. When he showed it to me, I mentioned that it was too bad the round hadn't hit a few inches farther over.

Whenever a fraudulent claim for a medal was made, it set a lot of teeth to grinding. Those of us who went to the field only wanted a safe passage home, and for the most part medals eluded us. But it hurt when they were presented to the undeserving.

All recon insertions were made either by helicopter or on foot. There was one insertion made that was an exception to the usual means of gaining access to enemy held territory.

On September 5th, Clubcar, under GySgt. Walter Webb, made a daring parachute jump into Happy Valley, west of Da Nang. The nine-man team from 1st Force had been assigned the mission of locating a Soviet-made missile launcher suspected of being hidden in the valley. The team made the jump at night from a 123 Caribou, a twin-engine cargo plane. Just prior to the jump, a storm blew in and winds up to thirty knots began gusting in the area of the drop zone. It was dark, cloudy, windy, and the plane was both off course and flying at an elevation higher than the one requested by the gunny.

The night it happened, several of us were gathered anxiously around a radio, monitoring the results. After word was sent back that the jump had been made, contact with the team was lost. After a long delay, we received a sitrep that the patrol had been badly scattered by the winds and was still trying to regroup and that some of the members were not accounted for, Gunny Webb among them.

When the team went out, all of the men but one remained in a tight stick. Moments after they exited the plane, a single chute turned and drifted off on its own course. Having missed the intended drop zone, the team landed in an area thick with trees and broken stumps. Several of the men landed in the trees, while others came down hard on the ground. They were a long time extricating themselves from the branches and getting organized. Gunny Webb, who was high in a tree and separated from the others, spent until dawn trying to get down from the tree, where he dangled sixty feet above the ground. At first light, he was able to untangle himself from his chute and slide down the trunk of the tree. However, due to an encounter with some VC in the area, the gunny was not able to rejoin the team. Injured, and after being chased into hiding by the VC, the gunny called for a medevac on his survival radio and was taken out late that day.

Eventually, all but one of the team members were accounted for. The corpsman, Hospitalman LaPorte, was missing.

After two other men, injured during the jump, were medevaced out, the rest of the team searched for LaPorte but could not find him. When the team was safely back at Camp Reasoner, and after an extensive air-rescue search had taken place, the corpsman still hadn't been found.

During the debriefing and investigation that followed, the mystery surrounding the corpsman's disappearance began to unfold.

It is believed that LaPorte intentionally turned his chute to drift away from the stick.

Although considered by the men who knew him to be a good man in the field, his behavior at times was strange and he was somewhat obsessed with the Vietnamese. He worked hard at learning the language and spent a great deal of time hanging around the Vietnamese workers in camp. On the night of the jump, LaPorte carried with him such a large amount of medical supplies he had to be helped onto the plane. It turned out later that the bulk of the supplies was made up of morphine, an anesthetic badly needed by the enemy.

LaPorte left a letter asking his buddies to take care of his things if he didn't come back. There were reports of another letter written by LaPorte espousing the cause of the enemy, that we were wrong intervening in Vietnam and that he was going over to the other side. I did not see either letter, and there is some question of the second one even existing.

Although there is no proof that LaPorte defected, many of us came to the conclusion that he had. Since the date of the jump, he has not been heard from, and none of the sightings of the handful of Americans who defected and began operating with the enemy have been confirmed as being Doc LaPorte.

As I worked in the S-2 shop, a feeling of uneasiness began to grow in me. I was not comfortable with the responsibility of sending men to the bush while monitoring their progress from the rear. Something was wrong with a system that sent so few men into combat while such a large number of us sat safely behind a desk as so-called support troops, of which there were vastly too many in Vietnam.

Also, the battalion was starting to fill up with senior first lieutenants and captains fresh from the States, who had little or no time in the bush, but were well versed in the trappings and vocabulary of military life and were quick to expound on any subject from firepower and death to courtesy and discipline. It was frustrating to hear them talk about war as though it were a series of chess moves played out in a drawing room and to listen to them go on about the behavior of the enlisted men off patrol. At night in the club, a favorite topic was to complain about some corporal or private having failed to salute or keep his uniform squared away or not respond with enthusiasm to a cleanup detail. These officers failed to understand that the men were giving their all in the field and had little left in them when they came in for their short three days of rest in the rear.

Coupled with that was the adoption of a battalion policy that reduced the time officers had to spend in the bush. Some were coming out after serving only four or five months, and sergeants and corporals were having to fill billets that should have been filled by officers.

There are things I do that even *I* cannot explain to myself, and late in September, I went to Colonel Steinmetz and asked to be returned to the field. The colonel said he would see what he could do about assigning me to a platoon, then asked why I wanted to go back in the bush. The XO, Major Timmons, a man I never got along with and who always hovered in the vicinity of the colonel, was descending on us as we spoke, so I mumbled something about time passing faster in the field and left it at that. When the colonel didn't press it, I saluted and left.

18

Toward the end of September, I met Roberta and the kids in Hawaii, and for five days we tried to forget about the war and resume life as a family. Our daughter Jodi was two and a half and all smiles and laughter and curly hair, and I couldn't hold her enough to make up for the months that had slipped by. Danny, at six months, was a huge kid who seldom cried or fussed and loved to be played with and carried about.

We stayed in army quarters at Fort DeRussey on the beach, and at first, Jodi didn't quite know what to make of all the sand and water. Wearing her swimsuit, dark glasses, and sandals, she would step gingerly across the sand, watching carefully each time she put a foot down, then shaking it free of sand the instant she picked it up. Unfamiliar with this new medium, she approached it with caution but soon mastered it and was happily digging up great shovelfuls and dumping them into her metal bucket. The water was a another matter, and I never succeeded in getting her to go in more than knee deep.

Hawaii was a new experience for all of us.

On the second day, I rented a car, and we began to tour the island, taking long drives through the mountains and along the coast. For Roberta and me, it was our first real honeymoon, made special by the kids being along. We made every moment count, and the time seemed to fly so fast we wanted to somehow reach out and stop it from going by.

It was, however, a strange period of time for me. There in Hawaii, life went on at its own quiet pace, and for the people passing by on the streets or around us in the shops

176

and restaurants, there was no war. It just didn't exist. People got up in the morning, had breakfast, went to work, played on the beach, took long walks in the parks, and slept undisturbed in clean, safe neighborhoods. While their lives went peacefully on, I couldn't let my defenses down. I watched constantly for anyone making a sudden move, sat with my back to the wall, would not enter a crowded room, or eat in a noisy restaurant. I very soon discovered that a backfiring automobile put me into an instant crouch as I looked for the source of the noise. It was only along the beach or in the quiet of the countryside that I seemed to relax.

Roberta and I spent hours trying to make up for the time we had lost. We talked quietly, made love, held each other close, and all the while, time seemed to race out of control toward our departure date.

We were fortunate then, because there were no antiwar protesters to mar the serenity of the island and ruin our time together. That entire specter had yet to raise its ugly head, and there in Hawaii the people around us were friendly and supportive, and we loved them for it.

Then came the day I had to put Roberta and the kids on a plane, and they were gone from me. It all seemed to have happened so fast. One minute they were there, then the next they were gone. Somehow it wasn't right.

On October 8, Bravo Company, 1st Recon, trucked out of Camp Reasoner and staged at 1/7's CP, located on Hill 41 at the east end of Charlie Ridge. The battalion CP was far enough from Da Nang so that every Vietnamese we passed either ignored us or gave us hostile looks. But by now, most of us were immune to their looks and answered with the finger.

I had been attached to Bravo Company for a patrol being led by Capt. Bill Warren, who was without question the finest commander I ever served under. It had been his idea to put together a company-size patrol and lead it along the entire ridgeline north of Mortar Valley, an area used as an infiltration route by both the VC and the NVA. All three of the company's platoons would be used for the patrol, and I was once again leading Dateline.

We were scheduled to move out at 0300 on the morning of the 9th, but during the night a monsoon-driven storm moved in with such force that the paddies surrounding Hill 41 began to flood, and our time of departure was postponed. At first light, I left the squad tent, where I had spent the night bailing water out of my cot and trying to keep the walls from collapsing, to look over our situation. The wind was still up, but the rain had fallen off to a drizzle. Bundled against the cold, I slipped and slid to the top of the hill and surveyed our surroundings. Overnight we had become an island. Water stretched in every direction for as far as I could see. Like something out of a fairy tale, a lake had magically appeared, and we were in the middle of it. For several minutes, I stayed on the hilltop and marveled at our newly created surroundings. Then I waded through the mud to the battalion CP, where I received official word that we wouldn't be going anywhere until the water subsided.

By 0930, we were lined up by platoons. Gunnery Sergeant Austin, the platoon sergeant, and I went down the line, checking the men, making sure they had everything and that their weapons were free of the mud that was already climbing above our boot tops and working its way up our trouser legs. Somewhere in there, I started coughing and couldn't stop. My stomach knotted up, and I went to my knees, doubled over in pain. It must have been a case of return-to-the-bush nerves, because the coughing soon stopped, and I was all right again.

Shortly after 1000, we set out on the long hump to the mountains. At the wire, we passed a night ambush, at last able to ford a stream at the base of the hill and come in. The men in the ambush party looked like drowned rats, and I could only imagine what their night out in the storm must have been like.

The water had drained off enough so that the paddy dikes were sticking out, forming paths that took us one way then another as we tried to maintain a course to the mountains.

Around noon, we ran into a creek that was overrunning its banks, and Captain Warren called a halt to find a crossing. After making several unsuccessful attempts to cross, he and I stripped to our undershorts and boots and entered the cold, rushing water to string a rope to the opposite bank. When we were in neck-deep and almost to the far side, one of the men accidentally fired an M-79 grenade launcher. When it went off, Captain Warren and I ducked beneath the surface of the water, thinking we had waded into an ambush. When we came up for air, someone yelled it had been an accident, and we both let loose with a long string of expletives.

Once the rope was attached on the opposite bank, the lead platoon crossed without incident and secured the far side.

While we were stopped, one of the men claimed he had been bitten by a snake, and since we couldn't prove otherwise, called in a medevac. Twice before, the same man had claimed illness or injury to avoid going on patrol and both times recovered with amazing speed. I suspected he would undergo a similar recovery as soon as he got back to the battalion area.

The drizzle had long since stopped, and the cloud cover sat at a thousand feet, and not a breeze blew. The air around us took on all the pleasantness of a boiler room in July. We were heavily loaded with weapons and equipment. Sweat poured from us. Breaks were few and far between, and although I had kept up my fitness program while working as the S-2, I found that I was completely unprepared for the long, grinding hike we were on.

We were being guided by a squad of 1/7 Marines led by a second lieutenant. Once we crossed the stream, we picked up a well-defined trail and stayed on it, moving rapidly and maintaining three- and four-meter intervals between each man.

In midafternoon, the grunts put us onto a trail leading into the mountains, bid us farewell, and departed to an ambush site a klick farther on in the lowlands.

If the hike through the flat ground had been bad, the mountains became grim. Captain Warren had a specific objective he wanted to reach by nightfall, and even though the pace had slowed because of the steepness of the terrain and the need to move with caution up the jungle trail, rest periods became almost nonexistent. I found myself gasping up every rise we came to and wanted desperately to flop down and stay there for an hour. The fact that the trail we were on was more stream than trail did not help. My feet were wet, cold, and being rubbed raw. A specimen of physical fitness I was not.

Toward dark, we reached the hill the CO wanted to spend the night on, and each platoon was assigned a section of perimeter to man. By the time the gunny and I had positioned the men and checked on them, it was dark. I joined the CP group, opened a can of C rations, and sat down to eat. It started to rain. And it kept on raining. We were harbored in an area of low, thick vegetation, and the few times the rain let up, the plants went right on dripping. I propped myself against a tree, wrapped up in a poncho, and tried to make the best of it.

Dawn came wet, foggy, gloomy, and miserable. I ate a C-ration candy bar and drank a can of cold coffee.

We saddled up and moved on.

Dateline had run point the first day, and we were assigned the same position on the second. I put out my point man and a backup and followed them with my primary tac radio operator, a new, quiet kid who didn't seem to like officers. Gunny Austin brought up the second squad, and the rest of the company followed, with Captain Warren somewhere near the middle of the column.

The trail was clear of obstacles and well defined, and the only hindrance to our movement was fighting the mud on the slopes. At times, our progress was marked with falls, curses, and downhill slides. Few of us were exempt from having our feet suddenly shoot out from under us and crashing to the ground, then sliding to a stop against a tree or rock.

Within a short time after we started, I found I was able to mentally detach myself from the rest of the company and treat our progress as though we were a ten-man patrol, off by ourselves. We moved in a guarded, watchful manner, scanning the trees and bushes and searching for trip wires as we went. The rest of the column plodded slowly along, but Captain Warren at no time came up on the radio to tell me to speed things up. Out front, I was the boss.

The rain had obliterated all signs of recent enemy activity. Although we failed to make contact that morning, I felt that Charlie was around. He just didn't know *we* were.

We passed through a graveyard of dead NVA, a dozen or more headboards with a name and a star carved on each one. A long way to come to die and never be heard from again, I thought. Nearby was an extensively developed ambush site that at one time housed an enemy platoon. I was glad only the dead were home that morning.

Early in the afternoon we took a break, and I climbed a tree to get a fix on our location. No sooner had I figured out where we were than I discovered the tree was a boiling ant-hill. I was covered with them, and they all seemed to be biting at once. I came crashing down out of the tree, slapping at the stinging creatures and stripping out of my clothes as I came. One particularly tenacious ant had me by the left testicle, and I couldn't get him off until my pants were down around my ankles and I was able to find him. The men nearby kept up a steady banter and whispered laughter as I danced and slapped and shook myself free of the last of the little monsters. When I had, my body was covered with small, red, itching welts that continued to sting. After I dressed and regained some of my composure, I reported our position to the captain.

We were nearly a klick short of where we thought we were.

I told Gunny Austin to pass his squad through and take over the lead position, and we moved out.

The second squad hadn't been on point for an hour when firing broke out, and one of the two dogs attached to the patrol to sniff out VC started yelping like it had been hit. I ran forward, passing the dog, which was unhurt and in the arms of its handler. The gunny was ahead behind some rocks.

He said a lone VC with a rifle had come down the trail, and he and the gunny spotted each other at the same time. By the time the gunny got his shots off, the gook was on the run and fast disappearing.

I sent four men up the trail. They moved up, threw a grenade into some rocks, and secured the top of a rise where the trail made a sharp turn to the right. I told the men behind me to drop their packs and follow me up the trail. Lance Corporal Legally, a thin, darkskinned Samoan, was in front of me on point. As we moved, our surroundings quickly changed from open and rocky to thick vegetation. We went up the trail cautiously but rapidly, not wanting the VC to get away, but at the same time fearing an ambush.

We were just moving into some overhanging trees when firing broke out, and Legally flew into the air, cartwheeled once, and landed at my feet. One of my men had mistaken him for the enemy and opened up as we passed in front of the group I had left at the bend. The instant Legally was hit, I knew what had gone wrong and was screaming "Cease fire!" at the top of my lungs. Then I yelled for a corpsman, dropped to my knees, and began cutting Legally's pack from him. I was shaking badly and kept saying, "You'll be all right, you'll be all right," over and over. He had been hit in the head, side, back, and leg from an almost point-blank range, but was conscious and alert. He kept calling me sir and telling me how badly he hurt, but he wasn't panicked or afraid.

I asked someone to call for a medevac.

By the time I got Legally's pack off, Doc Johnson, one of the corpsmen, had arrived and began working on him. Then a second corpsman arrived and together they set about saving his life. They hooked him up to an IV and began pumping plasma into him. Unable to sedate him because of the head wound, the corpsmen made him as comfortable as possible and kept talking to him to get his mind off the pain and keep him from going into deep shock. At one point, when they thought Legally was losing consciousness, they sat him up and began joking with him to keep him awake. Legally responded well and remained alert.

Captain Warren was soon up and took over, reading off the coordinates of our position to the medevac and bringing up the rest of the company. When the medevac came in, it was a large Jolly Green that hovered over us like a platform fixed in space. There wasn't enough room in the LZ for it to land, so it dropped a sling, and Legally and his gear went out by cable. Once he was safely underway, I calmed down and reported what had happened to Captain Warren. I told him I took full responsibility for the incident and that it would not have happened had I pulled the men out of the bend in the trail as I passed them. The captain impressed upon me the fact that he felt it was an accident and that I was not to blame myself for Legally having been shot. Easy to say, not so easy to do.

Lance Corporal Legally eventually ended up in the naval hospital in Oakland, California, where he recovered from his wounds.

Pete Badger's platoon took the point, and we moved out.

That night it rained. Three of us got together and used our ponchos to build a large hooch, and we were able to keep dry. In the morning, it was cold and foggy, but with the aid of a little C-4 explosive, I was able to heat up some water and cook a package of long-range rations, which came in a limited variety of dehydrated meals and weren't too bad when eaten hot. Usually, I would eat half a ration, seal the rest in its pouch and save it in a leg pocket for lunch. A long-range rat and a can of Cs would keep me going all day long.

Again, Pete took the point.

That morning, VC were on the trail, and Pete's point man spotted them just as they stepped out of some bushes. When the firing broke out, it all came from the front of the column. The VC tried to deploy and hold their section of the trail, but when Pete's machine gunner cut loose with what must have been the longest sustained burst in the history of modern warfare, they broke and scattered.

We were on the spine of a ridge, and although I could hear

people running below on our flanks, I couldn't see them and told the men to hold their fire for fear it might be our own men.

After the shooting stopped, some blood trails were found, and a booby trap was uncovered and blown in place. The entire action hadn't taken more than a few minutes, and we were on our way again.

We ended the third day on a hill named 502. It was covered with old NVA fighting holes and rotting bunkers. After checking them out, we moved into the holes and prepared to spend the night. The CO called the evening platoon-leaders' meeting and briefed us on the next day's movement. We would be swinging south toward Charlie Ridge.

It rained that night. All night. In the morning I was surrounded by ants. Flooded out of their nest, they had not only brought themselves but their eggs, as well, and had taken up a position next to mine. I carefully removed myself from their presence.

When we saddled up, a platoon that had yet to take point moved up to the lead position. It was led by a lieutenant who had a habit of delegating the more dangerous jobs to those of lesser rank. That morning was no exception. He buried himself in the middle of his trailing squad and let his platoon sergeant run point.

The Cong were out there, we just weren't finding them like we thought we would. From time to time, they would fire off a shot, and occasionally one of them would let out a yell, but the sounds were always at a distance. They knew we were around, but I don't think they had us pinpointed. Still, the terrain we were moving through offered countless ambush sites, and we were all on edge as we worked our way off Hill 502 and onto the next mountain. It was some of the spookiest ground I had ever worked, and at times I got so tightly wound up, you could have played me like a fiddle.

In a saddle on the next mountain, the trail forked, and we took the one heading south. It wasn't long before the trail gave out, and we were breaking brush. An Arc Light had gone off in the area, and each crater, with its surrounding stand of ripped and broken trees, made the going even more difficult.

We hit the bottom of the mountain and started up the side of another one that went on forever. Halfway up a ridge so steep we were crawling on our knees and pulling ourselves along by grabbing at saplings, the column stopped. No explanation for it came over the radio, it just stopped. After about fifteen minutes, the CO worked his way up to where I was and asked what the holdup was. I told him I didn't have a clue. He ordered me to come with him, and we climbed to the top of the ridge.

When we broke out on top, we found the lieutenant of the lead platoon resting against his pack, his pipe stuck between his teeth. The captain wanted to know just what the lieutenant had in mind, leaving the rest of the company hanging by its fingernails to the side of a mountain while he sat on his ass smoking a pipe!

While the captain chewed, I passed the word to get the column moving again, then climbed a tree to get a fix on our location. It was late in the afternoon, and when I spotted a grassy knoll about five hundred meters away, I told the captain it would be a good place to spend the night. I climbed down, and we headed out.

Just before sunset, we broke out of the jungle and onto the knoll. It was the first time we had been out of the forest in four days, and the relief I felt was profound.

The woods on the knoll proved to be an ideal defensive position, and we set in. Before dark, I took a squad out to check an open slope to our west. It was covered with old fighting holes and punji pits filled with rotting bamboo sticks incapable of penetrating a boot. In one of the pits, I found a short-handled scythe used to cut grass with and kept it for a souvenir. There were no signs indicating Charlie had been around for a long time, which puzzled us. We were in his neighborhood, yet he didn't appear to be home.

It didn't rain that night.

The next day, we dropped down into a valley and up the side of a high ridge. Due to an absence of trails, the going was rough, and the thick vegetation was difficult to penetrate. My platoon spent the day on point, and the work was exhausting. It wasn't until late in the day that we came to a well-used trail and were able to travel without fighting for every inch of the way. We were now going east toward Mortar Valley, moving down the final leg of the trip.

Just before dark, we set in on a hill that offered an excellent defensive position. Tired, I downed a can of peaches, rolled up in my poncho, and immediately fell asleep.

It didn't rain that night either.

Sometime around midnight, I woke up to artillery rounds pounding close to our position. I was so tired I could scarcely get my head off the ground to see what was going on. Rounds kept slamming in, the flash of each explosion lighting the area round us. Someone said we had gooks near the perimeter, but for the likes of me, I could not stay awake. I decided to let Captain Warren handle it and went back to sleep. From time to time, I would fade into a semiconscious state, hear more explosions, then fade out.

The next morning, Captain Warren told me a large number of VC had come down the trail we were camped on, and when they were discovered near us, he called in the artillery, which hammered most of the night. I couldn't believe I had slept through it!

We left the ridge and started down into a valley. Along the way, we entered a large grove of banana trees near an abandoned shack. Passing through the grove, I took out my K-bar and began slicing through the trees. Somewhere in my demented state of mind, I believed I was denying the enemy a food source and was leaving in our wake my own version of a scorched-earth policy. Soon, several of the men were slicing trees, and when we came out of the grove, most of them were down.

There were no trails, so when we found a clear-running mountain stream, we used it to take us to the valley floor. The water was sparkling clear, and I made the mistake of filling a canteen and drinking it without putting in a halazone tablet. A day later, I would be suffering terribly for that mistake.

Vegetation on either side of the stream was some of the thickest I had ever seen, and once in the water, there was no way out. We waded for hours, and our feet grew raw and our backs weary. What few breaks we took were spent standing in water up to our waists. On the valley floor, the stream widened and turned muddy. The going became easier, but we could still not find an opening in the impenetrable green barrier along the banks.

About 1300, we found a break in the wall and stumbled, soaked and tired, onto the grassy flatlands of Mortar Valley. There were still eight long kilometers between us and 1/7's CP.

We ate and moved on.

At the end of the valley, we spotted a grunt platoon sent out to lead us in. Without passing the word, I fired a pencil flare to mark our position. Everyone around me hit the deck and, as soon as they realized what the sudden pop had been, came up cursing. I apologized, sheepishly.

When we linked up with the grunts, they told us they had just killed a VC who was so old and battle-scarred he must have been fighting since the days of the Japanese occupation during World War II. Another VC was nearby, and the grunts thought they had him pinned in some rocks above us. They started firing at him with a 60-mm mortar, but I was too tired to watch and sat down to wring out my socks and rest my destroyed feet.

When we started out on the leg home, the grunts took off at a pace that just about killed me.

At 1/7's CP, the S-2 said he'd never seen humans so tattered and filthy and insisted on taking a picture of Captain Warren and myself. He said we looked like something out of a L'il Abner cartoon.

Back at Reasoner, I slept for twelve hours straight, then woke up to the worst case of the shits I had ever had in my life!

Welcome back to the field, I thought.

19

In Mortar Valley, I had received word over the radio that I would be taking over the 1st Platoon of Delta Company, recently moved up from Chu Lai. When I first arrived in country, the platoon was led by Ron Benoit, call sign Duckbill. Ron was now working for 1st Force, and very few of the original men were still with the platoon. Duckbill's last officer was a recent KIA, and the next man to take charge, a Staff Sergeant, had fallen apart in the middle of an ambush.

The morale of the platoon was such that the men had stated they would refuse to go to the field if the staff sergeant were left in command. However, the morale problem was not entirely the sergeant's doing, and like everything else, it had a history.

The last platoon leader, a very uptight and by-the-book mustang, had been a difficult man to work for. Prior to his taking command of the platoon, several of us had spoken to him about the need to listen to the more experienced members of the platoon and, until he got a feel for things, to follow their advice. In spite of our efforts, our words fell on deaf ears.

On patrol, the lieutenant began violating nearly every rule in the book. He stuck to trails and converted recon patrols into search-and-destroy operations, which is not the true function of small, basically unsupported, reconnaissance units. The men began to dread going out with him. When the lieutenant was killed during a fight with a company of NVA, I think his death was greeted with more of a sense of relief than loss.

A few weeks after the lieutenant was killed, the platoon sergeant walked the men into an ambush during a patrol out of Da Nang. Shortly after the team was inserted, the corpsman spotted a pair of VC watching them from a nearby hill. He reported the enemy's presence to the sergeant, who ordered the men to throw out some tear gas, then moved the patrol to another location.

The following day, the team was directed to move to an LZ for an extraction. The sergeant chose to go out using the same LZ they had come in on, a rice paddy surrounded by jungle-covered hills. Instead of approaching it with extreme caution, he picked the most direct route—a narrow draw leading down to the LZ. The enemy was waiting in prepared positions.

When the enemy opened fire, their initial burst hit the point man, Private First Class Heads, in the stomach. A private first class named Cronin was hit in one leg, and another private first class, Mike Leak, was hit in the chest, the round passing through one lung. The patrol was at that point, pinned down.

Heads's stomach wound was extensive, and in spite of the heavy fire coming from the enemy, the corpsman, Doc Stomp, went to his aid, trying to keep his internal organs from spilling out onto the ground. Stomp managed to hold everything in with a large battle dressing, but the wound was serious, made even more so by the fact that the bullet striking Heads had carried with it a large chunk of his belt buckle. He then went to work on the man with the chest wound.

Gradually, the patrol withdrew to a safer position, dragging its wounded with it. However, at this point, the platoon sergeant was in such a state of panic that he curled himself into a ball and began muttering incoherently. Leadership of the platoon fell to a lance corporal named Thompson, who called for a medevac and gunships.

When the gunships arrived, they began working over the area around the team, and a medevac came in. Unable to land, it hovered over the zone and began lifting the wounded out by a cable and sling. During the evacuation of the wounded, Pfc. John Porter was hit in the neck. The bullet severed the carotid artery, traveled down the spinal column, and lodged in a lung. Doc Stomp was able to stop the bleeding, saving Porter's life, but there was nothing he could do about the fact that Porter was now paralyzed and would remain so for the rest of his life. Porter was then medevaced.

Surrounded by a company-size force, the team held its ground, and the fighting went on for several hours. Gunships continued to make runs on enemy positions, and an attempt to extract the entire patrol by cable was undertaken. When the fire grew too intense for the choppers to take out everyone, those remaining on the ground were instructed to move to the LZ in the paddy. At that point, only three men were left on the ground—Cpl. Ihor Sulyma, LCpl. Robert Sylvia, and the corpsman, Doc Stomp. They threw what gear had been left behind when the wounded were evacuated into a pile, buried some sticks of C-4 under it, and lit the fuse.

Then they ran for it.

Down on the LZ, the gunships were working over the surrounding hills. As the three men broke from the jungle and raced through the mud for a waiting bird, they were chased by enemy fire. With the door gunners blazing back over their heads, the men reached the bird, scrambled on board, and were lifted safely away.

It had been a bad experience, and the survivors of the patrol declared to their company commander that they would refuse to go to the bush with the platoon sergeant, who had let them down when they needed him.

That had happened on the 12th of October. I was due to take command of the platoon on the 15th, and I knew the men would be giving me more than just the once over.

During our first meeting, the men impressed me as being closely knit and very capable. The platoon sergeant was another matter, but I had already been assured that once we completed an R & R stint at Ba Na, he would be transferred to a job in the rear.

I briefed the men on our assignment, telling them we would be relieving a grunt platoon that had been acting as security for what was now a joint army-Marine radio-relay station set up on the second floor of Le Grand Hotel de Tourane. After I described Ba Na and told them what we would be doing there, the men seemed eager to go.

Rain and fog kept us on LZ Finch the first day, but on the following, the weather broke, and we went in late in the afternoon.

During their stay at Ba Na, the grunts had tidied up the hotel, dug extensive fortifications and built log-and-sandbag bunkers, and used the surrounding chalets for target practice. The once quaint structures were now riddled with holes driven through by 106 recoilless rifle rounds. There wasn't much left of them.

The radio-relay station was housed on the second floor, where one of the rooms had been roofed with plastic and canvas, some cots installed, and four communicators lived with their radios. They were in contact with both Marine and army reconnaissance patrols working near the Laotion border. The army also kept a FAC in the air during the day as a backup for the teams they had in the field. Some of their patrols operated with as few as four men. These were usually dropped in at last light and stayed out for anywhere from one to four or five days. The four-man teams had a Huey slick plus gunships assigned to them so that if they got into trouble, help was immediately on the way. The Marine Corps didn't have that kind of backup capability, and if the birds were committed elsewhere and we were in trouble, tough.

The platoon occupying Ba Na was from 1/7. It was led by Lt. Warren McPherson, a Basic School classmate. Warren and his men had been on the mountain since September, when they came up to kick out a company of VC that had taken over the resort. Recon was the first to discover the VC were there, when they got shot out of the LZ on the tennis court. No one had been hurt, but it meant we couldn't field teams in Happy Valley until the VC gave up their residency.

The day after we arrived, the grunts were lifted out. They left behind some fifty thousand rounds of 5.56-mm ammunition, ten cases of fragmentation grenades, sixty pounds of C-4, and enough flares to celebrate the 4th of July with.

Before playing with any of the ordnance, we first had to reduce the size of the perimeter around the hotel. Counting the men running the radio relay and an ARVN communicator who didn't speak English, there were twenty-seven of us on the mountain. Not enough to occupy all of the positions of a sixty-man grunt platoon, reinforced.

I reorganized the defenses to include just the hotel. The tennis court to the edge of the woods was too big a chunk of real estate, so I had the men fill in the holes there and dig new ones closer in. Most of these were then interconnected with trenches. The north and south faces of the mountain were steep, making an approach from either extremely difficult. Also, the grunts had dumped a few thousand empty C-ration cans over the sides, making it impossible to climb either without creating a racket.

The men didn't much like the digging, but after three days of hard work, the positions were complete, and most of them had overhead cover adequate enough to keep out the elements.

At the time, we were still having trouble with our M-16s failing to extract. The only proven method to clear the chamber was to run a cleaning rod down the bore and knock out the spent cartridge, which is scary when you think about it. Since the grunts had left us so much 5.56 ammo, I decided to loosen the chambers of our M-16s by having each man fire a minimum of twelve hundred rounds through his weapon. If the weapons didn't work smoothly after that, I didn't know what to do.

We set up a range near the tennis court and, in groups of four, began shooting at the nearby trees. Each man would go through ten magazines of twenty rounds each, then fall back to reload his magazines. There was no target practice involved, we just shot. However, we soon discovered that if several of us concentrated our fire at the base of a tree, we could actually shoot it down. Trees started dropping right and left, some with trunks three feet in diameter. The minute one would start to go, we would all yell, "Timber!" followed by a mighty cheer.

When you are stuck on top of a mountain for days on end, you'd be surprised at the things you can come up with to entertain yourself.

The more rounds we fired, the better our weapons worked. By the time everyone had fired the prescribed twelve hundred rounds through their rifles, few of them were plagued with jamming. Still, I did not trust the M-16.

I next had the machine gunner drill each man in the care, cleaning, and firing of the M-60. It was an important weapon in the platoon, and I wanted everyone to know how to use it and to be able to carry out immediate action should it fail to fire.

We also practiced with the M-79 grenade launcher and a few LAAW rockets the grunts had left behind. No stone was left unturned in an effort to entertain ourselves. Lance Corporal Sylvia and I even experimented with building a large bomb made out of diesel fuel, a thermite grenade, and C-4. When Sylvia cut the fuse used to detonate an experimental version of our wonder weapon, he assured me we had plenty of time to reach the safety of a bunker before it went off. Twenty feet from the bunker, the bomb went off, nearly knocking us off our feet. I had counted on a bomb like the one we set off to fill a gap in our lines; it was designed to rain fire down on the enemy. Much to my dismay, the diesel fuel failed to ignite. We reinforced the gap with claymores.

Before we left Camp Reasoner, Doc Stomp had informed me that one of the men newly arrived from Okinawa had a raging case of the clap. He suggested I leave the man behind for treatment. I vetoed his suggestion and told him to take along whatever medication was necessary to treat the man. Daily, he went through the indignity of having to drop his pants in the hotel ballroom and take a shot in the ass, while the rest of us offered words of advice about the next time he got laid.

We had taken along extra clothing, but the monsoons were in full swing, and the nights on the mountain were bitterly cold. We kept a fire going in the fireplace to keep off the chill, but without any windows to close, the wind whipped through the building. The second floor leaked badly, and when it rained or a fog rolled in, it was difficult to stay warm and dry. Outside, it was impossible to stay either warm or dry. It usually started raining every afternoon about 1700 and didn't let up until 0400 the next morning.

The men in the bunkers were the ones to suffer the worst, and at night, I set up a system of rotating them indoors so they could warm themselves by the fire.

After ten days of rain and C rations, we were relieved and flown back to Reasoner. By then, the men and I had come to know each other, and I felt confident we would work well together.

At the time, Delta Company was being housed with the Motor Transport Battalion, about a half mile down the road from Camp Reasoner. With both Alpha and Delta now at Da Nang, Reasoner did not have the facilities to house the entire battalion. So Delta messed and slept with Motor T. While we were there, I was both patrol leader and acting company commander. When I was in the field, First Sergeant Banks, a Korean and World War II veteran, ran the company. He and I worked well together. The battalion XO and I didn't.

Early one morning, the XO showed up for an area inspection I didn't now about, was completely unprepared for, and couldn't have cared less if we passed or failed. The minute the XO discovered the hooches hadn't been cleaned and the company area policed, he went ballistic. One thing led to another, and we were soon embroiled in a sharp exchange of words. Finally, I told the major that if he didn't like what he saw he could get back in his jeep and leave. I had given up long ago trying to work for the man and wasn't going to start then. He left in a huff, threatening to report me to the battalion commander.

It was there at the Motor T Battalion that I got the only inspirational, gung-ho, kill-Cong speech I ever had in Vietnam.

While I was preparing for my next patrol (grease paint on,

gear packed), the hooch girl, who cleaned up and took care of the laundry, stopped in her work, shook her broom at me, and started yelling, "You go kill VC! Numba fucking ten. Kill Vietcong, no good!" By the time she was through, she had worked herself into a lather.

I told her I'd see what I could do, then stumbled outside and laughed myself silly.

It was the 2d of November, and we were inserted on Charlie Ridge north of Tam Hiep and the Song Vu Gia. The insertion was made in five CH-34s, ancient, lumbering birds that could carry no more that three or four combat-loaded troops. The LZ was too steep for the 34s to land and we had to jump six feet to the ground. One of the men, Lance Corporal Willis, twisted an ankle when he landed, and I decided to send him out on the next bird. It came in, off-loaded, and we threw Willis's gear on board. Then we boosted him up to put him on board. Halfway through the door, he got stuck. The gunner leaned forward to help pull him on board and, in the process, unplugged his headset. The pilot, thinking we had successfully loaded the man and not hearing anything to the contrary, took off. There they went, with Lance Corporal Willis dangling out the door. I yelled at Hostetler, my radio operator, to contact the pilot and tell him to put down at once. Meanwhile, the bird had flown over a deep ravine, and the distance between Willis and the ground was about six hundred feet. I started jumping up and down, hollering at the helicopter to get itself back here. But the last I saw of it was when it disappeared over the next ridge, with Willis frantically pedaling the air.

A few minutes later, I got word that the helicopter had set down and pulled Willis safely inside. I got my heart back in my chest, breathed a sigh of relief, and started the patrol up toward the tree line capping Charlie Ridge.

We hadn't been moving twenty minutes when a gook threw a grenade at us and took off running over a hill. The grenade failed to detonate. I felt the enemy was trying to pull us into an ambush and promptly changed course.

We began humping at right angles to the fingers coming

down from the ridge. The fog rolled in, and the rain came, and we went slipping up one side of a finger and sliding down the other. During one of our sliding descents, one of the men fell and his weapon discharged. I went back down the line and whispered a few choice words in his ear before going on.

Then, late that afternoon, while scouting the area around our harbor site, I nearly blew my foot off when the shotgun I was carrying discharged. The trigger caught on a magazine-pouch tab and cranked off a flechette round that left a large, smoking hole, inches from the end of my right foot. I swore, apologized to the man I had earlier chewed out, then vowed never to carry a shotgun on patrol again.

We had limited sightings near some villages that all had a name that sounded like Fuck—Fuck (1), Fuck (2), and Fuck (3). Fuckin' A!

But most of the time the fog was so thick that visibility was down to a few feet. Try spending a day staring into a fog bank sometime, you'll see just how exciting life can get.

When it did clear, we watched, and I tried to teach a new second lieutenant named Prilaman how to call in arty, but he was having trouble getting the hang of it—rounds kept landing where they weren't supposed to. He was clean, obedient, courteous, and kind; but he was also awkward and naive, and I worried about him. I don't know what eventually happened to him, but I hope he made it home in one piece.

It rained every night.

About the only thing remarkable about the patrol was the discovery of a huge, black granite outcrop upon which an artillery round had impacted and left a perfectly symmetrical pattern about eight feet in diameter. Years into the future, some wandering tribesman will no doubt stumble upon that rock and wonder at the god who chiseled out such an intricate design.

We had been told to police all of our trash and bring it back from the field with us—that way, Charlie will never know we were there. Only God knows where directives like that come from. So on the fourth day we came out, proudly carrying a burlap bag full of C-ration cans and gum wrappers. As we flew over Fuck (1), I yelled, "Heads up down there!" and kicked the bag out the door.

20

In November, I received word that Delta One would be the recon platoon attached to the new battalion landing team then being formed. The 3d Battalion, 1st Marines had been chosen to relieve the battalion currently afloat, and in order to bring it up to strength as an independent fighting force, units not normally found in an infantry battalion had to be added to it. Recon was one of those units. Word had it that the previous float passed its six months in a virtual state of R & R, executing landings and carrying out operations while sustaining very few casualties. There was no reason to suspect BLT 3/1 wouldn't have it just as easy.

Three weeks prior to going aboard ship, my platoon was pulled out of the field to begin an intensive training program involving scouting and patrolling, infantry tactics, first aid, radio procedure, and rubber-boat drill. I didn't know what to expect when we became part of 3/1, but I was prepared to operate as either a recon or infantry unit. I suspected we would be doing both. Because we were going afloat, most of the short timers were transferred out of the platoon, and six new men were assigned to bring it up to full strength. We needed time to train.

As part of the equipment assigned to us for the float, we received two, nine-man, inflatable rubber boats for river crossings and clandestine nighttime landings. However, me and my newly assigned platoon sergeant, Sergeant Woo, were the only ones who had trained in rubber boats. In the surf, they are difficult to maneuver and easy to capsize. Loaded with equipment, you go straight to the bottom when the boat suddenly overturns. During August, Force Recon had lost a man to drowning during a nighttime landing when their boat capsized in the surf. Not wanting to undergo a similar experience, I asked Captain Warren if he would set up a training program and teach us how to use the boats. He readily agreed.

The platoon moved onto China Beach, and for three days, we worked from early in the morning until dark, learning how to paddle and backpaddle in unison, turn, counter a broach, right a capsized boat, and read wave patterns. During our PT sessions, Captain Warren had us shoulder the boats and run up and down the beach while he counted cadence to keep us in step. "All part of the concept of teamwork," he insisted as we puffed and sweated along the shore.

It was exhausting but challenging work. In the end, we were skillfully launching in three- and four-foot waves and breaking through the surf line to the open sea. Getting through the surf is the most difficult and dangerous time in the water, and teamwork is essential. If your timing is right and you have read the waves correctly and everyone in the boat is pulling together and if the team leader is steering and working the bowline as he should, your chances of breaking through to deep water are good. But even when everything goes right, it can all go wrong when a wave comes along to either break on board or flip the boat over backward. In both cases, you end up in the water, clinging like crazy to your paddle because you've been told that if it gets loose in the surf to knife through the water like a missile, your instructor will personally shoot you.

Once beyond the surf line, you have to eventually come back to shore. And it is when returning to the beach that things often go wrong. The boat wants to ride the waves in, and the tendency is to let it ride for a quick return trip. However, about nine times out of ten, the stern tries to catch up with the bow, and once the boat turns, it starts to go over. At that point, it is very difficult to remain upright, and in you and your equipment go. It is better to brake with the paddles,

let the crest of the wave go by, then paddle after it rather than
try to ride it.

After making numerous daytime and two successful nighttime launches and returns, I felt confident we could handle
the boats if called on to do so.

In addition to the boats, I was also given a Mighty Mite,
which is a smaller, poorer version of the jeep. The tires were
bald, and it was hell to start, but it was all mine. I used it
mainly to get to the liaison meetings being held at 3/1's CP,
which was south of Da Nang in an area called the desert.
The road out was mined and booby-trapped nightly and had
to be swept by engineers daily. Whenever I drove down it, I
had the accelerator to the floor, thinking that if I hit a mine
the engineers missed, I should be travelling fast enough so
that it would only blow off the back half of the Mite, and I
would hopefully survive the experience. Fortunately, I never
found out if my theory worked or not.

At one of the meetings, I learned that we would be spending the first three weeks of the float at Subic Bay in the
Philippines. There the battalion would train in the field, do
live-fire exercises, have its weapons and vehicles repaired,
and be allowed to pull liberty. The news of a trip to the
Philippines was welcomed by one and all.

On December 2, 1967, the platoon was loaded onto two
six-bys, and we joined the convoy of tanks, jeeps, and trucks
headed for the Tien Sha loading ramp at Da Nang harbor.

The day was overcast and drizzling. The trip to Tien Sha
was slowed to a crawl by a vehicle ahead towing a Phantom
through the streets of Da Nang. As we crept along, hoards
of shouting kids attached themselves to the convoy, demand-
ing food and candy. Many of the troopers began entertaining
themselves by bouncing cans of C rations off the heads of
the swarming children. Some of the kids were staggered
by the blows they received, but as long as it was food being
thrown at them, they kept coming back for more.

There was a total of seven ships making up the float. They
included the *Navarro*, a troop transport. The *Vancouver*, an
LPD capable of landing troops and equipment by air and

water simultaneously. The *Alamo* and the *Whetstone*, both LSDs that launched amtracs and boats out of their well decks. The *Vernon County* and the *Windham County*, LSTs that ground ashore and dropped their bow ramps to off-load men and equipment. And the *Valley Forge*, an aircraft carrier commissioned right after World War II and later converted to helicopter use. All of the ships were used to house various elements of the battalion.

On the Tien Sha ramp, we loaded all of our gear and the Mighty Mite onto a Mike boat, which immediately set off for the *Valley Forge*. We were then flown out by helicopter to the carrier and assigned to our quarters. The troops were housed below the hanger deck in compartments crammed with tiered bunks. Marine lieutenants were housed forward of the hanger deck in quarters that, by shipboard standards, were spacious and comfortable. Bunks were stacked only three high, and each had a thick mattress, covered with clean sheets and blankets.

In the head, there was a long row of shower stalls, and hot-and-cold running water could be had by the mere turning of a handle. The sinks shone brightly, and there were real mirrors over them. But the real joy were the flush toilets. During my first trip to the head, I must have flushed a dozen times just to watch the water swirl magically away down the drain. They were genuine beauties, those gleaming porcelain bowls, and they came without the rising smell of two days' accumulation of shit and diesel fuel. It was a treat just to straddle one and sit.

Meals for the officers were eaten in the wardroom, where tables were covered with linen and the food brought to us on china plates, and at night, coffee was served and movies were shown.

We had reached the Land of Oz.

On the morning of December 3d, we set sail for the Phillipines.

When we cleared Da Nang Harbor, the wind came up, and the seas grew, and the ship began to rise and fall in a

long, slow, queasy rhythm. The excitement I felt about returning to a country I so fondly remembered was dampened
by a stomach that refused to adjust to the deck moving beneath my feet. Breakfast wanted to come back up, and lunch
was out of the question.

By dinner time, I was feeling well enough to eat but had
to go immediately back on deck to let the cool night wind
work its wonders. I stayed up late, watching the ship plow
the sea, pushing aside billions of microorganisms that let off
a phosphorescent glow when disturbed by our passage.

The next morning, we entered Subic Bay, sailing past the
isolated fishing village of Mabayo, where I had once spent
an afternoon diving in the clear water and entertaining the
kids on the beach with a camera filled with seawater, the
victim of a capsized banca. Past the jungle-covered mountains of the naval magazine area and Grande Island to our
berth at the end of the Cubi Point runway. Memories of the
eighteen months I spent flanking post in the jungle and pulling liberty in Olongapo and Manila flooded over me, and I
looked forward to walking the ground I once knew so well.

After we disembarked, we were assigned to quarters in
what had been the old Seabee quarters, halfway down the
hill from Cubi Point, quonset huts now maintained for transient battalions.

On December 7, we had our first liberty call. I dug a set
of civilian clothes out of my seabag and set forth to explore
Olongapo with Pete Badger and Carrol McBride, who had
been sent over by recon to attend scuba school.

Olongapo had changed.

Because of the war and so much money pouring into the
area, every sleazebag in the Philippines had gravitated to a
town that had always been wild but never sleazy. Where it
had once been safe to wander the back streets in a drunken
stupor, gangs of thieves and muggers now roamed. Where
bar girls had once whispered discreetly in your ear, "You
take me home, Joe?", it was now, "We go fuck. Five dollars
MPC for short time." And where floor shows had been sing-
ers and simple acrobatic or magic acts, nude dancers were

now picking up cupcakes with their snatches and feeding them to the audience. One sailor boasted he'd eaten five cupcakes that night and was going back for more. The guy must have had a real thing about pastry served up in a pussy. Mothers, if you only knew.

Everyone everywhere had a hand out, and where the popcorn vendors and flower girls once innocently lined our way back to the base, hookers waited, offering blowjobs in the back of a jitney. Pickpockets and shortchange artists were everywhere, and if you didn't mind your wallet, someone else would.

Most of the bars were crowded and noisy, and I soon left Pete and Carrol to explore on my own. I found a bar I used to hang out in behind the market place and climbed the stairs for a beer. It was out of the way and not crowded, but it hadn't escaped the sleeze factor. The girls were loud, obnoxious, and judging by the behavior of some, heavily into drugs. One girl in particular was alternately in a manic state and going down on sailors on the dance floor, with her girlfriends cheering her on, then deep into a depression, flying in tears to the arms of an older woman, where she curled up in her lap to sob and have her head quietly stroked. After a few minutes, she would jump up, bare her tits, and race after a newly arrived customer. It was like I had stepped into a freak show. But the bar was the same, and as I got farther into my beer, the memories were the same. The jukebox still had "Lonely Teardrops" by Jackie Wilson, and I played it over and over as I tried to remember all the faces I used to know and how it had once been.

But it was a different world, and like somebody said, there's no going back.

On the eighth, we crossed the bay for a live-fire exercise, practicing with mortars, machine guns, and sighting in our rifles. Far as we were from civilization, a couple of whores showed up and tried to ply their trade. Damn, they were ugly.

Back at camp, we threw our gear together and hit the boonies for three days of field training. Battalion hadn't figured

out what to do with us, and our role in the training exercise
was so vague that I turned it into a walkabout, and we never
saw another Marine unit. We swam in the Binitigan River,
explored the jungle, and wandered the foothills of Mount
Santa Rosa. At night, we camped on a hilltop, built camp-
fires, brewed coffee, and talked into the early morning hours.
We were on our own, and except for a radio link with battalion, independent of any outside forces. It was the first
peaceful moment I'd known since I left home.

Back in the battalion area, word came that we would be
pulling out for Vietnam on the 18th—our time had been cut
by almost a week. When the word was passed, a groan could
be heard from every part of battalion. The extra week in the
Philippines would have meant we would be on board ship for
the 25th, but by leaving on the 18th, there was time to die
before Christmas.

On the 14th, the battalion threw itself a party at the officers' club mainside. The following morning, I woke up with
one of the worst hangovers I'd ever had. At the morning
briefing, I learned that recon was going to be inserted across
the bay that afternoon to locate and establish an LZ for the
battalion's final training exercise.

With throbbing head and rolling stomach, I first set about
moving the platoon back on board the *Valley Forge*. Once we
moved all our gear onto the ship, I told the first squad to get
its gear ready for the exercise.

Late in the afternoon, we lifted off the flight deck in two
CH-46s and flew out across the bay. The exercise was supposed to simulate combat conditions as closely as possible,
and thinking the hike to the ground we were to secure for the
battalion LZ would be a breeze, I chose an insertion LZ
about two klicks away. It was nice grassy knoll from where
we would stride forth and reach our destination by dark and
sleep through the night.

The knoll was grassy, but the minute we stepped off it, we
found ourselves in a bamboo forest from which there was no
escape. Within minutes, we were drenched in sweat, filthy
and cursing the day we'd joined the Marine Corps. Move-

ment through the tightly woven walls of bamboo was next to impossible, yet move we had to. I had chosen the worst possible route to the battalion LZ. Each step taken involved thrusting out an arm, shoving aside the eight-foot-high shafts of bamboo, tripping over the lower growth, and having the shafts spring back and pummel the head, body, and legs. It was not unlike running a gauntlet. There were no paths to take in the tangled nightmare, and the instant the man ahead shoved through the wall, the hole he made closed and a new hole had to be made.

We thrashed, kicked, and cursed right through sunset and into the night. Then we kept on thrashing, kicking, and cursing. In the dark, we lost our bearings, stumbled, fell, and groped. A full moon came up and lighted the way, but still we could not break free of the mess I had walked us into. To add to our problem, we were contouring a steep hill, and instead of maintaining a direct heading, we kept plunging downhill off course.

We were soon out of water and sucking at our sweat-soaked T-shirts to keep our mouths from drying out. Around 2100, I called a halt to eat and take what moisture we could from the C rations we carried. Hung over, my head throbbing, I felt like I had taken the beating of my life.

Shortly after 2200, we broke out into a clearing. Below us, I could see the Agusuhin River, a creek by most standards, the water shimmering in the moonlight. We had gone little more than half a klick and ahead lay another forest of bamboo. I decided to head for the river and follow it as a way out of the nightmare we were in. Once we reached it, we filled our canteens, dropped in our halazone tablets, and drank until our stomachs ached. Then we began wading down river.

At 0100, we came to a grassy slope that led up over the ridgeline we would have to cross to reach the battalion LZ. We left the river and started up the slope. Throughout the march, I had called only a few, very brief rest halts, and all of us were by then staggering from fatigue. Near the top of the ridgeline, I called a halt, told the men we would take a two-hour break, and resume the march at 0400. I then set up a watch, with each of us taking fifteen-minute turns, and left instructions to be awakened for the last watch. I stretched out in the grass, pulled my poncho liner over me, and instantly fell asleep.

I woke up just as the sky was getting light. My watch said it was 0530. I jumped up and began yelling at the men, saying, ''Fifteen minutes! That's all you had to stay awake— fifteen lousy minutes!'' We saddled up and began a run over the top of the ridge. We reached the site of the LZ just as a scout helicopter flew over. I turned on my strobe light to let the pilot know we were in place and ready to land the battalion.

Having spent too much time in recon, I expected the battalion to come in one bird at a time, just like we did. The LZ I'd picked was ideal for that very purpose. We chopped down a tree in the zone, then waited on the edge to bring the battalion in.

Just before the sun broke the horizon, two platoons swooped in in a half-dozen flying machines. All headed for a huge field I'd failed to see in the dark. The birds landed together and off-loaded, not three hundred meters away. I tore my hat off my head and yelled, ''We're over here, you assholes! Remember us, recon? You wanted an LZ!''

Mad and more than a little frustrated, I headed the team up to the top of a hill, where we ate, then promptly fell asleep.

Three hours later, a grunt machine gunner crashed into our harbor site and, surprised, called out to his buddies, ''Hey, there's somebody already up here!''

''No shit,'' someone muttered, and we went back to sleep.

That afternoon, we were lifted back to the *Valley Forge*.

On the night of the 17th, a final liberty call was sounded for staff NCOs and officers. Much as I sympathized with the men who were denied liberty, I wasn't going to stay on board and spend an evening with them.

My sympathy was short-lived. The minute I stepped off the liberty launch at mainside, I saw Private First Class Padilla and Corporal Sulyma on the dock. As I looked around me, I saw three more men from my platoon. I asked Padilla, who was dressed in civilian clothes, what he was doing off the ship.

"Working party, sir," he answered.

I decided right then I didn't want to know any more and left for town.

Wandering from bar to bar, I again tried to recapture the place I had known nine years ago. But Olongapo had changed forever, and none of the bars held a familiar face or an old girlfriend, and when I went to look up the man who had been the tailor in our barracks on Cubi Point, his wife told me he had died of cancer. Sometime before midnight, I wandered into a bar near the main gate and listened to a band torture "Smoke Gets In Your Eyes" while couples shuffled drunkenly around the dance floor. It was a depressing scene, made more so when a sailor slammed a bar girl to the deck so hard she didn't get up for ten minutes. The couples just danced around her. When she came to, I helped her into a chair, finished my beer, and left.

On the liberty launch back to ship, I discovered half my platoon was on board. Secretly, I was proud of them for having figured out a way off the ship.

The next day we sailed for Da Nang. As we left Subic Bay, we picked up an escort of flying fish, and I watched them for over an hour as they broke from one wave and glided effortlessly to the next. It seemed so simple. Just spread your wings, leap into the air, and skim lightly over the surface of the water. Maybe if I joined them, I could learn how to fly and forget all about where we were going.

21

We hit Da Nang on the 19th, bounced out the next day and headed north. At a staff meeting on board the *Valley Forge*, we were briefed on an upcoming operation named Fortress Ridge, scheduled to kick off on the 21st. The CO decided to split the battalion into company-size units and spread them over a wide area north of the Cua Viet River. Lima Company would be going in just north of the river, not far from the sea. Mike Company was assigned to Red Beach, five klicks farther up the coast, while India and Kilo would be going into an area known as the dunes, three klicks inland. Recon was attached to Headquarters Company and would be securing LZ Eagle for the CP group. The area of the operation was about six kilometers south of the DMZ, along a coastal plain. The battalion would be going in via a combined sea/airborne assault.

We suited up in flak jackets and helmets, and in addition to our usual equipment, each of us carried an entrenching tool. Being wrapped in a flak jacket and helmet was comforting, but not enough so to ward off a case of preassault jitters. Packed into the walkways below the flight deck, waiting for our turn to go, that familiar feeling the executioner had his hand on the switch swept over me like a wave. Only three CH-46s were up and working, and the long wait for a ride to our LZ did little to lessen the anxiety.

We went in near a village called Giem Ha Trung, which was nestled in the sand dunes and surrounded by pine trees. Once we secured the LZ and the rest of Headquarters Company and the Howtars (breech-loaded 107-mm mortars on wheels) landed, we were ordered to check out the vil. I took the lead squad, with Cpl. Dan Hostetler as my primary tac radio operator, and Sergeant Woo brought up the rear with the second squad. Lance Corporal Shelby was on the artillery net. Twenty-six of us were present and accounted for, and we moved out, keeping ten- to fifteen-meter intervals between us.

The day was clear, sunny, and mild.

We approached the vil through the pines, using them to mask our movement. Whenever we ran out of trees, we stayed near the crest of the rolling dunes—I wanted to be up high if any shooting broke out. Near the outskirts of the vil, I sent four men up to secure a tall dune. Once they were in place, I moved the rest of the platoon up, sent Sergeant Woo and his squad around one end by way of some trees, and we had the vil in a vise. After watching for several minutes, I took Hostetler and eight other men into the vil for a closer look.

All seemed peaceful enough, but the folks at home were not exactly overjoyed to see us. We were greeted by everything from indifference to outright contempt. We started checking IDs, but the only thing we could read on them were the birthdates, most of which were grossly inaccurate. One toothless crone had a card saying she'd been born in 1951, which would have made her sixteen. But since it had her picture on it, who was I to dispute her age?

"The tropics must be hard on a body," Hostetler commented when we returned her card.

We looked in hooches, checked out family bunkers, and prodded haystacks and found nothing. Since the water table was about a foot and a half down, I didn't suspect much tunneling went on in the region, and we wasted very little time looking for them.

While we were searching the vil, Corporal Hostetler reported that India Company, under Captain Moran, was in contact with a large, dug-in NVA force near a village called Ha Loi Tay. Mike Company was moving over to assist. The NVA began shooting at both companies with artillery and rockets located in the DMZ. We could hear the fighting in the distance, but could not see the action. We were not called on to assist and went about the business of dealing with life in our small portion of the world.

When we finished searching the vil, we returned to the CP, where I gave a report on our patrol, then put the men to work digging in on the section of the perimeter assigned to us. When the holes were dug, we ate and listened to the Howtars firing in support of the companies in contact, which were trying to seal off Ha Loi Tay. However, their efforts were unsuccessful, and during the night the enemy packed up and left.

The next morning, we were sent to check on a village to the south. This time, we had a Marine interpreter and four ARVN scouts, dressed in tailored jungle fatigues, attached to us. If nothing else, they were pretty. As it turned out, the only thing they were adept at scouting were the village chickens, several of which they stole for their next meal. The locals were not at all happy about having their chickens stolen, and I ordered the Marine in charge of the scouts to pay for the birds.

When the ARVN weren't chasing chickens, they tried to throw their weight around in the village, but few of the people were having anything to do with them. Like monkeys, the four scouts seemed to be everywhere, and I thought that if there were any booby traps around, maybe these clowns would find them.

While we were in the vil, we bought a helmet full of rice to add to our evening meal. The woman who sold it to us was delighted with the sale, and I came away with the impression that the fifty cents we gave her was way over the going rate.

We stayed out for most of the day without making contact with the enemy, who seemed to freely roam through the area. That night on the perimeter, my men decorated a small pine tree with tinfoil and C-ration cans. Beneath the tree, they put empty C-ration boxes as presents. They laughed and joked while they decorated the tree, but once it was done, we all fell silent as thoughts of home rushed over us. I couldn't help wondering about Jodi and Dan and what Christmas morning would be like for them. But Christmas or no, in the two days we had been in the field, the battalion had already suffered eight killed and over twenty wounded, and deep down most of us believed it was only a matter of time before we got ours.

The next day, we were back in the vils. In one, Corporal Hostetler walked up to an eighty-year-old man shuffling along with the aid of a cane, looked him in the eye and said, "All right, buddy, I'm givin' you until noon to get out of town!"

I started laughing so hard I had to sit down.

We poked, prodded, and searched, but didn't find anything.

Early in the morning of the 24th, word came that the operation was securing and we would be returning to the ships. We were delighted with the news we would be on board for Christmas. We began back loading that morning. On the hanger deck of the *Valley Forge*, we were greeted by a pair of doughnut dollies with large round tits, serving doughnuts and coffee. They seemed so clean and out of place and unreal that many of us just stood and looked at them, dumbfounded.

While Sergeant Woo and I were collecting the platoon's ordnance, Private First Class Formella dropped a pop-up flare, and it went off with a loud bang. The flare shot out of the tube, caromed off the overhead, back down to the deck, up again, then started to race around the troop-filled compartment. We were falling all over each other trying to get out of its way. When it came to rest near a locker marked EXPLOSIVES, someone tried to kick it away but only succeeded in moving it closer to the locker. Finally, a black corporal grabbed a fire extinguisher and put it out.

I blew up at Formella, but he was so apologetic, I soon calmed down and let it go with a warning to be more careful.

Christmas day we had turkey with all the trimmings, and there was even a mail call. Roberta had sent me a Christmas card with a picture of Jodi and Dan on it, and when I opened the envelope and saw the photo, I had to go off by myself for a while.

We had a miniature Christmas tree in our quarters, a gift from someone's girlfriend. The mood was light, and most of us were in good spirits, but it was a day most of us would have liked to put aside and celebrate when we got home.

That afternoon, the colonel held a briefing for our next operation. This one was called Badger Tooth, and it would kick off the next morning. Again, it was a sea and airborne assault.

We went in about ten klicks south of the Cua Viet River, landing in an area of rolling sand dunes and very little vegetation. Again, the battalion was spread out and assigned to separate objectives. Within minutes after landing, most of the companies were taking fire, and the helicopters were getting shot at, but no casualties had been reported. Sniper fire even developed around the battalion CP, but it was sporadic and high.

We were operating within a few kilometers of Highway One, the Street Without Joy, a part of Vietnam that was never pacified.

The original plan called for the battalion to push inland, and at 1630, I received orders to recon an approach to the Song O Lau and find a crossing. The terrain on either side of the river was flat and under intensive cultivation, meaning flooded rice paddies. If the battalion was going to take its tracked vehicles when it moved, a route through the flooded lowlands would have to be found, which was the job assigned to us.

We set out for Highway 555 and a village named Nha Tho Nhut Tay, from where a dirt road leading to the river showed on the map. On the way to the village, I kept altering our course through the low shrub growth in an effort to throw off anyone trying to get a fix on us and set up an ambush. Unlike the jungle, we could be seen coming from half a klick away.

Near the village, I took our bearing on the steeple of a Catholic church, pockmarked with bullet holes and with the roof partly burned off. The church led us into the village and to the highway beyond. Around us, people drifted in and out of the scene, and a beautiful girl, dressed in a white *ao dai*, floated past a few yards away, holding her conical hat against the late afternoon sun. There we were, beings from another planet, and no one looked up to take notice.

We crossed the highway and followed a network of paddy dikes, feeling naked in the flat, open ground. Near the river, we entered a paddy and waded through knee-deep mud to a road leading to the river. At the river's edge, I passed the word to spread out and take a break. Corporal Hostetler and I sat down next to an old French bunker that once covered the ferry crossing. The sun was just touching the horizon, coloring the world around us a soft gold. For a while, I just sat and watched the water go by, thinking it was one of the most beautiful places I had ever seen.

We ate, then headed back, checking the road thoroughly as we went. If the battalion were going to cross here, they needed to know the condition of the road, which appeared to be good. As we went, I kept scanning the surrounding area with my binoculars. Halfway to the highway, I spotted several antennas and what I was sure were NVA soldiers near a building about one thousand meters east of us. The grunts had earlier taken sniper fire from a church near there. I called in the sighting, but was told by battalion they were probably friendlies and to return to the CP. Puzzled by the response and the fact that we were not told to check out the sighting more closely, I moved the platoon out, and we arrived at the CP at dusk. We moved into position on the perimeter and dug in.

Early the next morning, a grenade went off, waking me from a deep sleep. A few minutes later, the explosion was followed by a burst of rifle fire. Thinking we were being probed, I grabbed my rifle and proceeded to where the noise was coming from. A grunt sitting on the edge of a hole told me a gook had just been killed a few feet from our lines. He pointed in the direction the body lay. I walked over and in the early morning light was able to make out a body lying on its back with a cord showing from beneath it. Several of us sat and speculated as to the nature of the cord, thinking it might be the fuse to a satchel charge. Since the light was

Paul Young

bad, we decided to wait a while before investigating. When
we could see better, we ventured forth.

Whoever the guy had been, he now had a hole the size of
my fist in his chest, and his right arm was nearly severed at
the elbow. It hung on by a thin rope of flesh. Surprisingly,
there was very little blood. He was short, muscular, and
appeared to be about twenty-five years old. The cord coming
from beneath him was a rope tying his hands together.

After making a few inquiries, I learned that the dead man
had been brought in the night before by Kilo Company. In
the small hours of the morning, he had escaped. Hands tied
behind his back, he made it out of our lines and was almost
free when he was spotted in the dark and killed. In the after-
action report of the incident, the dead man changed status
from "one detainee without ID card" to "one VC KIA". It
must have been a battlefield promotion.

At 0800, I was ordered to mount my platoon on amtracs
and leave for the beach to investigate a possible radio trans-
mitter hidden inside a small freighter capsized just beyond
the surf line. After a twenty-minute ride, we reached the
beach, where I deployed the men in a defensive perimeter.
We were about six hundred meters south of a village named
Thon Tham Khe.

The freighter was lying on its starboard side, its bow toward the beach. Sergeant Woo, myself, and a communicator
from Headquarters Company, stripped down to our skivvies,
mounted one of the amtracs, and plowed out to sea. The
driver circled beyond the freighter, then back toward it. Thirty
feet off the stern, he reversed tracks to hold his position
against the incoming waves, and the three of us jumped into
the water and swam to the ship. Each of us was armed with
a pistol hung around our necks by a cord, but I couldn't help
thinking how little protection the pistol would offer if a gook
suddenly appeared and started shooting at us from the boat.

We reached the freighter and pulled ourselves on board by
a handrail. An antenna had been wired to the side of the
ship, and a piece of insulated wire leading from within was
attached to it. The antenna was so securely wired down that

we had to attach a rope to it and have the amtrac tear it away to get it down.

After that, Sergeant Woo and I dropped over the side and explored as much of the top deck as we could. Looking over the ship from the angle it was on, was not unlike entering a topsy-turvy world. In the head, sinks, toilets, and showers all lay in place on their sides, waiting patiently to be used. Ladders ran parallel to the surging waters, and deck hatches became portholes to dark, water-filled compartments. The main hatch leading to the hold was open and waiting, inches below the water line. In order to enter the hold, we would have to dive down, pull ourselves along a ladder, and pop up inside.

We tied one end of a safety line to an outside rail, and taking the other end, Sergeant Woo dove down and disappeared into the gloomy interior. Believing fully that I was about to have my brains blown out by an NVA radio operator inside, I took a deep breath and dove in after him. Halfway in, I surfaced in the passageway, took another breath, and kicked hard for the interior of the ship. When I broke the surface inside, I was holding my pistol out of the water and trying to look every which way at once.

The light leaking through to the hold was surprisingly good, and I immediately spotted Woo treading water a few feet away. When the adrenaline stopped pounding through me, I climbed onto a bulkhead and sat down to look over our surroundings. Sergeant Woo climbed up with me, and together we checked out every inch of the hold, but failed to come up with a radio or an operator to run it. Once we were satisfied the ship wasn't being used as part of a clandestine communications network with Hanoi Hannah behind the dials, we dove back through the hatch and swam out to the waiting amtrac.

Back on the beach, I returned the pistol I had borrowed to its owner, Private First Class Forman, who seemed rather proud of it and had been reluctant to part with it when I asked for a pistol to use. It was an old, sorely cared for piece, but Forman assured me it was a real shooter. After I gave it back to him, he aimed it at a nearby stick and fired. Nothing. He fired again. Nothing. When he flipped open the cylinder and looked down the barrel, he discovered that both bullets were firmly lodged inside.

"A real piece you've got there," I commented.

While we were on the beach, a large crowd of Vietnamese began to gather nearby. They soon numbered one hundred or more, and all of them carried personal belongings of one kind or another. I radioed their presence to battalion, stating that something was up because the people seemed to be making some sort of an evacuation and were now taking up residence in a stand of pine trees.

All of them were coming from the village to the north—Thon Tham Khe.

Battalion radioed back not to worry about it and to return to the CP.

I was concerned enough about the sighting to report it again when we returned to the CP around 1000. The after-action report reads, "271010H—Recon platoon returns from checking reported antenna. It was a piece of scrap metal resembling an antenna." The "piece of scrap metal" *was* an antenna. But more important is the absence of both my reports of the people on the beach. The after-action report does not mention either.

By 1100, Lima Company was in a world of shit in Thon Tham Khe.

Lima had actually been in the village the day before, sweeping through it at dusk. The presence of trenches and enemy fortifications were noted, but since no special emphasis had been placed on a careful search of the village, the company moved through quickly. Their pace was accelerated even more so when a gunship spotted some NVA to the north of the village and took them under fire—killing several of the fleeing soldiers—and the company moved out to join in the fray.

Undiscovered in Thon Tham Khe was a heavily armed NVA battalion (the 116th), which had gone to ground the moment Lima Company entered the village. The NVA did not engage the Marines in a fight, and somehow remained hidden until Lima Company passed through.

Near dark, Lima and Mike companies linked up and spent the night in a village northwest of Thon Tham Khe.

On the morning of the 27th, the two company commanders discovered that Lima had come too far north, and Lima set out to return to Thon Tham Khe. When the company arrived, the NVA were waiting for them. They let the lead platoon of Lima walk into their lines before initiating an ambush that inflicted such heavy casualties the platoon was nearly wiped out. In some cases, the fighting was so intense it became hand to hand.

Captain Hubble, the Lima company commander, did what he could to deploy his remaining platoons and called for naval gunfire support from the USS *O'Bannon*, which began firing the mission.

Tragically, the battalion commander, who was over a thousand meters from the scene of the fighting, began putting pressure on Captain Hubble to get up and take the enemy head on.

Captain Hubble continued to bring down naval gunfire on the enemy. In addition, two separate air strikes were made on Thon Tham Khe. But the NVA were dug in and concealed, and it was impossible to assess the damage done by either naval gunfire or air.

The fire coming from the village did not let up, and every attempt on the part of the Marines to maneuver was met by interlocking fields of fire and mortars, and no progress was made by Lima Company.

Kilo and India Companies were moved into blocking positions at the southern end of the village, and Mike Company was told to take up a position on Lima's left flank. While the companies were moving into place, the battalion commander continued to put pressure on Captain Hubble to get up and go kick some ass. The colonel seemed convinced that Lima was up against a force small enough to be overwhelmed if the captain maneuvered aggressively.

Pinned down in a long, narrow trench, Captain Hubble

gathered together some of the men around him and asked them what they thought about a frontal assault. The consensus was to stay put and hammer the NVA with supporting arms until an advantage could be gained and the company was better able to maneuver. However, the pressure coming from the colonel had become so intense that Captain Hubble was given what was tantamount to an order to assault the enemy position. Instead of heeding the advice of those around him, the captain got his men on line, gave the command to charge, and came out of the trench shooting.

At that point, all hell broke loose as the Marines were met by a devastating volume of fire. They were not on their feet for more than a few seconds, and the charge did not carry more than a matter of feet beyond the edge of the trench. Captain Hubble and some twenty-six other Marines were killed outright. Those who weren't killed either fell wounded or immediately went to ground to escape being killed.

If the battlefield had been confused before, it now fell completely apart as communications went dead, platoons lost contact with each other, and fire control was lost.

When Mike Company moved over to Lima's left flank, it too came under heavy fire and was pinned down. At the southern end of Thon Tham Khe, Kilo also found itself under heavy fire.

While the fight was going on, I sat near the CP group, monitoring the action over Hostetler's radio. Sometime after Captain Hubble was killed, a very scared, very alone Marine came up on the air and reported that the captain and everyone around him were dead. He wanted desperately for somebody to please get him out of there. I didn't know who the kid was, but I sure felt for him.

When the 81-mm mortars firing in support of the battle ran out of ammunition, the CP and the mortars packed up, mounted the amtracs and moved closer to Thon Tham Khe, where the CP was reestablished and the mortar section resupplied. We were left behind and told that the tracs would return for us.

No tanks had been brought ashore for the operation, and

they were called for now. However, of the five tanks assigned to the float, one was back at Da Nang for repairs, and one wouldn't start and had to be left aboard ship. Of the three that headed for the beach in landing crafts, one was driven off the boat in such deep water it sank to its antenna and had to be retrieved later. The two remaining tanks made it in to support Mike Company and were able to knock out several bunkers before nightfall.

Late in the afternoon, the amtracs returned to pick us up and take us to the southern end ofd Thon Tham Khe, where we dug in.

After dark, the men of Lima and Mike Companies crawled out to retrieve their dead and wounded and move them to an LZ for evacuation. It took most of the night to gather in the casualties.

That night, an attempt was made to seal off the village, but a large gap was left on the western side.

We waited out the night, knowing an assault would take place in the morning and assuming we would be part of it.

Spooky was on station most of the night, and when he ran out of flares, the USS *O'Bannon* fired illumination and continued to hammer the village with its guns.

In the morning, air came on station and began to soften the vil with napalm and 250-pound bombs. After the airstrike, naval gunfire resumed.

At 1130 hours on the 28th, India and Kilo left their holes and began the assault. Recon was left with the CP group to watch.

The attack went off like a textbook example of an assault against a fortified position. The minute air left station, the Marines came out of their holes and moved on the objective while mortars and naval gunfire pounded the enemy positions. As the Marines drew near their objective, the gunfire shifted to targets deeper in the village, and the troops went in, guns blazing.

The only problem was, the 116th NVA Battalion had slipped away during the night, taking all of their dead and wounded with them. India and Kilo swept the objective, tak-

ing one wounded but failing to make significant contact with
the enemy.

The mystery of where the 116th went and how they got out
plagued the battalion for most of the day. Some even speculated they left by sea, using the village fishing boats to effect
their departure. Eventually, their escape route was discovered in the gap between the companies to the west. We did
not see the 116th again. A synopsis of the battle published in
U.S. Marines in Vietnam, 1967 includes a statement that an
ARVN battalion, operating farther to the north, discovered
over one hundred bodies from the 116th abandoned in the
dunes. But I do not recall hearing any such report at the time
and am skeptical about the statement and feel it was made to
make a bad situation look better.

The facts are, that on December 27, 1967, 3d Battalion,
1st Marines suffered forty-eight dead and eighty-six wounded
in the battle for Thon Tham Khe, and very few dead or
wounded NVA were accounted for in the village.

Adding to the agony of the affair was a statement by the
battalion commander that no medals would be handed out
for Operation Badger Tooth. I have no idea what motivated
such a statement, but many heroic deeds were performed
that day, and many men went unrecognized for performing
those deeds.

After the sweep of the village, we were moved to the
northern end to man an outpost three hundred meters from
the perimeter. From there, we patrolled to the north.

On the 29th, we took a man in his late thirties prisoner.
He was unarmed, but was headed toward the CP when we
found him gathering up some of the gear left on the battlefield. We tied his hands and blindfolded him and brought
him with us. On the way back to the CP, we discovered a
dead NVA soldier lying face down in a steam; a school of
small fish was nibbling at his nose and lips. Two of the men
dragged him out of the water and rolled him over. He looked
like the ultimate prune.

Near the beach, we found the body of a young male clad

in black pajamas. His hands were tied behind his back, and he had been bayoneted. For the last day and a half, it had been raining and blowing hard, and the body was almost completely buried by the sand. I noted its location on my map, and we moved on.

At the CP, we turned our prisoner over to an interrogation team, then went back to our outpost.

The rain came down hard all that afternoon, and we hooched up as best we could to keep dry. Sergeant Woo was able to stay out of the elements by curling up inside a small, concrete shrine on our hill.

While Hostetler and I were huddled together under our ponchos and trying to keep the wind from carrying everything we owned off the hill, he made another one of his comments, which were becoming classic at this point.

"You know, Lieutenant," he said, "it's too bad we aren't fighting the French."

I couldn't let that pass without at least asking why. When I did, he said, "Because these Vietnamese women are so fucking ugly."

When the rain slowed to a drizzle, we built a fire to get warm. No sooner did we have it going than word came over the radio that General Cushman was flying in for a visit. Not only were we to put the fires out, but we were to police the battlefield.

We put the fires out and cleaned up the area, but the general failed to arrive.

It continued to rain.

The companies were still making limited contact with the enemy, but for all purposes, Badger Tooth was over and done with.

At 1800 on the 31st, a truce was to go into effect, and the war was supposed to stop for a day. Meanwhile, the battalion would commence backloading. But foul weather and high seas prevented us from returning to the ship, and on January 1st, we sat on the beach, enduring some of the worst weather I had ever been exposed to. Sand was in everything, and we were soaked to the skin by the wind-driven rain. My teeth chattered, and I shook uncontrollably from the cold as we waited for a break in the weather.

Late in the afternoon, the rain stopped, and the sun peeked through the breaking clouds. Everywhere along the beach, men started building bonfires to dry out by and get warm again. By nightfall, most of us had managed to dry our clothes.

We deployed in a wide perimeter and dug in. After the wind blew the clouds away, it turned bitterly cold. My fox-hole was full of water, which kept me from curling up in the bottom to stay warm, so I sat cross-legged, wrapped in my sleeping-bag cover. Toward midnight, I was so cold, I started lighting heat tabs and dropping them between my legs. With my face left in the cold air to avoid inhaling the fumes from the heat tab, the rest of me got nice and warm under the cover. When the tab burned out, I fell onto my side and went to sleep. About every twenty minutes, the cold would wake me up, and I would light another tab.

Thus the night passed.

On January 2, we went back on board ship.

22

Back on board ship, the mood was subdued. Too many men had been killed and wounded for it to be otherwise, and if the fact that more of us would suffer a similar fate hadn't sunk in before, it did now. Still, we weren't living out life as though there were no tomorrow. We shook off our losses as best we could and continued the march.

On January 5th, I received orders to transfer my platoon to the USS *Whetstone*, an LSD (Landing Ship Dock). We were in Da Nang Harbor at the time, and the transfer was made from the *Valley Forge* by Jacob's ladder to a bobbing LCVT (Landing Craft Vehicle Tank). Carrying all of our weapons and gear on our backs made the trip down the rope ladder not only difficult but dangerous, and some of the men became tangled in the ladder, which had a tendency to throw your feet up to the level of your head, regardless of which direction you were climbing in. However, once the first two men were down, they were able to stabilize the ladder by holding it tight as the LCVT rode the swells, and we made the transfer without injuries.

On board the *Whetstone*, the platoon was assigned to quarters shared by an amtrac platoon under Lieutenant Metziger, and an Ontos platoon under Lieutenant Brown; the former being possessed of a sense of humor as twisted as mine. Metziger was forever telling me my luck had run out and that I was the next officer in line to be killed in action. To which I replied, "Watch the pins, Metziger. Watch the pins." Meaning that his track would hit a mine, and his legs would be blown off. Later, he did hit an underwater mine that very

nearly blew his legs off and threw him into the Cua Viet.
Had it not been for a quick-thinking Marine who dove in
after him, Metziger would have drowned. The Ontos, a thin-
skinned, land-roving, tracked vehicle mounting six 106-mm
recoilless rifles and carrying a crew of three, fared no better
when it came to mines. A charge that would only take the
track off a tank would destroy an Ontos. Given my prefer-
ences, I would rather walk than ride either the amtrac or the
Ontos.

Being the senior Marine officer on board, I was assigned
to a room by myself, while Metziger and Brown bunked
together. The naval officers on the *Whetstone* were consid-
erably less stuffy than those on the *Valley Forge*, and we were
made to feel right at home.

The *Whetstone* was basically a floating dry dock for small
boats and amphibious vehicles. Two-thirds of its hull was an
open well deck, where LCVTs and Mike boats were stored
aft, and the Ontos and amtracs were stored forward. When
the Ontos were to be deployed in an operation, they were
driven onto the front-loading Mike boats and LCVTs, which
would then take them ashore. Once they were loaded, the
ship's aft gate was lowered, and the flotation compartments
were flooded to sink the well deck. When the deck was
flooded, the boats floated free and backed out into the open
sea. The amtracs just fired up their engines and drove down
the heavy wooden deck to the rising waters and plowed in,
each loaded with a squad of Marines. Once ashore, the amtracs dropped their ramps, and the men inside came out running. Many of them seasick.

While we waited on board, word came daily about an
impending operation, but no briefings were held and nothing
in writing was passed on. An investigation was held to look
into the disastrous Operation Badger Tooth, and there was a
lot of blame shifted from one end of the ranking hierarchy
to the other, but to my knowledge, nothing came of it.

I quickly grew tired of shipboard life, and when I heard
the *Whetstone* was sending an LCVT and a Mike boat to Hue

city to pick up some heavy equipment, I volunteered my platoon to go along as a security force.

On January 10th, we boarded the boats at 0700, the well deck was flooded, and we bobbed out to sea, bits of flotsam alongside the looming *Whetstone* and the rest of the ships making up the float. However, once we were underway and free of the large ships, our flotilla didn't seem so small, and we became a force unto ourselves.

Pushed along by an onshore breeze, we made good time riding the long, rolling swells to the Thuan An estuary. Once through the estuary, we wound our way through a maze of fishing weirs to the mouth of the Hoi Loc Khoai and on to the Song Huong, better known as the Perfume River. The trip to Hue would take about three hours, so there was nothing for us to do but sit back and take in the scenery of the flat, green countryside, a welcome relief from the endless horizon of the sea.

The Perfume was murky and brown and, in some places, over half a kilometer wide. But it was loaded with sandbars and for the most part shallow. The coxswain of the LCVT, which carried most of the platoon, had to be careful to stay in midchannel to keep from running aground.

On the LCVT, we had plenty of room to walk about in, and the ride was smooth. The Mike boat, with its flat bottom and high bow, caught every wave and ripple in the river and sort of bounced its way along.

An hour up river, a Vietnamese family pulled alongside in a fishing boat driven by a coughing one-lunger, a pair of eyes painted on the bow to ward off evil spirits. One of the men took a picture of them with a Polaroid, motioned for them to extend their long-handled fishing net, and dropped the photo in it. Grinning and admiring the photo, the family swung away and headed across river, which was dotted with a hundred similar boats.

Again, I found myself intrigued by the exotic beauty of the land and the people in it.

Near Hue city, the banks of the river became crowded with houses rising on stilts above the water. Small, paddle-driven boats darted everywhere near the shore. Most were laden to the freeboard with goods destined for market, while others bobbed high, transporting a mother and child perilously from one shore to the other.

We ground to a halt on the mud ramp near the university bridge, where Andres Vaart, a lieutenant along for the ride, and I debarked and headed for a look at the city.

We walked down broad, tree-lined boulevards, admiring the women with their long black hair and flowing *ao dai*s, longing to touch them, but failing to get even a look cast our way. People on bicycles everywhere passed us by.

At an army compound, we stopped in the officers' club for a beer. The looks there told us we weren't welcome, but we stayed anyway. The club smelled of wax and Brasso and polish, and a bank of slot machines lined one wall to break the monotony of such a remote hardship post. The officers were dressed in freshly starched uniforms, and their boots shone so you could see your face in them. They talked of girlfriends in the city, groused over their working hours, and cast disdainful looks at us, the intruders, with our jungle boots faded white and our patched fatigues and the haunted look in our eyes. It was a depressing place, and after a few beers, we left and returned to the boats.

When we got back, the troops were hanging over the sides, entertaining and being entertained by a flock of kids paddling small boats woven from bamboo and sealed with pitch. My men were throwing coins and cans of C rations into the water, and the kids were diving for them, then returning to the surface, grinning from ear to ear and holding whatever prizes they had gathered from the muddy waters. They dove and swam about and scrambled in and out of their boats like hyperactive ducks.

While I was watching them, I managed to lose my balance and fall overboard into the strong-smelling waters of the Perfume. My camera was in a leg pocket, and I grabbed for it the instant I hit the water. I had it out and was holding it over my head when I surfaced, hoping it hadn't been damaged. I was greeted by a chorus of loud cheers, whistles, and hoots from my platoon and half the sailors on board the LCVT.

Embarrassed, I climbed out of the water and reboarded the boat, where the cook dried out my camera in his oven. It worked fine afterwards, and the film in it developed clearly but with watermarks running through the pictures.

We left Hue late in the afternoon and were soon running out of light. I passed the word to the men to keep their weapons handy, with magazines in place, chambers empty.

At last light, we were still four klicks east of the mouth of the Hoi Loc Khoai, which led to the estuary and the sea. All hands were alert in the growing dark, watching the near bank of the river, when someone tried to mortar us. The rounds were off by a hundred or more meters, and before the gooks could adjust, it was suddenly dark.

A few minutes later, a wooden fishing boat cut between the LCVT and the Mike boat and opened up with an automatic weapon, sending a long stream of green tracers over our heads. I have no idea what the people in that boat had on their little minds, but we immediately took them under fire with our M-16s and some ancient M-1s carried by the sailors.

Then one of the sailors jumped up behind a pair of twin twenty-millimeter cannons mounted aft, loaded the weapon and fired. Bang. The gun went off just once, then quit. I had admired it earlier, noting it had several coats of lead-based paint plastered to it and wondering when it had last been fired. The sailor took immediate action to clear the weapon, but failed to get it to work.

In spite of our return fire, the fishing boat was still cruising along and shooting at us.

A sailor on board the Mike boat opened up with the .50-caliber machine gun mounted on the coxswain's box and began dancing rounds all over the water, blinding us as the tracers skipped wildly over the surface.

Just then, our boat ran aground, and we were stuck fast on a sandbar. Fine, I thought. We have now lost our maneuverability and make a fine target out here in the river.

The coxswain of the Mike boat shifted into reverse to avoid ramming us as one of my men shoved the sailor off the fifty, took control of the gun, and began walking rounds across the water and up the stern of the fishing boat. It literally blew apart as the rounds chewed it to pieces, throwing large chunks of wood into the air. The boat went up by the bow, capsized, and began to float, bottom up. No one came to the surface to ask for help.

The moment the boat was shredded, Andy Vaart and I yelled for the troops to cease fire. My men stopped immediately, but the sailors kept on banging away with their M-1s, and we had to go down the line yelling at them to get them to stop shooting. They'd, by God, come all this way and were going to have something to write home about!

We were still stuck on the sandbar. The coxswain revved the engines and attempted to back off, but we didn't move. He kept at it. Out on the river, dozens of fishing boats were now carrying lanterns raised on poles, the people on board signaling their whereabouts so we wouldn't mistake them for the enemy. Then a sort of long moan spread across the water which I took to be a we-really-don't-want-anything-to-do-with-this plea.

The coxswain revved and swore and rammed the boat into forward then back into reverse, repeating the sudden change of gears several times. Slowly the boat began to break loose from the sandbar. Just as it came free, a small, shallow-draft patrol boat appeared out of nowhere, the men on board asking if we needed help. The patrol boat carried enough weapons to sink the *Whetstone*. Each man carried a rifle, plus a pair of twin twenties were mounted up front, and an 81-mm mortar was bolted down amidships!

The coxswain said he would appreciate it if they would get us back into the channel and stay with us to the mouth of the river in case we ran aground again. With the patrol boat leading, we putted back on course and were soon underway.

By the time we cleared the estuary, the moon was up, and we made good time back to the *Whetstone*. We docked at

2200 and were debriefed by the ship's executive officer. After the debriefing and a sandwich, I took a shower and hit the rack, glad to be back on board.

23

There is not a whole lot you can say about floating around at sea. You're out there with all this water, and pretty soon you find out just how entertaining the little things in life can become. Fishing boats bobbing corklike in the sea a hundred miles from land are always good for a lean on the rail and twenty minutes' worth of spitting over the side. A refueling tender at work is good for at least thirty minutes, but if you're really desperate, you can watch for the two or three hours it takes to fill the ship's tanks. Dolphins are nice. Seagulls can be either taken or not.

We floated from the DMZ to Da Nang, and from Da Nang to the DMZ, waiting for word of our next operation. None came, but I knew there *had* to be another one before I went home. My date of departure for the States was around the 10th of February, and I was sweating out the days. But I was also worried about my platoon because a replacement officer had not been assigned to take command after I left. Two grunt platoon commanders had put in requests to take over the platoon, but both had been turned down by the colonel. He had his priorities—line companies came first. I just chose not to see his point of view and was more than a little irritated with his decision.

On January 22, officers from throughout the battalion were summoned to the *Valley Forge* and briefed for an operation named Badger Catch. It was to kick off on the following day. The mission assigned to the battalion was to clear the north bank of the Cua Viet, from the coast to a village five klicks inland named Mai Xa Thi, located next to Jones Creek. Although there was a large Marine unit on the coast just south of the Cua Viet, the NVA and local VC units had taken over the area north of the river. Heavy contact was expected.

On the morning of the 23d, we went in. This time, the battalion took everything it owned with it. Headquarters Company was set down north of a village named Xom Con Tong, about two klicks in from the sea. While the company was getting organized, I sat down with Dan McEvily, a Basic School classmate, to do a map study of the area. As we were getting oriented, two artillery rounds impacted one hundred meters away. Not realizing it was the NVA shooting at us, I commented to Dan that somebody was really off target, then went back to studying the map. Two more rounds came in, then the firing stopped.

We were back in the sand dunes again, and I was ordered to take my platoon out to check on some villages to the north. We moved out, taking with us an officer fresh out of Basic School, who had been recently assigned to take over my platoon. His name was Lieutenant Kapp, and although he seemed capable, I wanted to turn the platoon over to a more experienced officer.

We poked and prodded through our assigned vil, while Corporal Hostetler kept up a running commentary on his exploits in the Philippines. It seems he had fallen in love with a bar girl, who had introduced him to the wonders of oral sex.

"I've never met a girl like her, Lieutenant. I'm even thinking about extending so I can get a tour at Subic Bay to be with her. What do you think, sir?" Hostetler asked as we made our way past one foul-smelling hooch to the next.

"The Marine Corps will probably want six years of your life for a duty station like that. Once they know you want something, they go for blood," I said.

"Maybe, sir, but if you saw this girl, you'd know she's worth it. She's beautiful. And she says she loves me."

"I'm sure she does," I said, not wanting to burst his bubble about the devotion of bar girls.

We walked deeper into the village. Hostetler fell silent as he mulled over the decision to extend or not. Unsure what to do, he then asked, concerned, "Can you catch the clap from eating pussy, Lieutenant?"

I laughed so hard, things started coming out of my nose.

We continued to search the village but failed to turn up anything significant.

Back at the battalion CP, I received orders to take out a patrol that night to make a reconnaissance of the village of My Loc, Kilo Company's objective for the next day. We were to determine whether or not the enemy occupied the vil.

I decided to limit the number of men going to twelve and would use the first squad plus Sergeant Woo for the patrol. We reorganized our equipment so we would be traveling as light as possible, checked our weapons, and rubbed on grease paint.

At 2030 hours, we left the battalion perimeter to begin the two thousand-meter trek to My Loc. We would be traveling through the dunes, which, aside from some scattered clumps of pine trees, offered very little in the way of concealment. No moon and a heavy overcast kept us in near total darkness most of the time, but an outpost to the north, called C-4, was being probed, and had a Spooky on station that was dropping flares every few minutes. To avoid being caught in the light, we dropped to our knees and froze every time a flare went off. The oscillating light caused the pines scattered over the dunes to come to life and march along our front and flanks; the effect of which was unnerving, and we were soon seeing an NVA behind every tree.

A few hundred meters from the battalion perimeter, I caught sight of some men running across the face of a dune. There were no more than fifty meters between us, and I was sure they were NVA but didn't open fire for fear they were a stray grunt patrol on its way in. I hissed at the men to get down, then hollered out a loud, "Who goes there!'' I was answered by a short burst that passed harm-lessly overhead.

"You son of a bitch!" I yelled back, angry with myself for calling out something so stupid as, "Who goes there!" and not shooting in the first place.

By then I was convinced they were NVA, but they had disappeared into some pines, and we had nothing to shoot at. I called the battalion CP and told them they had people headed their way, then got the patrol moving again.

As we threaded our way through the dunes and pines in a stop-wait-start approach to the village, I kept our bearing by constantly checking the luminous dial on my lensatic compass and keeping track of a tree line bordering the village of Xom Con Tong to our south. Whenever a flare went off over C-4, I could see the tall trees near the village. Thus, we were able to stay on course.

To keep from being silhouetted on the skyline, we stayed in the valleys and along the faces of the dunes. I didn't like being down low but felt that if we were going to complete our mission unseen, we would have to forget about keeping to the high ground. We had enough firepower to hold our own, but I did not want to get caught out in the dunes in a firefight.

About 2300, we found ourselves in a graveyard on the outskirts of My Loc. I gave the signal to get down, and on our hands and knees, we approached the village. When we could hear voices, I called a halt, split the patrol into three sections, and sent two of them crawling off at forty-five de-gree angles from me, then moved my section forward to a low rise. I got out my binoculars and tried to penetrate the darkness in the vil. A few hundred feet away, a lone lantern shone brightly, but I could not see any movement around it. I could hear people digging and talking, but had no way to determine how many of them there were.

We had been in position about ten minutes when a grenade went off. A few minutes later, the section on the right came scurrying in. The men in it reported they had run into a listening post and a grenade had been thrown at them. No one was hurt.

The section on the left came in, and we pulled back to a pine-covered dune to hold a whispered discussion on what we had found. Neither of the sections was able to see anything going on inside the vil, but they had all heard voices and digging. The presence of an LP convinced us that enemy troops were in the village, but just how many was anyone's guess.

I altered our return route so we wouldn't be covering the same ground twice, and we made our way back as cautiously as we had gone out, arriving at the battalion CP shortly after 0200. The CP was operating out of two amtracs, and I reported to Major Shannon, the S-3, who was still awake. I told him that although we hadn't seen anyone inside the village, I was certain the enemy was there.

Afterwards, we went into our position on the line and slept. When the sun came up, we continued working the villages to the north.

Kilo Company was assigned to take My Loc and that afternoon ran into stiff resistance. The company dug in and began pounding the vil with air and arty, determined not to repeat the mistakes made during the fight for Thon Tham Khe on Operation Badger Tooth.

As Kilo deployed at the edge of a vil east of My Loc, a platoon sergeant was wounded and went down in the open between the lines. Two attempts to reach him were beaten back by small-arms fire. The sergeant called out for his buddies to leave him until after dark and then come for him. A second lieutenant, new to the battalion, decided to give it one more try and went out to get the sergeant but was shot dead. After dark, a rescue party crept out and brought in the wounded man and the dead lieutenant.

Things had not gone well for Kilo the first day, and the enemy position was proving to be a tough nut to crack. That night, the battalion S-3 jumped down my throat, claiming I had reported that the village of My Loc was not occupied by the enemy. I jumped right back and told him that was not what I had said and that he damn well knew it! We exchanged a few more words, then the major stalked back to his amtrac, unwilling to admit he was wrong. Since then, I have been plagued by the thought that the major passed on information to Kilo Company that a night reconnaissance of My Loc found the village to be cleared of enemy forces and Kilo went in unprepared. I hope that was not the case, but as the situation would have it, I never learned what information Kilo received prior to the fight for My Loc.

On the 26th, the struggle for My Loc was still going on and Kilo, under Capt. John Regal, was making good use of all the available supporting arms and steadily taking possession of the vil. Late in the morning of the second day, they had kicked out the NVA and gone in. The CP followed them in at 1400, and shortly after dark, cold and shivering in the damp night air, we began loading onto amtracs to move to My Loc.

As we were loading, one of the men from Headquarters Company sat down next to the exhaust vent, called a dog house, on top of one of the tracs, and leaned against it for warmth. Within a few minutes, the M-16 ammunition in his pack began exploding from the heat given off by the exhaust, sending bits and pieces of his pack flying through the air. As the rounds cooked off in rapid-fire succession and the man turned and twisted frantically to rid himself of his pack, a lance corporal next to him wrenched the pack off his back and threw it as far as he could. Those of us around the pack scrambled to get away from it, afraid it might have a grenade in it which the rounds would set off. Standing well away from it, we watched as the ammunition continued to go off for another minute or so, shredding the back half of the pack. When no large explosion occurred and things settled down, we finished loading the trac and started out across the dunes.

We cut through the village of Xom Con Tong to the banks of the Cua Viet and headed west along the shore. As we went, riding on top of the tracks, we passed hooch after hooch that had been destroyed and burned down during the fighting. Glowing embers winked eerily at us in the dark like a thousand yellow eyes. I was amazed at the total destruction of the place.

When we arrived at My Loc, I reported to the Headquarters Company commander and was told to take a patrol back to the area we had just left and set up an ambush in case any of the enemy came snooping around the abandoned CP site.

Shit!

We moved out at 2200 in a thick fog rolling off the river. The sky was overcast, the moon had evaporated, and C-4 wasn't calling for flares. We could scarcely see our hands in front of our faces.

Four hundred meters out of My Loc, I turned around to check on the patrol. Aside from the point men and Hostetler, who was glued to my ass, the rest of the platoon was gone. I hissed out a call to them, but failed to get an answer. I told Hostetler to raise the rest of the platoon on the radio and find out where it was. "Somewhere behind you," came the reply. I told them to move along the heading we had set out on and keep coming until they linked up with us. Then the four of us sat down in the dark and waited.

Twenty long minutes went by before the point man for the trailing group emerged from the fog. I took a head count, got the platoon on line, and we set out again.

Ten minutes later, I looked back, and the platoon was gone again! I told Hostetler to get on the horn and wake somebody up back there. When the platoon rejoined us, I went down the line telling each man not to lose sight of the man in front of him, and if he had to, hang onto his pack!

Five minutes later, we were separated again.

At that point, our travels had brought us to the edge of a graveyard. Frustrated, worried we would get involved in an intramural firefight in the fog, I decided then and there to call a halt to this blundering through the night. When the rest of the platoon caught up with us, I told Sergeant Woo to deploy the men in the graveyard, then established a CP inside a large walled-off area, the entrance to which was decorated by a pagodalike structure and a concrete dragon. I plopped down next to the dragon and gave Hostetler the first of several phony location reports to call in and told him to wake me in half an hour so I could give him another.

I would have preferred to have reported to battalion exactly what our situation was and that we were basically lost in the fog, but honesty would only have been met by an insistence that I get off my ass and get on with the mission. So I lied.

The false location reports went on until 0300, when I was told to return to My Loc.

The sun found us dug in in a potato field not far from the CP, which was set up in amtracs bristling with antennas. Most of my platoon was either asleep or gathered around a well, trying to clean up and shave.

By 1000 hours, the sun was beating down with a vengeance, and we were trying to find what little shade we could. Lieutenant McEvily was hooched up under a poncho, and I wandered over to get out of the sun and speculate with him just when the battalion adjutant would be cutting orders for us to go home. Dan McEvily and I had left the States in the same overseas draft, and our return would be at the same time or close to it. In other words, we were short and counting the hours.

I had just gotten comfortable when two artillery rounds slammed into the potato field, and we were suddenly all assholes and elbows. I scrambled on all fours to the nearest hole, arriving there right after Dan and immediately before his radio operator. I landed hard on Dan, flattening him in the bottom of the hole. Then his radio operator landed on me. The three of us managed to fill a one-man hole neatly to the brim just as a fire for effect hammered in. With rounds landing everywhere around us, the three of us were so closely packed together, we would have been arrested had the circumstances been anything other than what they were.

Rounds kept coming in, and the only thing I was able to do about it was to make sure air was going in and out of my lungs and that I kept breathing, but even then I wasn't sure that was always the case.

After about five minutes, the fire lifted, and I raced back

to my platoon, where I had left my helmet and flak jacket—two items I badly felt the need of.

When I got there, Hostetler popped out of the hole we had dug earlier and, wide-eyed, inquired just what that had been all about. I told him I was sure the enemy had a forward observer in the area and to pass the word that no one was to stray far from a hole unless ordered otherwise.

It was then I noticed Lieutenant Kapp, my replacement, lying between two furrows and told him he had better start digging now. He looked at me and shook his head without saying a word and didn't get up.

I put on my helmet and flak jacket, sat down on the edge of my hole, and told Hostetler to find out what he could about this incoming artillery business.

A few minutes later, he reported that there was so much traffic over the airwaves he couldn't get much in the way of information, but word had it the enemy guns were shooting from inside the DMZ.

During the lull, Hostetler said, ''Lieutenant, did you know that Carter's got a girlfriend named Rose Bush? Now who would name a kid Rose Bush? That's almost as bad as Lady Bird Johnson.''

He managed to get a smile out of me that time.

Then from up north we heard the guns go off. Someone yelled, ''Incoming!'' and it was assholes-and-elbows time again. Hostetler beat me into the hole, and I wound up on top of him, swearing I'd be the first one in next time.

Whoever was out there calling the shots brought them right down on top of us, filling the air with metal, dirt, and parts of nearby hooches. I curled myself into a ball and tried to crawl inside my helmet. Teeth clenched, eyes squeezed shut, I kept telling God what a great guy I'd be if He would only get us out of this in one piece.

When the firing finally lifted, there wasn't one of us in that field that didn't have a changed outlook on life and our thousand-yard stares had reached out a little farther than they had been.

When ten minutes went by and nothing came in, several

wounded Marines were brought up to be medevaced. They were placed under a tree not far from the hole Hostetler and I were occupying. One of the Marines had taken a piece of metal in the spine, and his limbs flopped uncontrollably as he was carried to the LZ. Legs kicking, back arched, he bucked and twisted like a chicken with its head cut off. Moments later, when the next fire for effect came in, he was still out there. One of the wounded got up and raced for cover, but the others had no choice but to lie where they were. I felt sorry for them out in the open, but there wasn't much I could do about it. When the firing stopped, they seemed to be all right, but no more wounded were left out in the open again.

During that third time around, one of my men went a little crazy and got out of his hole and started running around in the open with rounds impacting all around him. From behind me, someone yelled, "Hey, Lieutenant, Evans is out of his hole and running around in the field!"

I wasn't about to go get him and yelled back for someone to tackle him and drag him into a hole.

A few seconds later, I heard a thud followed by a string of curses.

"He's still trying to get out of his hole, Lieutenant. What do we do with him?"

"Shoot him full of morphine and sit on him until he calms down!" I yelled.

This time, I had beaten Hostetler to the bottom of the hole, and as he clung to me he said, "You know, Lieutenant, this artillery shit won't hurt you unless it actually lands on top of you."

After a long pause, a less confident voice asked, "Will it?"

Sorry as the situation was, I couldn't help but laugh.

The fire coming into the potato field had started at one end and walked the length of the field, through the mortar section, past us, and beyond to the CP, still housed in the amtracs. With their long antennas sticking high above the hooch the tracs were trying to hide behind, they made a target no self-respecting forward observer could pass up.

As the fire shifted to the CP group, I lifted my head above the edge of the hole to watch. A communicator was in the process of ripping out antenna cables as the tracs jockeyed to clear the area. It gave me no small amount of satisfaction to know that the CP was getting its share of the shit.

About 1500, I was told to get ready for another night patrol. Battalion didn't yet know where we were going, but to be ready when the decision was made.

The incoming had slacked off in the afternoon, and I couldn't help but think the NVA FO had been dislodged from his position and could no longer observe My Loc. Also, India Company had run up against an NVA battalion to the northwest in a village named Lam Xuan (1), and the NVA artillery fire had been shifted to hit India.

Just before dark, our patrol was canceled, and that night I was able to catch up on some sleep.

The next day, I was ordered to move the platoon toward Lam Xuan (1) to provide protection for two tanks that had been damaged by mines. We saddled up and moved twelve hundred meters to a place where the dunes gave way to a sea of rice paddies that stretched to the DMZ and beyond. Two tanks sat in a natural roadway in the sand, each had a track blown off. They had followed the obvious route to Lam Xuan (1) and paid the price.

I placed the platoon in a defensive perimeter, and we dug in. A klick away, India was trying to break into Lam Xuan (1), and I watched the battle through my binoculars. India's CO was using all his supporting arms, plus a few Ontos and their 106 recoilless rifles, to hammer the NVA inside the vil. A tank, bogged down to the turret in a paddy, was just outside the vil, its gun angled skyward.

As I watched, a lone tank left the battle, headed our way, tearing across the paddies at full speed. Two hundred feet from us, it bogged down as it tried to climb a muddy dike. The driver, a black lance corporal, climbed out and threw up his hands in resignation. He walked over to us and reported that he was the sole survivor of his crew, the rest had been medevaced.

Later, a fourth tank and three amtracs joined us, and I worked them into our defenses. I told the tank commanders to load their guns with flechette rounds as we got ready for the night.

When darkness came, it didn't really get dark. The night was continuously lighted by tracers, flares, and blossoming explosions.

Shortly before midnight, my listening post was hit with a grenade and one man was slightly wounded. The listening post came in, and for the rest of the night, we were shot at by sniper fire and some automatic-weapons fire. Since we could not see where it was coming from, I passed the word not to shoot unless a target presented itself. None did, and at first light, the firing stopped.

Early that morning, a tank retriever came out and hauled away the two tanks with their tracks blown off. Later, it came back for the one stuck in the paddy.

After several unsuccessful attempts to pull the tank out, the retriever plus three amtracs cabled together and in one mighty heave managed to free the stuck tank. The cables were disconnected, and the tank driver maneuvered to reach solid ground. He backed up, turned, and promptly ran over a mine that lifted the front of the tank three or four feet into the air and peeled off a track. The instant the tank came to rest, the driver shot out of the hatch, his feet churning. He hit the ground and didn't stop running until he was a good one hundred yards from his machine.

One of the amtrac drivers began jumping up and down, pointing at the tank and yelling, "Goddamn, we were right there! Right there!"

No one had been hurt during the incident. I turned to the men and told them we would be there a while longer and that they may as well eat.

By noon, the retriever had hauled away the last of the stricken vehicles.

Our time in the dunes had given us a reprieve from the

incoming artillery, but once back in My Loc, we were again under its umbrella. But by now, we were all keenly attuned to the rumbling fire coming from the DMZ, and the instant we heard it, took to our holes. If we were quick, we could be in a protected position before a round announced itself with a sharp crack and shattering explosion. However, when our own artillery was firing, we couldn't hear a thing from the DMZ and didn't know the enemy was firing until the rounds began impacting among us. It was a tense situation to say the least.

Most of the incoming was being directed at India Company, which was still working over Lam Xuan (1), but the NVA never seemed to forget us and cranked rounds our way whenever they felt the urge.

We moved out of the potato field to a new position near the river and dug in next to some hooches that offered protection from the sun. Most of the hooches in My Loc were either concrete and tin or had some concrete and tin worked into their construction, and the village was a cut above most of the ones I had seen in Vietnam. The hooch we were next to was still standing and had somehow survived the battle unscathed.

That afternoon, Sergeant Woo and I went over to the battalion LZ to pick up some supplies and catch up on the latest word about the fight for Lam Xuan (1). While we were there, a helicopter came in and dropped off some supplies and the battalion supply officer, strode handsomely around the area in spit-shined boots, starched fatigues, and shining brass. Everything he wore was brand-spanking-new, right down to his flak jacket and camouflaged helmet cover. He went about the business of supervising the unloading of the helicopter with a confident, proud-to-be-here-in-the-field-with-you-fellas look on his face.

About then, the NVA threw in some artillery rounds, and the look on his face changed from ain't-this-wonderful to utter horror. I dove into a hole and lost sight of him, and when the firing lifted, I climbed out. The supply officer was long gone. I don't know whether he went up in a cloud of smoke, swam or ran back to the ship, but like magic, he was gone. It was a trick I wished I could master.

We spent the night in relative quiet.

Late the next day, I wandered through what was left of My Loc, struck by the tragedy of our surroundings. Few of the houses had gone undamaged during the fighting, and many were burned to the ground. In one house, its roof blown off and only three walls standing, I found a picture of a man and his family dressed in their Sunday best. The mother and children were smiling, but the father wore a more stern look on his face. It was not unlike many of the photos I had seen of Vietnamese families, but for a long time I sat in the house staring at it, wondering what had happened to the family I held in my hands. Were they all dead, or had they managed to escape before the fighting began? One thing was certain, if they were alive, when they came back home they sure as hell weren't going to like what they found. Before I left, I put the photo carefully back on a shelf.

It was the 29th of January, and I was due to go home in less than two weeks. However, no word of my being pulled from the field had arrived.

I was at a point where the war ceased to have any meaning for me, and I just wanted to go home. Vietnam had become like a movie you sit down to watch after it's started and leave before it's over. There's no beginning and no end, just the in between part where you pick up a few stray threads and try to make sense out of it. But no sense ever seemed to come of it because we kept fighting over the same ground and giving it back. No cities were ever liberated, and no citizens thronged to cheer us on, and no beautiful women ever threw themselves on us unless it was for money.

I wanted out, but I felt guilty as hell about leaving. I had a deep sense of commitment to the men in the platoon and worried about what would happen to them. Lieutenant Kapp had disappeared that day in the potato field, and I had not seen him since, nor did I know where he went. Word had come that he did not want a recon platoon. So until an officer was assigned, Sergeant Woo would be in command after I left. He was capable as a platoon sergeant, but didn't carry the clout of an officer, a clout that was needed to protect the men from those of the hi-diddle-diddle, straight-up-the-middle school of thought and who tended to get a lot of people killed.

After wandering through the vil, I rejoined the platoon on the perimeter, where we sat guarding the CP from an enemy that never came. India pushed the NVA out of Lam Xuan (1), and now Lima and Kilo were hammering away at them in Lam Xuan (2), farther to the north. Somewhere out there, there had to be a Lam Xuan (3) to fight over.

At 1800 hours on January 29, the Tet truce went into effect, but nothing changed. The NVA kept throwing in artillery, and we kept throwing it back. Earlier, something had told me there wouldn't be a truce anyway.

Dan McEvily had returned to the ship that day, and I kept wondering when the call for me to go would come. I told myself they wouldn't leave me in the field until my relief came, but then I wasn't so sure about that.

At 2300 that night, a call came over the radio to have my gear packed and to be on the LZ in the morning to return to the ship. I couldn't believe it. I was finally coming out. Later I learned that Dan had gone to the battalion adjutant and told him to get me out of the field because we had come in country at the same time, and the deed was done. I am eternally grateful to Dan for that.

At first light, the NVA threw in a few wake-up rounds, but they were closer to the CP than us, and no one was hurt.

I made the rounds, shaking hands with the men in the platoon, who were all happy for me. But there was a look of when-does-my-turn-come on their faces, and knowing some of them wouldn't make it, I couldn't help but feel guilty again about leaving.

After I said good-bye, I gathered up my gear and went to the LZ. At 0800, a CH-46 medevac popped over a tree line and touched down, its ramp already lowered. As I ran on board, a wounded Marine lying on a stretcher looked up at me and smiled, and the pilot turned around in his seat, grinning, to give me a thumbs-up. They knew I was going home.

We lifted off, staying low, and skimming the tree tops to the coast. When we came to the beach, we gained altitude for the trip back to the *Whetstone*. As we climbed, I looked back at the country that had held me for so long, thinking I had left Vietnam forever.

I didn't know how wrong I was.

Since Vietnam

After Leaving Vietnam, I was stationed at the Marine Corps Recruit Depot, San Diego, California, for seven months, working with drill instructors and recruits as a company series officer. From there, I was sent to language school at Monterey, California, for a six-month course in Spanish. After Monterey, I was stationed at Camp LeJeune, North Carolina, with the interrogation and translation unit for two years. Deciding not to make a career of the Marine Corps, I was discharged with the rank of captain in 1971.

My family and I returned to San Diego, where I attended San Diego State for a year to complete the requirements for an elementary teaching credential. Shortly after receiving my credential, we moved to Bishop, California, where my wife, Roberta, and I raised our children and have taught for the last nineteen years, including a teaching year in England on a Fulbright Scholarship.

Jodi, our oldest daughter, is a graduate of Cal Poly, San Luis Obispo. Dan, our oldest son, attends the University of Nevada, Reno. Our youngest daughter, Teri, is married and attends Montana State University at Bozeman. Our youngest son, Brian, lives and works in San Luis Obispo, California.

In my spare time, I write, sculpt metal, and work on old cars. Roberta loves to paint, work at needlecraft, and is an avid gardener. Both of us love to travel.

Follow the riveting, true-to-life account of survival and death in one of the most highly skilled units in Vietnam.

FORCE RECON DIARY, 1969

by
Bruce H. Norton

Published by Ivy Books.
Available in your local bookstore.

The confusion...
the horror...
the truth...

=VIETNAM=

*one of the most controversial
periods of U.S. history*